THE
ULTIMATE
BARTENDER'S

D1005864

BARNES
&NOBLE
BOOKS
NEW YORK

1000

FABULOUS RECIPES FROM
THE FOUR SEASONS
RESTAURANT

THE
ULTIMATE
BARTENDER'S
GUIDE

FRED DuBOSE
WITH
GREG CONNOLLY
CHARLES CORPION
JOHN VARRIANO

THE ULTIMATE BARTENDER'S GUIDE

For information contact:
Silver Lining Books, 122 Fifth Avenue, New York, NY 10011
212 633-4000

Publisher: Barbara J. Morgan
Design: Richard J. Berenson
Berenson Design & Books, Ltd., New York, NY
Production: Della R. Mancuso
Mancuso Associates, Inc., North Salem, NY

Library of Congress Cataloging-in-Publication Data is available on request.

ISBN 0-7607-3980-3

Printed in China

First Printing

YOUR HOME BAR
LIQUEURS
APÉRITIFS
CHAMPAGNE/WINE
PUNCHES
SHOTS
FROZEN DRINKS
HOT DRINKS
NONALCOHOLIC
BAR BITES

SCOTCH
BOURBON
WHISKEY
GIN
VODKA
RUM
TEQUILA
BRANDY

WELCOME

F YOU WANT TO LEARN how to mix drinks with a certain amount of panache, who better to guide you than the bartenders at one of New York's most famous restaurants? With *The Ultimate Bartender's Guide*, experts Greg Connolly, Charles Corpion, and John Varriano invite you to try your hand at duplicating their creations. They also enourage you to drop by Park Avenue and 52nd Street for a taste of the unique Four Seasons experience. If you're unable to visit in person, this book is the next best thing.

Some of the guide's thousand-plus drinks are old standards with a Four Seasons twist, but many more are brand-new. Sprinkled throughout these pages are assorted tips on techniques and buying, interesting facts about the origins of spirits and liqueurs, and glimpses of the beautifully appointed restaurant where Greg, Charles, and John work their magic. The "Your Home Bar" chapter (page 9) helps you get off on the right foot with advice and instructions on everything from stocking your home bar to shaking a drink to garnishing it. As a bonus, the "Bar Bites" chapter (page 227) serves up 12 hors d'oeuvres for parties, compliments of the chef.

The Four Seasons is housed in a landmark building (see page 152), designed by Mies van der Rohe and an essential stop on any tour of Manhattan architecture. Like the building, the restaurant's

*The Four Seasons
Restaurant bartenders:
(left to right)
Charles Corpion,
Greg Connolly,
and
John Varriano*

striking interior (the work of architect Phillip Johnson) has been granted landmark status. Since the mid-1980s, the reputation of the restaurant has grown to legendary proportions under the guiding hands of Managing Partners Alex von Bidder and Julian Niccolini and Executive Chef Christian Albin.

Yet the stars of this book are the bartenders, native New Yorkers all. Charles Corpion followed in the footsteps of his father, who tended bar at New York's Copacabana in the 1950s. Head bartender Greg Connolly was enshrined in the Bartender's Hall of Fame but modestly says he's "a husband and father first." John Varriano is a successful painter who became a bartender back in his "starving artist" days. Together, the men have 45 years of bartending experience, the fruits of which they now invite you to enjoy.

AN AMERICAN ORIGINAL

In *Straight Up or On the Rocks*, author William Grimes relates how the immortal journalist and critic H. L. Mencken "once claimed that he and a friend hired a mathematician to compute how many cocktails could be made from the ingredients available at a respectable bar. The total was 17,864,392,788. 'We tried 273 at random,' he reported, 'and found them all good.'"

That is the nature of the cocktail, an invention with American ingenuity written all over it. In fact, the mixed drink was born in the bars and taverns of the United States in the 19th century—hardly a surprise, given our forebears' penchant for taking the customs and traditions brought from the Old World (in this case, the way to consume alcohol) and turning them into something new.

That spirit of invention pervades *The Ultimate Bartender's Guide*, as it does virtually every bartending guide ever written. Of course, the creations of bartenders Greg Connolly, Charles Corpion, and John Varriano reflect their preferences for certain ingredients—preferences that grew not only from experiment-ation but also from their knowledge of which drinks Four Seasons customers have enjoyed most over the years.

You will no doubt do the same, making an adjustment here and there to tailor any cocktail in this or any other bartending guide to your own taste. There's also no need to always follow the mixing directions to the letter. Mixing a drink directly in the glass when the recipe calls for shaking may not give it the finesse it would have had, but the result will still be perfectly drinkable.

Naturally, the same applies to bar equipment. When stirring a drink with ice, it matters not whether you do it in the mixing glass of a shaker or in a tall iced-tea tumbler—only one example of the leeway you have when turning out those marvelous inventions we know as cocktails. So browse through this book, see what strikes your fancy, and start adding some real dazzlers to your home bartending repertoire.

To your health!

YOUR HOME BAR

TOOLS OF THE TRADE

Your success as a home bartender doesn't depend on having lots of bar equipment (required for Scotch and soda: glass, ice, and hand for pouring), much less every kind of liquor known to man. Still, there are a few home bar essentials you'll want to stock up on.

EQUIPMENT

The good news is that you probably already have much of the equipment you need—a large glass for mixing, a corkscrew, a blender, measuring spoons, and the like. But adding a few tools to your cabinet is a small yet worthy investment, not only improving your mixed drinks but enhancing your reputation as a host in the bargain.

COCKTAIL SHAKER

That gleaming martini shaker seen in so many 1940s movies may be synonymous with glamour, but it has a rather ordinary name: the standard, or regular, shaker. The other choice is the Boston shaker, the one used by most professional bartenders.

STANDARD SHAKER
These are available in stainless steel and aluminum; stainless steel is preferred because it keeps the drink colder. Most models come with a built-in strainer.

BOSTON SHAKER
The two halves of this shaker (a mixing glass and a stainless steel shell) fit together end to end. You'll need a separate strainer when using a Boston shaker.

STANDARD SHAKER

BOSTON SHAKER

JIGGER

The double form of this glass or stainless-steel measuring tool has a small cup on one side (usually 1 ounce or 1 1/2 ounces) and a larger cup on the other (usually 2 ounces). Single and double jiggers also come in other sizes but top out at 3 ounces. Some jiggers are fitted with long handles.

MEASURING SPOONS AND CUPS

Unless you own two or three jiggers of different sizes, you will need a set of measuring spoons (1 tablespoon equals 1/2 ounce). The spoons also come in handy when a drink recipe calls for 1/4- or 1/8- teaspoon amounts of a spice or syrup. Measuring cups are needed when making punches and other drinks in quantity.

MIXING GLASS

In this guide, "mixing glass" usually refers to the mixing glass of a shaker (see page 10), but you can mix a cocktail's ingredients in any large glass. Some pitchers are also intended as mixing glasses, in which case they may come with a stirring rod.

ICE BUCKET AND ICE TONGS

An ice bucket will keep ice colder when you're preparing several drinks for a party. You'll also want to use ice tongs or a scoop, not your hands, to transfer ice to a glass or shaker—obviously, the more hygienic approach.

ICE SCOOP

A second advantage of an ice scoop is that you can use it as a measure. One heaping scoop of small ice cubes is roughly the right amount to add when shaking or stirring a cocktail.

BAR SPOON OR STIRRING ROD

Use a bar spoon (or any other long-handled spoon) or a glass stirring rod when chilling a drink by stirring (page 19). Bar spoons are also used for layering drinks (page 20).

STRAINER

If you don't own a shaker with a built-in strainer, add a strainer to your list. Shown above is the spoon-shaped Hawthorne strainer with a spring coil at the head. It fits inside the top of your mixing glass, and the coil strains the drink as you pour.

JUICER

Hand-held wooden or metal citrus reamers come in handy when you need to juice only one lemon. But the most common citrus juicer is a two-piece plastic or stainless-steel type with a reamer plate set atop a bowl that collects the juice. A third choice is an electric juice extractor. Extractors, which come in several models, will liquify or puree virtually any kind of fruit.

MUDDLER

A wooden bar muddler is used to crush ingredients like cherries and mint leaves, often right in the bottom of the cocktail glass. The tool has a broad end that's either rounded or flat. An iced-tea spoon could also be used to crush ingredients, though not as effectively.

PITCHER

A pitcher is usually needed when you're serving drinks in quantity. Pitchers can also serve another purpose: A medium-sized, straight-sided glass pitcher can be used as a mixing glass for drinks stirred with ice.

ODDS AND ENDS

The well-stocked home bar also makes room for some of
the following appliances and items.

BLENDER
For making margaritas,
daiquiris, and other
frozen drinks

BOTTLE OPENER
To pop the top off bottled
soft drinks

CAN OPENER
The punch type, for opening
cans of fruit juice or liquids

CHAMPAGNE STOPPER
To keep champagne bubbly
while mixing drinks that
call for it

CITRUS STRIPPER
A tool that cuts 1/4-inch
strips from citrus rinds

CITRUS ZESTER
For zesting the rinds of
lemons, limes, and oranges

COASTERS
To protect wooden tabletops

CORKSCREW
Choose from several styles

CUTTING BOARD
For when you slice lemons
and other garnishes

FUNNEL
For putting liquids back
into a bottle when you've
overmeasured

ICE CRUSHER
This manual or electric
appliance isn't as expensive
as it may sound

KNIFE
A small paring knife is used
for cutting garnishes—and the
sharper it is, the better

NAPKINS
To use as coasters, insulate
an ice-filled rocks glass, or
simply add a nice touch

STRAWS
For certain iced drinks

SWIZZLE STICKS
For stirring drinks in the
drinking glass

TOOTHPICKS, COCKTAIL
Long, sometimes decorative,
plastic picks for spearing
garnishes like olives

VEGETABLE PEELER
For peeling garnishes or
stripping citrus rinds

WINE CHARMS
For hooking around wineglass
stems so partygoers know
which glass belongs
to whom

GLASSWARE

Because most people have just two or three kinds of bar glasses, only the most gung-ho home bartender is going to stock the cabinet with every choice under the sun. As a matter of fact, anyone can get by with a wine or martini glass for drinks served straight up and a rocks or highball glass for those on ice. Still, any bartending guide worth its salt is going to show you what is available.

A picture of one of the thirteen kinds of glasses shown on these two pages appears beside each recipe in this guide, just in case you choose to serve your mixed drinks "by the book."

ROCKS/ OLD-FASHIONED

Rocks glasses hold from 5 to 10 ounces, with a 5- or 6-ounce glass the most versatile.

HIGHBALL/COLLINS

Technically, the highball is the larger of these two, but both range from 8 to 16 ounces.

MARTINI

Nowadays, martini glasses range from a 6-ounce glass to a huge 16-ouncer (too much of a good thing?).

WHITE WINE

Sizes range from 5 to 10 ounces, but the most practical size for a white wine glass is 6 to 8 ounces. Forms vary from balloon shaped to straight sided to tulip shaped.

RED WINE

The larger size of this balloon glass allows wine to breathe. Sizes typically range from 8 to 14 ounces.

ROCKS HIGHBALL/ MARTINI WHITE WINE RED WINE SHERRY
COLLINS

SHERRY

The smallest of the wine glasses holds from 4 to 6 ounces. It can also be used for liqueur-based drinks.

FLUTE

This glass is elongated to keep champagne bubbly and typically holds 6 ounces.

TULIP

Named for its shape, this glass usually holds 8 ounces.

SNIFTER

The snifter comes in several sizes and is the traditional vessel for brandy served neat; its large bowl is cupped in your hand to warm the contents. Snifters can also be used for some cocktails.

LIQUEUR

These vary in shape and generally hold 3 to 5 ounces.

SOUR

Whether tulip shaped or straight sided with a rounded bottom, this glass usually holds 5 to 6 ounces.

MARGARITA

While most margarita glasses have a narrow neck above the stem, some are balloon shaped. Capacity ranges from 12 to 16 ounces.

SHOT

This 2-ounce glass is used for drinking shots but can also be used as a measuring tool when mixing cocktails.

FLUTE   TULIP   SNIFTER   LIQUEUR   SOUR   MARGARITA   SHOT

THE WELL-STOCKED BAR

The list of spirits shown here gives an idea of what you might need at one time or another. Buy large bottles of whatever you use most, and remember that the higher the quality, the better your finished product—so go for the best you can afford. In the interest of moderation, we also suggest that you check the proof (see box).

Also listed are the mixers and flavorings most frequently used in this guide—including fresh sour mix—many of which are elaborated on in Mixers Et Cetera (pages 22–24).

SPIRITS

- Apéritifs of choice
- Bourbon
- Brandy
- Cognac
- Gin
- Liqueurs of choice
- Rum (light and dark)
- Scotch (blended and single malt)
- Tequila (silver and gold)
- Vermouth (dry and sweet)
- Vodka (including flavored)
- Whiskey (Canadian, Tennessee, and rye)
- Wine (white, red, and rosé)

MIXERS

- Bottled water (still and sparkling)
- Club soda
- Cream
- Cream of coconut
- Fresh sour mix (see page 23)
- Fruit juices
- Soft drinks
- Tomato juice
- Tonic water

FLAVORINGS

- Bitters
- Grenadine and other syrups
- Fruit purees
- Roses lime juice
- Sugar
- Tabasco
- Worcestershire sauce

Check the Proof

Proof gauges the strength of a spirit. The proof listed on the bottle is twice the percentage of alcohol—in other words, 100-proof liquor contains 50 percent alcohol. Why should you check the proof when buying liquor and other spirits? Obviously, because drinks mixed with 80 proof will be much kinder to you and your guests than those mixed with 150 proof products. The same goes for wine, the strength of which is shown on the label as the alcohol percentage—usually 11.5 to 14.5 percent.

THE PERFECT DRINK

The next few pages tell you how to perform other tasks (most of them easy) on your way to the perfect mixed drink. Remember that the quality of a cocktail is measured by the way the flavors blend and the freshness of the ingredients, not by its color or a fancy garnish.

TECHNIQUES

When it comes to mixing drinks, practice doesn't always make perfect. More important is paying attention to what you're doing. A drink that's been mismeasured or gets watered down while being prepared is just another libation, not the winner you aspire to create.

SHAKEN OR STIRRED?

Whether to shake or stir a drink is one of the finer points of mixing, and choosing one over the other isn't going to make or break your drink. Still, the common procedure is to shake drinks that have sugar, cream, and fresh sour mix. Clear drinks served chilled and straight up are generally stirred, though shaking won't hurt them (not surprisingly, the idea that shaking will "bruise" gin is a myth).

Shaking or stirring chills and slightly dilutes a drink—and while a little dilution is desirable, too much will affect the taste. That's why we recommend pouring the ingredients into the mixing glass or shaker *before* adding the ice—a departure from normal procedure.

How much ice to add? Enough to fill the shaker at least half full. And take note: When shaking or stirring, use only ice cubes, not crushed ice; the latter melts faster and can result in a too-watery drink.

SHAKING Pour ingredients (with the exception of club soda, champagne, soft drinks, and other sparkling beverages) over the ice in the shaker glass or container. Fit the stainless-steel shell over the glass—or, if using a standard shaker, secure the lid tightly.

When shaking, hold the shaker with both hands (one at each end), grip tightly, and put plenty of pressure on each end. Eight to ten vigorous shakes are sufficient to mix the ingredients and chill the drink without diluting it. (Shake no more than two cocktails at a time in a shaker holding 16 ounces or less.)

STIRRING While most of the recipes in this guide specify a "mixing glass" for stirring, we use the term in the broadest sense. It matters not whether you use a pitcher, the glass of a shaker, or any other container. Just make sure it's big enough to keep the ingredients from sloshing over the sides.

Pour the specified ingredients into your mixing glass and stir vigorously for about 20 seconds with a stirring rod, bar spoon, or any other long-handled spoon. Time yourself, since stirring for longer than 20 seconds will dilute the drink.

STRAINING AND POURING

Pour a drink (or drinks) immediately after shaking or stirring it with ice—again, to keep it from becoming watery.

STRAINING Drinks that are served straight up aren't necessarily the only ones that need to be strained. When a drink is poured onto crushed ice, you want to shake or stir it with regular ice and then strain it onto its faster-melting counterpart. On-the-rocks drinks with muddled ingredients also usually need to be strained.

POURING CONTENTS Some of this guide's iced-drink recipes direct you to pour the contents of the shaker or mixing glass—ice and all—directly into the glass. Unlike the ice in the drinking glass, that in the shaker gets a head start on absorbing the drink's flavors— a good thing. Still, the choice is yours, so don't think the directions for pouring have to be followed to the letter.

STIRRING IN THE DRINKING GLASS

When mixing a drink directly in the glass, you need stir only once or twice with a swizzle stick or spoon. A carbonated beverage tends to mix the ingredients because it bubbles, but a gentle stir once any club soda, sparkling water, or soft drink is added is still a good idea.

MUDDLING

To muddle fruits or herb leaves is to crush or mash them with a wooden rod called—you guessed it—a muddler. What's the point? To release scents and flavorful aromatic oils. Muddling is often done directly in the bottom of the drinking glass, as when a cherry and orange slice are muddled in some versions of the Old-Fashioned; the same goes for the mint leaves and sugar in a mint julep. Various shaken or stirred recipes call for straining out the muddled material.

BLENDING

When blending frozen drinks or smoothies, use crushed ice. The amount of ice to use varies, but the less that goes into the blender, the slushier the drink will be. Another tip: Frozen drinks and smoothies will keep their texture longer if you chill the drinking glass beforehand.

Put the ingredients, not ice, in the blender first. (If fruit is included, process it before adding anything else.) Add crushed ice, then make sure the jar lid is on tight before you throw the switch. Process the contents for about 15 seconds, starting at slow speed and gradually increasing to medium.

FLOATING AND LAYERING

A few recipes call for floating or layering a spirit on another, which requires gauging their relative weights. Check the alcohol volume on the label: the lower it is, the heavier the product. The reason? Because low-proof products contain sugar and are consequently more syrupy.

When FLOATING alcoholic beverages, pour a light one such as schnapps or sloe gin very slowly down the inside edge of a glass containing a heavier spirit—usually a liqueur. Otherwise, use the tool needed for layering drinks: a bar spoon.

LAYERING means topping one ingredient with another until a pretty rainbow effect is achieved. The only layered drinks in this guide are found in Shots (pages 195–202), but you might want to try layering some of the drinks in other chapters, too.

Pour the heaviest ingredi-

ent in first, then place the tip of the bowl of a bar spoon (back side facing up) so that it touches the inside of the glass just above the liquid. Slowly pour the next ingredient over the bowl of the spoon so that it flows very gradually into the glass. Repeat with the remaining ingredients.

CHILLING GLASSES

The simplest way to chill glasses is to put them in the refrigerator for 30 minutes or so or in the freezer for 10. This method is hardly practical when turning out drinks in quantity, so if you're having a party try one of these methods instead:

• Put crushed ice in a glass and let it stand for about 5 minutes, then discard the ice and wipe the glass dry.

• Put ice cubes in the glass and fill with water. After 3 or 4 minutes, discard the contents and wipe the glass dry.

FROSTING GLASSES

Give summery iced drinks something extra by frosting the glasses. To frost, dip a glass in cold water, shake off the excess, and put it in the freezer for at least an hour.

The following tip may be stating the obvious, but here goes: The proper way to hold a frosted martini glass is by its stem, lest you melt the ice and spoil the effect.

About Ice

In this guide, the word "ice" refers to cubes. Crushed ice is specified as such and is listed with the ingredients. Naturally, ice cubes don't melt as fast as crushed ice, which explains why they are the ice of choice when mixed drinks are shaken.

To turn ice cubes into crushed ice, put them in a heavy plastic bag, wrap the bag in a dish towel, and pound away with a mallet or rolling pin. (You'll probably have to do the same with a bag of ice bought at the supermarket.) Don't overdo it, because the smaller the pieces, the faster they will melt. You could also invest in a manual or electric ice crusher; some models of electric crusher are surprisingly inexpensive.

Some tips for freezing and using ice:
• Keep ice from absorbing unwanted odors by making it (preferably with bottled, not tap, water) shortly before you use it.
• Use the ice in the shaker for another drink only if the drink is the same, since traces of the previous ingredients remain.
• The cubes used by most professional bartenders are smaller than the standard size—about 1" x 1" compared to 2" x 1 1/2". Home stores sell ice trays that enable you to freeze cubes in a variety of sizes and shapes (heart-shaped cubes, anyone?), so you may want to buy a few to use for mixed drinks only.

(See also Fruit-Juice Ice Cubes for Punch, page 193.)

FROSTING RIMS

When you want to frost the rim of a glass with sugar or salt you can moisten the rim (the first step) in one of two ways: 1) Rub a wedge of citrus fruit around the rim (yes, you can use the garnish) or 2) dip the rim into water, juice, or liquor and shake off the excess. (You could also dip your finger into a liquid and run it around the rim, but this shortcut is not quite as effective—not to mention less appetizing.) Then simply dip the rim into a saucer of superfine sugar or salt.

STEAMING GLASSES

To steam a glass is merely to heat it. A warm glass brings out the spirit's aroma—the reason brandies are often served in steamed glasses.

To steam a glass easily, fill it with hot water and let it sit for a minute or two. Discard the water and wipe the glass dry.

MIXERS ET CETERA

Here's a rundown on mixers and other ingredients that show up in the recipes of *The Ultimate Bartender's Guide*, with some tips on how to get the best out of them and what to look for when buying.

APPLE, PINEAPPLE, AND TOMATO JUICES

Refrigerated apple and pineapple juices are always better for using in mixed drinks than the bottled sort. Tomato juice usually comes only bottled or canned, so be sure to choose a better brand.

BITTERS

Under the "bitters" umbrella fall any aromatic mixtures based on the distillation of herbs, seeds, barks, roots, and flowers. But this broad definition also includes such apéritifs and digestifs as Campari and Fernet-Branca, drinks in their own right. Bitters called for in this guide are those dashed into the drink as an accent—Angostura bitters and Peychaud's bitters, to name two.

Bitters for flavoring are sold in the condiments section of most supermarkets. If you have trouble finding them, you can order some brands online.

CITRUS JUICES

The fresher the juice used, the better the finished cocktail. Choose good-quality refrigerated orange juice over bottled or frozen, and don't even consider taking a shortcut by buying lemon juice or lime juice in one of those squeezable fruit-shaped plastic containers.

Juicers for lemons, limes, and oranges vary from hand-held citrus presses and reamers to motorized juice extractors. (See also Juicer, page 12, and The Big Squeeze, page 32.)

Whether to strain the pulp out of orange juice is a matter of taste, although pulp-free orange juice will keep your glass looking neater as you drink your cocktail.

CREAM AND MILK

When our recipes call for cream (light or heavy), they mean what they say. Suit yourself, but substituting half-and-half or milk will end in a less sumptuous drink. (See also Whipped Cream, page 24.)

Likewise, when a recipe calls for milk, use whole milk, not lowfat or skim; in all but milk punches and shakes, the amounts called for in a typical recipe are not going to affect your waistline.

CREAM OF COCONUT

Popular brands of this rich, sweet mixer include Coco Lopez, Coco Casa, and Goya. Do not confuse cream of coconut with coconut milk or even coconut cream, both of which are less rich.

FRUIT PUREES

The fruit purees called for in some of this guide's recipes don't necessarily have to be prepared at home in your blender or food processor. (If you go that route, just be sure to wash the fruit first, cut it into fairly small pieces, and check for any stray bits of leaf or stem before you puree it.) Canned and frozen purees, including those from Milne and Ravifruit, are available in gourmet stores and online.

SOFT DRINKS

Lemon-lime soft drinks like Sprite and 7-Up are the ones most commonly mixed into cocktails, though cola and root beer are sometimes used as well. To keep them from going flat in the glass, add soft drinks last and then stir very gently.

SOUR MIX, FRESH

Many of our recipes specify an ounce or so of fresh sour mix, which can be made in quantity and kept in the fridge for about a week. And why would you bother making it fresh when you can buy a dried sour mix? Because it tastes fresher, tarter, and more natural.

When making fresh sour mix, you'd be wise to follow the Four Seasons bartenders' lead and use only fresh-squeezed juice. Frozen lemon juice will do in a pinch, but only if it is unsweetened.

The Four Seasons recipe for a pint:
2 cups freshly squeezed lemon juice
1/2 cup superfine sugar
1/4 cup pasteurized egg white

Combine the ingredients in a shaker or lidded jar.
Shake well. Pour into an airtight container and
store in the refrigerator.

Use only pure pasteurized egg whites, such as those made by Eggology, not the flavored yellow brands meant as whole egg substitutes. Dried egg whites, including Just Whites, will work just as well when mixed with water according to directions.

SUGAR

Recipes that call for sugar specify superfine sugar, which dissolves faster when shaken with liquids. Some drinks that are mixed directly in the glass call for powdered sugar, which dissolves even faster.
For frosting glass rims with sugar, see page 21.

SYRUPS

The fruit syrups called for in this guide's recipes aren't sold at the corner grocery, but you can find them with a little effort. The most widely used, the nonalcoholic pomegranate syrup **grenadine,** is available in many supermarkets and liquor stores. It is also sold online, as are fruit syrups (including those from Torani and Monin) made specifically for mixing into drinks—hot coffee included.

WATER

Water, water everywhere . . .
   Club soda is carbonated with carbon dioxide, while **sparkling water** is naturally carbonated in a spring. **Seltzer** technically refers to the water that comes from the German town of Nieder Selters, but all three of these terms have become interchangeable.
   Whatever you call them, carbonated waters that come in bottles must have their tops screwed back on tightly, since they can lose their punch in a matter of hours.
   When **still water** is specified in a cocktail recipe, you're better off using commercial bottled water, not tap water.

WHIPPED CREAM

When topping a drink with whipped cream, there's no reason not to use whipped cream from a can. But not so fast: For after-dinner drinks served at dinner parties, fresh whipped cream crowning a hot drink will no doubt be noticed and appreciated by your guests.

GARNISHES

A garnish not only imparts a bit of extra flavor to a cocktail but gives it an artful flourish. The range of choices is wide, but make sure a garnish is in proportion to the glass: A strawberry perched on the rim of a small liqueur glass is not only impractical but looks silly.

CHERRIES

All recipes in this guide specify maraschino cherries, also called cocktail cherries—the sweet, bright red fruits that come in a jar. They are dropped into the drink whole.

CHOCOLATE

A candy store or chocolatier is the place to find the long, narrow chocolate **sticks** that can be used to garnish drinks. **Shavings** can be scraped from a block of sweet chocolate with a knife.

FLOWERS

Among the small blooms that can be floated on a drink are plumeria (the flower used for Hawaiian leis) and nasturtium or pansy (both edible). Flowers can also be tucked along the edge of frozen drinks.

FRUIT GARNISHES

Wash unpeeled fruits before slicing. Cut fruit **slices** from 1/4 to almost 1/2 inch thick; to perch a whole or halved slice on the glass rim, make a cut from the outer edge to the center.

To cut **wedges**, slice the fruit lengthwise in half, then lengthwise into quarters or eighths (see also page 53). To cut long **spirals** of peel (an out-there garnish to hang on tall glasses), begin at one end of the fruit and use a citrus stripper or sharp paring knife to cut around and down the fruit, creating a continuous spiral.

Fresh pineapple, peach, mango, and similar fruits can be cut into **spears** for garnishing tall iced drinks. Using a sharp knife, cut a

Making a Citrus Wheel

For holiday parties, you could add a few citrus wheels to hot cider or mulled wine. Cut a lemon or orange into slices almost half an inch wide and insert whole cloves at equal intervals into the peel of each slice. Then float the wheels in the serving bowl.

fruit chunk into slices just under 1/2 inch thick, then cut each slice into spears of the same scant 1/2-inch thickness.

Small fruits can be used **whole** or **halved**. A strawberry, minus leaves and stem, can be dropped right into the drink. A whole strawberry (with or without leaves) or apricot can be perched on the glass rim: Just cut a small slit in the bottom of the fruit to secure it.

OLIVES

Pitted green olives are the standard garnish for drinks, but that doesn't mean you can't use olives stuffed with everything from a bit of anchovy to an almond. Just make sure the stuffing isn't going to spoil your drink's taste. A jalapeño-stuffed olive in a martini made with sweet vermouth is hardly a marriage made in heaven.

ONIONS, COCKTAIL

The Gibson and its variations may be one of the few cocktails that call for them, but you can try cocktail onions in a Bloody Mary or any other savory drink. These pickled pearl onions are found in most grocery stores and some liquor stores. Unless the label on the bottle shows them to be pickled with vermouth, flush the onions with water before using or the pickling brine will taint the drink.

SPICES

The most effective way to dissolve a spice in a drink is to shake it with the other ingredients. Nutmeg and cinnamon are the two most often used, and then usually in creamy drinks or mulled wines.

TWISTS

Narrow slices of citrus peel are called twists because they're twisted over a drink to add a bit of aromatic oil. Twists can also be used to rub the rim of the glass, lending still more flavor. At The Four Seasons, twists are wider and shorter than the traditional sort. This larger piece is not only easier to twist but also releases more oil.

• For a traditional twist, cut the fruit in half lengthwise. Use a sharp paring knife or a citrus stripper to cut the rind lengthwise into 1/3-inch strips.

• To create a Four Seasons–style twist, use a sharp paring knife to cut an ovoid piece of rind about 2 inches x 1 inch.

Hold the twist between the thumb and fore-finger of both hands and give it a sharp twist over the drink; if you look closely, you'll see a fine spray of oil (you'll certainly smell it, at least). Then drop the twist into the drink.

DRINKS FOR ALL SEASONS

Some cocktails seem to come into their own at certain times of the year—so if you're looking for the perfect cooler for a hot day or a warming one when it's cold, scan these lists, complete with page numbers. Summer and spring drinks are interchangeable, of course, as are those suited to fall and winter—but the restaurant isn't called The Four Seasons for nothing.

SPRING

VODKA
Ashley's Punch *186*
Birth of Venus *79*
Bluebird *80*
Cello's Dream *82*
Cîroc Rocks *82*
Creamy Dream *84*
Dirty Blonde *84*
Headless Horseman *86*
Island Delight *88*
Lucasta *89*
Mudslide *92*
Percolator *93*
Rendezvous *94*
Russicano *94*
Snow Storm *96*
Strawberry Blast *209*
Swiss Alps *97*
Topaz *98*
Vanilla Punch *194*
White Licorice *102*

RUM & TEQUILA
Acapulco Fizz *128*
Aztec Gold *79*
California Sky *129*
The Coliseum *107*
Donkey Express *108*
Frozen Daiquiris *110–111*
Frozen Margaritas *131*
Golden Island *112*
Italian Cooler *113*

Mexican Holiday *135*
Polly's Choice *116*
Raindrop *136*
Sour Thorn *124*
Spring Break *138*
Strawberry Whip *138*
The Vera Cruz *142*
Yo-Ho-Ho *218*

WHISKEYS
Catch-22 *53*
Connolly Cooler *54*
Four Seasons Whiskey Sour *54*
French Connection *47*
Irish Coffee *216*
Irish Cooler *55*
Irish Punch *190*
Karen's Cocktail *55*
Mounted Cop *58*
Scotch Mist *38*
Scotch Rickey *40*
Seaside *59*
Whiskey Mint Cooler *60*

GIN
The Academic *62*
Ascot *63*
Damsel *66*
Fairy Tale *68*
Florentine *68*
Kate's Fave *70*
The Monk *72*

SUMMER

Belle of the Ball *177*
Champagne Bleu *177*
Chateau Kiss *158*
Cranberry Cocktail *178*
Creamy Nut *148*
De Chirico's Delight *160*
Ginicot *149*
Indian Summer *215*

Mediterranean Kiss *171*
Minty Apple *216*
Newton's Apple *163*
Sour Grapes *153*
Southern Pleasure *165*
Sweet Apple *153*
Vanilla Kiss *166*
William Tell *154*

WINTER

VODKA
Cello's Dream *82*
Creamy Dream *84*
Godchild *85*
Lucasta *89*
Monkey *92*
Mount Etna *92*
Swiss Alps *97*
Tannhauser *97*
Truffle *98*
Velvet Hammer *98*
White Licorice *102*

RUM & TEQUILA
Banana Cream Pie *105*
Bloody Maria *129*
Foxy Squirrel *109*
Gentle Juan *132*
Gold Leaf *132*
Hot Sour *132*
Lemon Meringue *113*
Mint Chocolate Cup *114*
Rummy Meditation *119*
Rummy Southern Belle *120*
Rum Rico *121*
Sour Emperor *123*

WHISKEYS
Blackstone *52*
Blushing Scot *34*
Bourbon Kiss 1 and 2 *43*
Bourbon Milk Punch *45*
Hot Buttered Bourbon *215*
Park Avenue Sour *58*
Southern Cream Pie *50*
Tennessee Traveler *217*
TNT *50*

GIN
Astoria *63*
Bilbo B. *64*
Bloody Brit *64*
Carousel *65*
Faust *68*
Green River *70*
Pink Lady 1 and 2 *73*

WINE COCKTAILS, LIQUEURS, & SUCH
Annie's Cherry Pie *212*
Brandied Port *177*
Brandy Alexander *145*
Brandy Runner *146*
Café Mystique *147*
Café Royale *213*
Court Jester *160*
Licorice Delight *163*
The Matador *181*
Port Pleasant *182*
Red Pagoda *217*
Spiked Hot Chocolate *217*
Tipsy Earl *217*
Toasted Almond *166*
Toasted Monk *218*
Vanilla Dream *154*

WHERE'S IT FROM?

The cocktail was born and bred in America, but it draws on ingredients from virtually every corner of the world. At The Four Seasons, one of the questions bar patrons ask most often is where a certain product originated. So we'll give you the answers, too.

LIQUEURS & OTHER PRODUCTS

Agavero *Mexico*
Alizé *France*
amaretto *Italy*
Angostura Bitters *Venezuela, later Trinidad*
anisette *France*
applejack *United States*
Armagnac *France*
B & B *France*
Baileys Irish Cream *Ireland*
banane, crème de *France*
Bénédictine *France*
cacao, crème de *France*
calvados *France*
Campari *Italy*
cassis, crème de *France*
Chambord *France*
Chartreuse *France*
Cherry Heering *Denmark*
Cognac *France*
Cointreau *France*
curaçao, blue *Curaçao*
Cynar *Italy*
Drambuie *Scotland*
Dubonnet *France*
Fernet-Branca *Italy*
framboise *France*
Frangelico *Italy*
Galliano *Italy*
Godiva liqueurs *Belgium*
Goldschlager *Switzerland*
Grand Marnier *France*
grenadine *Grenada*

Harveys Bristol Cream *England*
Irish Mist *Ireland*
Jägermeister *Germany*
Kahlúa *Mexico*
kirschwasser *Germany*
kümmel *Netherlands*
Lillehammer *Denmark*
Lillet *France*
limoncello *Italy*
Malibu rum *Barbados*
Midori *Japan*
noyaux, crème de *France*
ouzo *Greece*
Pernod *France*
Peychaud's Bitters *New Orleans*
Pimm's No. 1 *England*
Poire William *Switzerland, France*
Punt e Mes *Italy*
sambuca *Italy*
schnapps *Denmark, Germany*
Southern Comfort *New Orleans, later Louisville*
Strega *Italy*
Tia Maria *Jamaica*
triple sec *Curaçao*
Tuaca *Italy*
Unicum bitters *Austria*

EQUIVALENTS

If you've misplaced the jigger and have to rummage through the drawer to find your measuring spoons, this chart will come in handy. Starting with a dash and ending with a gallon (the latter of concern only when you're preparing drinks in large quantities for a party or a holiday punch), the chart also serves as a basic reference.

BAR MEASUREMENTS

Amounts in this chart run from smallest to largest

AMOUNT	EQUIVALENT	EQUIVALENT
1 dash	1/16 teaspoon	
2 dashes	1/8 teaspoon	
4 dashes	1/4 teaspoon	
1 teaspoon	1/6 ounce	1/3 tablespoon
1/2 tablespoon	1/4 ounce	1 1/2 teaspoons
1 tablespoon	1/2 ounce	3 teaspoons
1/4 cup	2 ounces	4 tablespoons
3/8 cup	3 ounces	6 tablespoons
1/2 cup	4 ounces	8 tablespoons
3/4 cup	6 ounces	12 tablespoons
1 cup	8 ounces	16 tablespoons
1 cup cream	2 cups whipped	10 heaping tablespoons
Pint	2 cups	16 ounces
Quart	2 pints	32 ounces
Gallon	4 quarts	128 ounces

The Big Squeeze

How much juice you get from citrus fruits depends, naturally, on their size and variety. There are also a couple of ways to maximize the amount of juice: 1) Extract the juice when the fruits are at room temperature, not straight from the fridge. 2) Rolling the fruit back and forth a few times on the countertop will make it yield more juice because it helps loosen the pulp from the pith. Below are the approximate amounts you can expect.

1 grapefruit, medium sized	1 cup juice
1 orange, medium sized	3–4 tablespoons juice
1 lemon, medium sized	2 tablespoons juice
1 lime, medium sized	4 teaspoons juice

SCOTCH

SCOTCH

It's the smokiness of Scotch, no doubt, that makes Scotland's fabled whiskey the spirit of choice among the suave. For that, they can thank the peat fires used to heat the malted barley in the mix.

BASIC GODFATHER

Enjoy it or else

- 2 ounces Scotch
- 1 ounce amaretto

Pour Scotch and liqueur into glass filled with ice and stir.

BENSON EXPRESS

Named for a longtime Four Seasons regular

- 2 1/2 ounces 25-year-old Macallan Scotch
- Club soda

Pour Scotch into ice-filled glass. Serve with club soda as a chaser.

BLUSHING SCOT

Tinted with red grenadine

- 2 ounces Scotch
- 1 ounce Godiva White Chocolate Liqueur
- 1/2 ounce light cream
- 1/4 teaspoon grenadine

Combine ingredients in mixing glass. Add ice, shake, and strain into glass.

BOBBY BURNS MARTINI

A toast to Scotland's revered poet

- 2 ounces Scotch
- 1 ounce sweet vermouth
- 1 teaspoon Bénédictine
- Lemon twist for garnish

Pour Scotch, vermouth, and liqueur into mixing glass. Add ice and stir to chill. Strain into glass and garnish.

FANCY SCOTCH

With triple sec, orange liqueur flavored with peels from sweet and bitter oranges. Though the name means "triple dry," the taste is quite sweet

- 2 ounces Scotch
- 1/2 ounce triple sec
- 1/2 ounce fresh sour mix
- 1 dash bitters of choice

Combine ingredients in mixing glass. Add ice, shake, and strain into glass.

How the Four Seasons Was Named

It was a book of haiku meditations on time and change that gave Joseph H. Baum the idea to name a new restaurant "The Four Seasons." A visionary young hotelier who in 1952 joined Riker's Restaurant Associates (RA), Joe Baum was among those charged with creating what would become a temple of haute cuisine. The poetry struck a chord, he recalls, because "everything we wanted to do with the restaurant represented change. What is more foodlike and sophisticated than the seasons and what they bring to New York?... The theatrical season; the social season, the fall, spring, summer.... The happy idea of the seasons let us create an enduring style instead of a contemporary fashion."

RA asked their personnel to offer ideas for names based on the seasons, reaping such contenders as "Table of the Four Seasons" and "Season-o-Rama" (the latter no doubt quickly discarded). The name eventually chosen was shorn of excess, in perfect keeping with the simplicity and elegance of the 24,000-square-foot space in Mies van der Rohe's landmark building.

 ## SCOTCH OLD-FASHIONED

Fruity and sweet

- 1 teaspoon superfine sugar
- 1 slice orange
- 1 maraschino cherry
- 1 dash bitters of choice
- 2 1/2 ounces Scotch
- Still water

Muddle sugar, orange slice, cherry, and bitters in bottom of glass. Fill with ice, pour in Scotch, and top off with water.

 ## SCOTCH ON THE GRILL

A Grill Room specialty

- 3 ounces Scotch
- 1/2 ounce sweet vermouth
- 3 dashes Angostura bitters
- Lemon twist for garnish

Combine ingredients in mixing glass. Add ice and stir to chill. Strain into glass and garnish.

 ## SCOTCH ON THE ROCKS

The whiskey in all its naked glory

- 2 1/2 ounces Scotch

Fill glass three-quarters full of ice and add Scotch.

 ## SCOTCH RADKE

"The usual" for a regular named Radke: a super-premium brand

- 2 ounces Johnnie Walker Blue Label
- Club soda

Pour Scotch into glass filled with ice. Serve with club soda on ice as a chaser.

SCOTCH RICKEY

Zest for a summer day

- 2 1/2 ounces Scotch
- Juice of half a lime
- 3 ounces club soda
- Lime twist for garnish

Pour Scotch and juice into glass filled with ice. Add club soda, stir gently, and garnish.

SCOTCH SOUR

If you like, forgo the sour glass and serve on the rocks

- 2 ounces Scotch
- 1 ounce fresh sour mix
- Maraschino cherry for garnish
- Orange slice for garnish

Combine Scotch and sour mix in mixing glass. Add ice and shake. Strain into glass and garnish.

SCOTCH STINGER

Minty mixology

- 2 ounces Scotch
- 1/2 ounce white crème de menthe
- Mint sprig for garnish

Stir Scotch and liqueur in ice-filled glass, then garnish.

SCOTCH STREET

A few steps from Easy Street?

- 1 1/2 ounces Scotch
- 1/2 ounce Southern Comfort
- 1/2 ounce fresh sour mix
- Orange slice for garnish
- Maraschino cherry for garnish

Combine liquid ingredients in mixing glass. Add ice, shake, strain into glass, and garnish.

SUMMER SCOTCH COCKTAIL

Graced with grapefruit juice and vermouth

- 2 ounces Scotch
- 1/2 ounce dry vermouth
- 2 ounces grapefruit juice
- Lime slice for garnish

Combine Scotch, vermouth, and juice in mixing glass. Add ice and stir to chill. Strain into glass and garnish.

TIPPERARY SCOTCH COCKTAIL

The original Tipperary calls for Irish whiskey

- 1 ounce Scotch
- 1 ounce sweet vermouth
- 1 ounce green Chartreuse
- Maraschino cherry for garnish

Combine Scotch, vermouth, and liqueur in mixing glass. Add ice and stir to chill. Strain into glass and garnish.

BOURBON

BOURBON

America's own prized whiskey is made from corn mash—and, as y'all can't help but know, is closely tied to the South. The real thing is distilled from a corn, malt, and rye mash that has to contain at least 51 percent corn; it is then aged in charred new oak barrels.

BABYLON SOUR

*Serve straight up
or on the rocks*

- 2 1/2 ounces bourbon
- 1 ounce fresh sour mix
- 2 dashes bitters of choice
- Lemon twist for garnish

Combine bourbon, sour mix, and bitters in mixing glass. Add ice and shake. Strain into glass and garnish.

BEEKMAN PLACE

*Inspired by the nearby
good address*

- 3 ounces Very Old Barton bourbon
- 1 ounce Southern Comfort
- 2 dashes orange bitters

Combine ingredients in mixing glass. Add ice, stir to chill, and strain into glass.

BOURBON AND SODA

Bourbon with a bit of fizz

- 2 1/2 ounces bourbon
- 1 ounce club soda

Pour bourbon and soda into ice-filled glass and stir gently.

BOURBON AND SPRITE

Fizz plus lemon-lime

- 2 1/2 ounces bourbon
- 1 ounce Sprite
- Lime slice for garnish

Pour bourbon and Sprite into glass filled with ice. Stir gently and garnish.

BOURBON BREEZE

Floating your way

- 2 ounces bourbon
- 1/2 ounce blue curaçao
- 1 ounce lemon juice

Combine ingredients in mixing glass. Add ice, stir to chill, and pour contents into glass.

BOURBON CREAM FLOAT

Sorry . . . no ice cream

- 2 ounces bourbon
- 2 ounces Godiva Liqueur
- 1/2 ounce heavy cream

Combine bourbon and liqueur in mixing glass. Shake, strain into glass, and top with cream.

 BOURBON GODFATHER

The Don puts on a southern accent

- 2 1/2 ounces bourbon
- 1/2 ounce amaretto

Pour bourbon and liqueur into ice-filled glass and stir.

 BOURBON JOHN COLLINS

Another drink named John Collins calls for Scotch

- 2 ounces bourbon
- 1 ounce fresh sour mix
- Club soda
- Orange slice for garnish

Pour bourbon and lemon juice into glass filled with ice. Top with club soda to taste, stir gently, and garnish.

 BOURBON KISS I

For chocolate addicts

- 2 ounces bourbon
- 1/2 ounce dark crème de cacao
- 1/2 ounce white crème de cacao

Combine ingredients in mixing glass. Add ice, stir to chill, and strain into glass.

 BOURBON KISS 2

A.k.a. the Bourbon Chocolate Martini

- 1 1/2 ounces bourbon
- 1/2 ounce dark crème de cacao
- 1/2 ounce Godiva Liqueur

Combine ingredients in mixing glass. Add ice, stir to chill, and strain into glass.

 BOURBON MANHATTAN

A sophisticated Southerner

- 3 1/2 ounces bourbon
- 1/2 ounce dry vermouth
- Maraschino cherry

Combine liquid ingredients in mixing glass. Add ice, shake, and strain into glass. Add garnish.

BARTENDER'S TIP When mixing a drink that is shaken or stirred, Four Seasons bartenders pour the ingredients into the mixing glass of the shaker *before* filling it with ice. Adding the ice last has two advantages: First, you can measure the amounts more precisely as you pour ingredients into a mixing glass; second, your cocktail will be less likely to get watered down.

A Bar Regular: The Creative Muse

The creative dynamos working their magic behind the bar at The Four Seasons continuously reaffirm that necessity is the mother of invention. "I'd like something with gin," says a visitor, "and don't be afraid to get original." Another volunteers that he loved a drink in Aspen last month but recalls only a couple of ingredients. So the bartenders often find themselves inventing drinks to match what a customer *thinks* he had. To the mixologists' credit, customers usually prefer the

drinks served at The Four Seasons to those they remember—a tribute to the expertise of John Varriano, Greg Connolly, and Charles Corpion.

Of course, every new invention needs a name. Some of the drinks are labeled for Four Seasons regulars who have particular tastes, while others are named for customers who have requested a certain variation on a cocktail. A Mr. Ogdon ordered Scotch "his way" for so long that the Ogdon Special is now on the bar menu.

Other names come straight from the bartenders' fertile minds, with the following only three examples of dozens:

• Greg Connolly drives to and from The Four Seasons over the Queensboro Bridge, where traffic gets notoriously slow. What better to call his sloe gin–based cocktail than the logjam's alternate name: The 59th Street Bridge?

• John Varriano, who has a background in art, not only paints but admires the works of Pablo Picasso—hence the name for his cocktail laced with blue curaçao and, "for elegance," a splash of Pernod: The Blue Period.

• Charles Corpion became a topographical "equal opportunity namer" when he decided what to call his variations of the vodka cocktail Sex on the Beach. He labeled one Sex in the Mountains, the other Sex in the Valley.

BOURBON MILK PUNCH

With a touch of cinnamon

- 2 ounces bourbon
- 2 ounces milk
- 1 teaspoon
  superfine sugar
- 1/8 teaspoon cinnamon
- Cinnamon for sprinkling

Combine ingredients in mixing glass. Add ice and shake. Pour into glass and sprinkle with more cinnamon if desired.

BOURBON MIST

Bourbon, ice, and more ice

- Crushed ice
- 3 1/2 ounces
  Ten High bourbon

Fill glass with crushed ice and pour in bourbon. As ice settles, top up glass with more ice.

BOURBON OLD-FASHIONED

A classic cocktail heads south

- 1 teaspoon
  superfine sugar
- 1 orange slice
- 1 maraschino cherry
- 3 dashes
  Angostura bitters
- 2 1/2 ounces
  Maker's Mark bourbon
- 1 ounce club soda

Muddle sugar, orange, cherry, and bitters in bottom of glass. Add ice and pour in bourbon. Top with soda and stir gently.

BOURBON PIE

Rich and inviting

- 1 ounce bourbon
- 1/2 ounce dark
  crème de cacao
- 1/2 ounce
  crème de banane
- 1/2 ounce milk

Combine ingredients in mixing glass. Add ice, stir to chill, and strain into glass.

BOURBON PUNCH FIZZ

A low-alcohol drink with the slightest hint of fruit

- 1 ounce bourbon
- 1 splash fruit juice
  (orange, lemon, lime,
  pineapple, or grapefruit)
- Club soda
- Pineapple spear
  for garnish

Pour bourbon into ice-filled glass and add splash of juice. Top with club soda to taste, stir gently, and garnish.

BOURBON RICKEY

Yet another limey named Rickey

- 2 1/2 ounces bourbon
- 1/2 ounce lime juice
- Club soda
- Lime slice for garnish

Pour bourbon and juice into glass filled with ice. Top with club soda to taste, stir gently, and garnish.

BOURBON SOUR

*Tart but pleasing,
whether drunk straight up
or on the rocks*

- 3 ounces bourbon
- 1 ounce fresh sour mix
- Orange slice for garnish
- Maraschino cherry
  for garnish

Combine bourbon and sour mix in mixing glass. Add ice, shake, strain into glass, and garnish

CAESAR

A predinner treat

- 3 1/2 ounces bourbon
- 1/2 ounce Campari
- Lemon slice for garnish

Pour bourbon and Campari into glass filled with ice. Stir and garnish.

CUSTER'S LAST STAND

*Does battle with boredom.
The grenadine in this drink is
a nonalcoholic pomegranate
syrup that found its calling as
an addition to cocktails*

- 1/2 ounces
  Jim Beam bourbon
- 1/2 ounce grenadine
- 1 ounce lemon juice
- 3 dashes
  bitters of choice
- Lemon wedge for garnish

Pour all ingredients except garnish in glass filled with ice. Stir and garnish.

D. L. COCKTAIL

*Street-smart Charles
reveals a recipe kept on
the down low until now*

- 2 1/2 ounces bourbon
- 1/2 ounce sweet vermouth
- 1/2 ounce lemon juice

Pour all ingredients into glass filled with ice and stir.

DUBONNET MANHATTAN

*Take your pick of regular
Dubonnet or red*

- 3 ounces bourbon
- 1/2 ounce Dubonnet or
  Dubonnet Rouge
- 1/2 ounce dry vermouth

Combine ingredients in mixing glass. Add ice, shake, and strain into glass.

EDIE'S CHOICE

A bourbon stinger

- 2 ounces bourbon
- 1/2 ounce white
  crème de menthe

Combine bourbon and liqueur in ice-filled glass and stir.

EQUALIZER

"Dessert" after a big meal

- 2 ounces bourbon
- 1/2 ounce white
  crème de menthe
- 3 dashes Grand Marnier

Combine ingredients in mixing glass and proceed as in Dubonnet Manhattan.

FRENCH CONNECTION

Deux liqueurs française

- 1 1/2 ounces bourbon
- 1/2 ounce Pernod
- 1/2 ounce dark crème de cacao
- 1 ounce heavy cream
- Nutmeg for sprinkling

Shake with ice, strain into glass, and sprinkle nutmeg.

 ## HEADLESS JOCKEY

A Kentucky take on the Headless Horseman

- 2 ounces bourbon
- 1 dash bitters of choice
- Ginger ale

Pour bourbon into ice-filled glass. Add bitters, top with ginger ale, and stir gently.

 ## KENTUCKY KISS

Simple and smooth

- 2 ounces bourbon
- 4 ounces apricot nectar

Combine ingredients in ice-filled glass and stir.

 ## LOUISVILLE SLUGGER

Step up to the plate and sip

- 1 1/2 ounces bourbon
- 1/2 ounce orange juice
- 1/2 ounce pineapple juice
- Club soda

Pour bourbon and juices into ice-filled glass. Top with club soda to taste and stir gently.

 ## LULU'S FIZZ

Specialty of a Kentucky "hostess with the mostest"

- 2 ounces bourbon
- 2 ounces light rum
- 1/2 ounce fresh sour mix
- 3 dashes bitters of choice
- Club soda
- Maraschino cherry for garnish

Combine bourbon, rum, sour mix, and bitters in mixing glass. Add ice, shake, and pour contents into glass. Top with club soda to taste, stir gently, and garnish.

MANHATTAN COWBOY

A little bit country, a little bit man-about-town

- 2 1/2 ounces Maker's Mark bourbon
- 1/2 ounce Southern Comfort
- 1/2 ounce orange juice
- 1/2 ounce lemon juice
- Orange twist for garnish

Pour bourbon, Southern Comfort, and juices into ice-filled glass. Stir and garnish.

 ## THE MIDTOWN

Named for our very large neighborhood

- 1 ounce bourbon
- 1/2 ounce Harveys Bristol Cream
- 1/2 ounce Grand Marnier

Pour ingredients into mixing glass. Add ice, shake, and strain into glass.

MINT JULEP

The Four Seasons is located nowhere near Kentucky horse country, but that doesn't mean our bartenders aren't well acquainted with the authentic recipe for this legendary drink of the South. They also had the nerve to develop their own version—and, to much raising of southern eyebrows, even serve mint juleps in a tulip glass rather than a silver or pewter julep cup. Less elegant? Perhaps. Less impressive? Not in our Yankee opinion.

FOUR SEASONS MINT JULEP

Plain mint is preferred over peppermint or spearmint

- 6 sprigs mint
- 3 ounces bourbon
- 2 ounces fresh sour mix
- Crushed ice

Muddle mint in bottom of mixing glass. Add ice, bourbon, and sour mix. Shake and strain into glass filled with crushed ice, then serve with a straw.

DIXIE JULEP

The mint is on the side

- 2 1/2 ounces bourbon
- 1/2 teaspoon superfine sugar
- Crushed ice
- 3 mint sprigs for garnish

Combine bourbon and sugar in mixing glass. Add ice, shake, and strain into glass filled with crushed ice. Garnish with mint and serve with a straw.

CLASSIC MINT JULEP

For die-hard traditionalists

- 4 mint sprigs
- 1 teaspoon superfine sugar
- 2 teaspoons still water
- Crushed ice
- 2 1/2 ounces Kentucky Gentleman bourbon
- Mint sprig for garnish

In the bottom of a julep cup or highball glass, muddle mint and sugar with water. Fill with ice and add bourbon. Garnish with mint and serve with straw.

MOCK MINT JULEP

No muddling required

- Crushed ice
- 2 ounces bourbon
- 1/2 ounce white crème de menthe
- Mint sprig for garnish

Fill glass with crushed ice. Pour in bourbon and liqueur, stir, and garnish.

MISSION IMPOSSIBLE

A few sips, and who can say what might happen?

- 3 ounces bourbon
- 1/2 ounce lemon juice
- 1 dash bitters of choice
- 1/2 ounce still water
- Lime slice for garnish

Combine bourbon, juice, bitters, and water in mixing glass. Add ice and shake. Strain into glass and garnish.

PLYMOUTH ROCK

A libation unknown to the Pilgrims

- 2 1/2 ounces bourbon
- Juice of half a lemon
- Juice of half a lime
- 2 dashes orange bitters
- Club soda
- Lime slice for garnish

Pour bourbon and juices into ice-filled glass. Add bitters and stir. Top with club soda to taste, stir gently, and garnish.

PROHIBITION EXPRESS

Do not mix in the bathtub. The Italian liqueur sambuca, made from elderberries, gives this drink its licoricy flavor

- 2 1/2 ounces bourbon
- 1 ounce sambuca

Pour bourbon and liqueur into ice-filled glass and stir.

RUSTY SPIKE

Pointing southward

- 3 ounces bourbon
- 1 ounce Drambuie

Pour bourbon and liqueur into ice-filled glass and stir.

SEX IN THE MOUNTAINS

If a popular vodka cocktail can be called Sex on the Beach, why not this?

- 1 1/2 ounces bourbon
- 1 ounce peach schnapps
- 1 ounce orange juice
- 1/2 ounce cranberry juice

Combine ingredients in glass filled with ice and stir.

SEX IN THE VALLEY

Ditto

- 1 1/2 ounces bourbon
- 2 ounces peach schnapps
- 1/2 ounce triple sec
- 1/2 ounce pineapple juice
- 1/2 ounce cranberry juice

Pour ingredients into glass filled with ice and stir.

SOUTHERN BREEZE

With a captivating scent of fruit

- 2 ounces bourbon
- 1/2 ounce Southern Comfort
- 1/2 ounce orange juice
- 1/2 ounce cranberry juice

Combine ingredients in ice-filled glass and stir.

SOUTHERN CREAM PIE

Have a slice

- 2 1/2 ounces bourbon
- 1 teaspoon superfine sugar
- 1/2 ounce light cream
- 1/8 teaspoon nutmeg

Combine ingredients in mixing glass. Add ice, shake, and strain into glass. Sprinkle with more nutmeg, if desired.

SOUTHERN SETTLER

Meant for the morning after

- 2 ounces bourbon
- 1 ounce 7-Up or Sprite
- 1 ounce club soda
- 2 dashes bitters of choice

Combine ingredients in glass filled with ice and stir gently.

STATUE OF LIBERTY

In honor of the Lady of the Harbor's French origins

- 3 ounces bourbon
- 1/2 ounce Cointreau
- 1/2 ounce grenadine
- Maraschino cherry for garnish

Combine liquid ingredients in mixing glass. Add ice, shake, strain into glass, and garnish.

SWEET BOURBON MANHATTAN

A good late-night choice

- 3 1/2 ounces bourbon
- 1/2 ounce sweet vermouth
- Maraschino cherry for garnish

Combine liquid ingredients in mixing glass. Add ice, shake, strain into glass, and garnish.

THOROUGHBRED

With lemon-lime fizz

- 2 1/2 ounces Ten High bourbon
- 1 ounce fresh sour mix
- 1 ounce orange juice
- Sprite

Combine first three ingredients in mixing glass. Add ice, shake, and pour contents into glass. Add Sprite to taste; stir gently.

TNT

An explosion of licoricy-orange flavor

- 2 1/2 ounces bourbon
- 1/2 ounce anisette
- 1/2 ounce orange liqueur

Combine bourbon and liqueurs in ice-filled glass and stir.

THE FOUR SEASONS

WHISKEY COCKTAILS

WHISKEY COCKTAILS

Scotch and bourbon aren't the only whiskeys on the block, of course. Bartenders at The Four Seasons make good use of Irish whiskeys (lacking the smokiness of Scotch but still nice and malty); light-bodied Canadian blends; and Tennessee, rye, and other homegrown whiskeys.

ALGONQUIN

Created at the eponymous hotel by the late David Grinstead, who ended his distinguished bartending career at The Four Seasons

- 1 1/2 ounces whiskey of choice
- 1 ounce dry vermouth
- 1 ounce pineapple juice
- 1 ounce club soda

Pour whiskey, vermouth, and juice into mixing glass. Add ice and stir to chill. Strain into glass, top with club soda, and stir gently.

BLACK ROCK

Named for the investment company across 52nd Street

- 1 1/2 ounces Jameson Irish whiskey
- 1/2 ounce blue curaçao
- 1/2 ounce cognac
- Maraschino cherry for garnish

Combine whiskey, liqueur, and cognac in mixing glass. Add ice and shake. Strain into glass and garnish.

BLACKSTONE

In honor of yet another neighborhood firm

- 2 ounces whiskey of choice
- 1/2 ounce dry sherry
- 1/2 ounce fresh sour mix
- Maraschino cherry for garnish

Combine whiskey, sherry, and sour mix in mixing glass. Add ice and shake. Strain into glass and garnish.

BLUE MONDAY

Our whiskey version of the vodka classic—a toast to the weekend that was

- 2 ounces whiskey of choice
- 1/2 ounce blueberry brandy
- 1/2 ounce fresh sour mix
- Maraschino cherry for garnish

Pour whiskey, brandy, and sour mix into mixing glass. Add ice and shake. Strain into glass and garnish.

BOILERMAKER

A blast from your college past

- 1 ounce whiskey of choice
- 12 ounces beer
  of choice, chilled

Pour beer into glass,
top with whiskey, and stir.

CATCH-22

Half Irish, half Scottish

- 1 1/2 ounces Irish whiskey
- 1 1/2 ounces Scotch

Combine whiskeys in glass
filled with ice and stir.

CATSKILL COCKTAIL

Mountain cherry-picking

- 2 1/2 ounces whiskey
  of choice
- 1/2 ounce cherry brandy
- Maraschino cherry
  for garnish

Combine whiskey and brandy
in glass filled with ice. Stir
and garnish.

- - - - - - - - - - - - - - -

BARTENDER'S TIP Fruit
garnishes for cocktails
aren't just for looks—
nor are they something
to skimp on. That's why
bartenders at The Four
Seasons cut a wedge of
lemon or lime no less
than an inch wide. Slices
of lemon and orange are
also cut a bit wider—
close to half an inch.

- - - - - - - - - - - - - - -

CHARLES'S WARD EIGHT

*One of our bartenders
reinterprets an old favorite*

- 2 ounces
  Canadian whiskey
- 1/2 ounce fresh sour mix
- 1/2 ounce grenadine
- Crushed ice
- Orange slice for garnish

Pour whiskey, sour mix,
and grenadine into mixing
glass. Add ice and shake.
Strain into glass filled with
crushed ice, then garnish.
Serve with straw, if desired.

CITY STORMER

*A swirl of whiskey and
two liqueurs*

- 1 1/2 ounces whiskey
  of choice
- 1/2 ounce white
  crème de menthe
- 1/2 ounce dark
  crème de cacao

Pour whiskey and liqueurs into
ice-filled glass and stir.

COMMODORE

For imbibing on your yacht

- 2 ounces
  whiskey of choice
- 1/2 ounce Drambuie
- 1 ounce fresh sour mix
- Orange slice for garnish

Combine whiskey, liqueur,
and sour mix in mixing glass.
Add ice and shake. Strain into
ice-filled glass and garnish.

CONNOLLY COOLER

Created by . . . and named for . . . bartender Greg

- 1 1/2 ounces Tennessee whiskey
- 1/2 ounce lime juice
- 1/2 ounce orange juice
- Ginger ale
- Lime twist for garnish

Combine whiskey and juices in mixing glass. Add ice and shake. Strain into ice-filled glass, top with ginger ale to taste, stir gently, and garnish.

EAST RIVER COCKTAIL

Potent and olivey

- 2 1/2 ounces whiskey of choice
- 1/2 ounce olive juice
- 3 olives for garnish

Pour whiskey and olive juice into glass filled with ice. Stir and garnish.

52ND STREET COCKTAIL

Beneath the awning at No. 99: our front door

- 2 1/2 ounces whiskey of choice
- 1/2 ounce Southern Comfort
- Maraschino cherry for garnish

Pour whiskey and Southern Comfort into glass filled with ice. Stir and garnish.

THE 59TH STREET BRIDGE

Why the name? See page 44

- 2 ounces whiskey of choice
- 1/2 ounce Drambuie
- 1/4 ounce sloe gin

Pour whiskey, liqueur, and sloe gin into mixing glass. Add ice and shake. Strain into glass filled with ice and stir.

FOUR SEASONS SHAMROCK

Erin go bragh

- 2 ounces Irish whiskey
- 1 ounce dry vermouth
- 1 teaspoon green crème de menthe

Pour ingredients into mixing glass. Add ice, stir to chill, and strain into glass.

FOUR SEASONS WHISKEY SOUR

Our take on a classic

- 2 1/2 ounces Crown Royal whiskey
- 1 1/2 ounces fresh sour mix
- Crushed ice
- Orange slice for garnish
- Maraschino cherry for garnish

Combine whiskey and sour mix in mixing glass. Add ice and shake. Strain into glass filled with crushed ice and garnish.

HUDSON RIVER COCKTAIL

Savored by New Yorkers on either side

- 2 ounces
  whiskey of choice
- 1/2 ounce dry vermouth
- 1/2 ounce orange juice

Combine ingredients in mixing glass. Add ice, shake, and strain into glass.

IRISH COOLER

A spiked soft drink

- 2 1/2 ounces
  Irish whiskey
- 12 ounces
  7-Up or Sprite
- Lemon slice for garnish

Pour whiskey and soft drink into glass filled with ice. Stir gently and garnish.

IRISH FIXER

Tonic for the morning after. Irish Mist liqueur, based on an ancient formula, is flavored with honey and herbs

- 2 ounces Irish whiskey
- 1/2 ounce Irish Mist
- 1/4 ounce orange juice
- 1/4 ounce lemon juice
- Crushed ice

Combine whiskey, liqueur, and juices in mixing glass. Add ice, shake, and strain into glass filled with crushed ice.

KAREN'S COCKTAIL

The favorite of our restaurant manager

- 2 1/2 ounces
  blended whiskey
- 1/2 ounce anisette
- 1 dash Angostura bitters
- Lemon twist for garnish

Combine liquid ingredients in mixing glass. Add ice and stir to chill. Pour contents into glass and garnish.

LYNCHBURG LEMONADE

From Jack Daniels's Tennessee hometown

- 2 ounces Jack Daniels
  Tennessee whiskey
- 1/2 ounce triple sec
- 1 ounce fresh sour mix
- 1 1/2 ounces Sprite
- Lemon slice for garnish
- Maraschino cherry
  for garnish

Combine bourbon, triple sec, and sour mix in mixing glass. Add ice and shake. Pour into ice-filled glass and add Sprite. Stir gently and garnish.

THE MANHATTAN

Most chroniclers hold that The Manhattan Club, now located at the edge of the Theater District, is the birthplace of this 1870s rye whiskey "martini." The cocktail was a staple for the upper crust in the Gilded Age, and J. P. Morgan reportedly enjoyed a daily dose after the market closed. The Manhattan was jiggered into countless variations even back then, but the original consisted of equal parts rye and vermouth topped off with a dash of orange bitters.

FOUR SEASONS MANHATTAN

Stripped down but potent

- 2 1/2 ounces rye whiskey
- 1/2 ounce sweet vermouth
- Maraschino cherry for garnish

Pour whiskey and vermouth into mixing glass. Add ice and shake. Strain into glass and garnish.

DRY MANHATTAN

With dry vermouth and lemon

- 2 3/4 ounces rye whiskey
- 1/4 ounce dry vermouth
- Lemon twist

Pour whiskey and vermouth into mixing glass and proceed as in Four Seasons Manhattan.

PERFECT MANHATTAN

Sweet, dry . . . yin, yang

- 2 1/2 ounces rye whiskey
- 1/4 ounce sweet vermouth
- 1/4 ounce dry vermouth
- Lemon twist for garnish

Pour whiskey and vermouths into mixing glass and proceed as in Four Seasons Manhattan.

OLD-FASHIONED MANHATTAN

A marriage of two classics

- 1 maraschino cherry
- 1 orange slice
- 2 1/2 ounces rye whiskey
- 1/2 ounce sweet vermouth

Muddle cherry and orange slice in bottom of glass. Fill glass with ice, pour in whiskey and vermouth, and stir.

JONES BEACH MANHATTAN

Named for the oceanside playground on Long Island

- 2 ounces rye whiskey
- 1/2 ounce
  sweet vermouth
- 1 ounce orange juice
- Orange slice for garnish

Pour liquids into glass filled with ice. Stir and garnish.

SWEET MANHATTAN

With maraschino liqueur

- 2 1/2 ounces rye whiskey
- 1/4 ounce
  sweet vermouth
- 1/4 ounce maraschino
- Maraschino cherry
  for garnish

Pour whiskey, vermouth, and liqueur into mixing glass, then proceed as in Four Seasons Manhattan.

CHAMBORD MANHATTAN

A touch of black raspberry

- 2 1/2 ounces rye whiskey
- 1/2 ounce Chambord
- Maraschino cherry
  for garnish

Pour whiskey and liqueur into glass filled with ice. Stir and garnish.

DEE DEE'S MANHATTAN

Named for a customer who likes it tart

- 2 ounces rye whiskey
- 1/2 ounce
  sweet vermouth
- 1 ounce cranberry juice
- 2 drops lemon juice
- Orange slice
  for garnish

Combine liquid ingredients in glass filled with ice. Stir and garnish.

MOUNTED COP

*In honor of New York's
finest . . . and their steeds*

- 2 ounces whiskey of choice
- 1/2 ounce white
  crème de cacao
- 1/2 ounce heavy cream
- Nutmeg for sprinkling

Pour whiskey, liqueur, and
cream into mixing glass. Add
ice and shake. Strain into glass
and sprinkle with nutmeg.

OLD-FASHIONED

*So famous it lent its name
to a bar glass*

- 1 orange slice
- 1 maraschino cherry
- 1/2 teaspoon
  superfine sugar
- 2 1/2 ounces
  whiskey of choice
- 1 splash still water

Muddle fruit and sugar in
bottom of glass. Add ice and
pour in whiskey. Top with
water and stir.

OPENING NIGHT
COCKTAIL

Curtain up, light the lights!

- 2 ounces
  whiskey of choice
- 1 ounce Cointreau
- Lemon twist for garnish

Pour whiskey and liqueur
into glass filled with ice.
Stir and garnish.

PARK AVENUE
SOUR

*An homage to the high-
powered boulevard where
our famous building stands*

- 2 ounces whiskey of choice
- 1 ounce fresh sour mix
- Maraschino cherry
  for garnish
- Orange slice for garnish

Pour whiskey and sour mix
into mixing glass. Add ice
and shake. Strain into
glass and garnish.

PARKING METER

Ticking with flavor

- 2 1/2 ounces whiskey
  of choice
- 1/2 ounce lemon juice
- 1 dash Tabasco

Combine ingredients in mixing
glass. Add ice, shake, and pour
contents into glass.

RUSTY SCREW

*The Rusty Nail meets
the Screwdriver*

- 1 1/2 ounces
  whiskey of choice
- 1 ounce Drambuie
- 1/2 ounce orange juice
- Orange slice for garnish

Combine whiskey, liqueur,
and juice in ice-filled glass.
Stir and garnish.

RYE FIZZ

Bubbly and sweet. Pungent Angostura bitters were created in Venezuela by a German surgeon who immigrated to the country in 1918

- 2 1/2 ounces rye whiskey
- 1/2 teaspoon sugar
- 1 dash Angostura bitters
- Club soda
- Lemon twist for garnish

Combine whiskey, sugar, and bitters in mixing glass. Add ice, shake, and strain into ice-filled glass. Top with club soda to taste, stir gently, and garnish.

SEASIDE

Whiskey with a touch of gin

- 1 1/2 ounces whiskey of choice
- 1/2 ounce gin
- 1/2 ounce fresh sour mix
- Crushed ice
- 3 sprigs fresh mint for garnish

Combine whiskey, gin, and sour mix in mixing glass. Add ice and shake. Strain into ice-filled glass and garnish.

7 AND 7

Simple yet timeless

- 2 1/2 ounces Seagrams 7
- 12 ounces 7-Up or Sprite

Pour whiskey into glass filled with ice. Top with soft drink and stir gently.

SMITHTOWN

For Greg's Long Island town

- 1 1/2 ounces Jamesons Irish whiskey
- 1/2 ounce dry vermouth
- 1/2 ounce sweet vermouth
- Lemon twist for garnish

Pour whiskey and vermouths into ice-filled glass. Stir and garnish.

SUBWAY CAR

Usually fast, sometimes "sloe"

- 2 ounces whiskey of choice
- 1 ounce sloe gin
- Olive for garnish

Combine whiskey and sloe gin in glass filled with ice. Stir and garnish.

TAXI CAB

More orange than yellow

- 2 ounces whiskey of choice
- 2 ounces orange juice
- 1 tablespoon lemon juice
- Lemon twist for garnish

Combine whiskey and juices in mixing glass. Add ice and stir to chill. Strain into glass and garnish.

WHISKEY DRIVER

Not limited to golf days

- 2 ounces whiskey of choice
- 1 1/2 ounces orange juice
- Orange slice for garnish

Combine liquids in ice-filled glass. Stir and garnish.

WHISKEY

WHISKEY FIZZ

Effervescent and sweet

- 2 1/2 ounces rye whiskey
- 1/2 teaspoon sugar
- 1 dash Angostura bitters
- Crushed ice
- Club soda

Combine whiskey, sugar, and bitters in mixing glass. Add ice, shake, and strain into glass filled with crushed ice. Top with club soda to taste and stir gently.

WHISKEY GODFATHER

Hold the Brando impersonation

- 1 ounce whiskey of choice
- 1 ounce amaretto

Pour whiskey and liqueur into ice-filled glass and stir.

WHISKEY MINT COOLER

With a touch of lemon

- 1/4 ounce lemon juice
- 5 mint leaves
- 2 1/2 ounces whiskey of choice
- Mint sprig for garnish

Muddle lemon juice and mint leaves in bottom of glass. Add ice and pour in whiskey. Stir and garnish.

WHISKEY ORCHARD

For apple aficionados

- 2 ounces whiskey of choice
- 1 ounce apple brandy
- Apple slice for garnish

Pour whiskey and brandy into ice-filled glass and garnish.

WHISKEY PRES

Short for "Presbyterian". . . and light on the liqueur

- 2 ounces whiskey of choice
- Club soda
- Ginger ale

Pour whiskey into glass filled with ice. Top with equal parts club soda and ginger ale. Stir gently.

WHISKEY STINGER

Minty and cool

- 2 1/2 ounces whiskey of choice
- 1/2 ounce white crème de menthe

Combine whiskey and liqueur in an ice-filled glass and stir.

GIN

GIN

Though gin was invented by a Dutch chemist in the mid 1600s—as a medicine, no less—the English introduced it to the world. In fact, in the eyes of people everywhere this juniper berry–flavored spirit is wrapped in the British flag. It also comes in a number of varieties, with dry gin the most favored. Hail Britannia!

THE ACADEMIC

*Galliano and orange . . .
a study in good taste*

- 2 ounces gin
- 1/2 ounce Galliano
- 1/2 ounce orange juice

Combine ingredients in mixing glass. Add ice, stir to chill, and strain into glass.

ANDROMEDA

*Bit of a rocket-booster,
with gin and four liqueurs*

- 2 ounces gin
- 1 ounce
  Southern Comfort
- 1/2 ounce sloe gin
- 1/2 ounce Chambord
- 1/2 teaspoon
  blue curaçao

Combine ingredients in mixing glass. Add ice and stir to chill. Pour contents into glass or strain into martini glass.

ANGEL'S BREAST

White, whiter, whitest

- 2 ounces gin
- 1 ounce white
  crème de cacao
- 1 ounce Godiva
  White Chocolate Liqueur
- 1 ounce light cream

Pour ingredients into mixing glass. Add ice, shake, and strain into glass.

APOLLO

*Fit for a Greek god. The word
"cacao" in the liqueur's name
is French for cocoa*

- 2 1/2 ounces gin
- 1 ounce white
  crème de cacao
- 1/2 ounce blue curaçao

Combine ingredients in mixing glass. Add ice, stir to chill, and strain into glass.

APPLE SOUR

Enjoy straight up or iced

- 2 ounces gin
- 1 1/2 ounce
  sour apple liqueur
- 1 ounce fresh sour mix

Combine ingredients in mixing glass. Add ice, shake, and strain into glass.

ARCHBISHOP

A religious experience

- 2 1/2 ounces Boodles gin
- 1/2 ounce Bénédictine
- 1 dash bitters of choice

Combine ingredients in glass filled with ice and stir.

THE ARTHUR

Named for Camelot's king

- 2 1/2 ounces gin
- 1/2 ounce Grand Marnier
- 1 teaspoon lemon juice
- Orange twist for garnish

Pour gin, liqueur, and juice into mixing glass. Add ice and stir to chill. Pour contents into glass or strain into martini glass, then garnish.

ASCOT

No extravagant hat required

2 1/2 ounces gin
1/2 ounce sweet vermouth
2 dashes Angostura bitters

Combine ingredients in mixing glass. Add ice, stir to chill, and strain into glass.

ASTORIA

A jewel in Queens's crown

- 2 ounces gin
- 1 ounce white
  crème de cacao
- 1 ounce light cream

Pour ingredients into mixing glass. Add ice, shake, and strain into glass.

ASTOR PLACE

Downtown haunt of the hip

- 2 1/2 ounces gin
- 1/2 ounce Galliano
- 1 dash bitters of choice

Combine ingredients in mixing glass. Add ice, stir to chill, and strain into glass.

ATHENA

For the goddess inside

- 2 ounces gin
- 1 ounce white
  crème de menthe
- 1 ounce light cream

Pour ingredients into mixing glass. Add ice, shake, and strain into glass.

AVENUE B

Way down in Alphabet City

- 2 ounces gin
- 1 ounce white
  crème de cacao
- 1/2 ounce Drambuie

Combine ingredients in mixing glass. Add ice, stir to chill, and strain into glass.

BEE LINE

*Nectary toast to an
NYC subway line*

- 2 ounces gin
- 1/2 ounce
  peach schnapps
- 1/2 ounce
  apricot brandy

Combine ingredients in mixing
glass. Add ice, stir to chill, and
strain into glass.

BETTE'S CHOICE

*The favorite of a regular. The
licorice-flavored Pernod, from
France, succeeded absinthe as
the bohemian drink of choice*

- 2 1/2 ounces gin
- 1/2 ounce Pernod
- 1/2 teaspoon grenadine

Pour ingredients into mixing
glass. Add ice, stir to chill,
and strain into glass.

BILBO B.

One rich little Hobbit

- 2 ounces gin
- 1 ounce Scotch
- 1/2 ounce dark
  crème de cacao
- 1/2 ounce heavy cream

Combine ingredients in mixing
glass. Add ice, shake, and pour
contents into glass.

BLEECKER STREET

*As enticing as Greenwich
Village's street of wonders*

- 2 1/2 ounces gin
- 1/2 ounce Grand Marnier
- 1/2 ounce lime juice
- 1/2 teaspoon
  superfine sugar
- Orange twist for garnish

Combine gin, liqueur, juice,
and sugar in mixing glass.
Add ice and shake. Strain into
glass and garnish.

BLOODY BRIT

Cheers, mate!

- 2 1/2 ounces Beefeater
  dry gin
- 3 ounces tomato juice
- 5 dashes
  Worcestershire sauce
- 3 dashes Tabasco
- Oyster for garnish

Combine liquid ingredients
in ice-filled glass, stir, and
garnish with raw oyster.

BLUE SKY

Tinted with blue curaçao

- 2 ounces gin
- 1/2 ounce blue curaçao
- 1/2 ounce
  orange liqueur

Pour ingredients into glass
filled with ice and stir.

GIN

BRAVEHEART

British gin, Scottish whiskey

- 2 1/2 ounces
  Gordon's London dry gin
- 1 teaspoon Scotch
- Lemon twist for garnish

Pour gin and Scotch into mixing glass. Add ice and stir to chill. Strain into glass and garnish.

CAROUSEL

May set you spinning

- 2 ounces gin
- 1 ounce white crème de cacao
- 2 dashes grenadine
- 1 ounce light cream

Combine ingredients in mixing glass. Add ice, shake, and strain into glass.

BRONX TALE

A variation on the classic Bronx Cocktail

- 2 ounces gin
- 1 ounce orange juice
- 1 teaspoon dry vermouth

Combine ingredients in mixing glass. Add ice, shake, and strain into glass.

CATAPULT

Hook feet around chair legs while sipping

- 2 ounces gin
- 1 ounce vodka
- 1 ounce Campari
- 1 ounce orange juice

Combine ingredients in glass filled with ice and stir.

BROOKLYN NITE

Good times across the bridge

- 2 ounces gin
- 1 ounce dark rum
- 1 ounce Cointreau
- 1 teaspoon lemon juice

Pour ingredients into ice-filled glass and stir.

CENTURY

A timeless mix

- 2 ounces gin
- 1 ounce grapefruit juice
- 1/2 ounce Chambord
- 1/2 ounce triple sec

Combine ingredients in mixing glass. Add ice, shake, and strain into glass.

GIN

CHANDELIER

With plenty of sparkle

- 2 ounces gin
- 1/2 ounce dry vermouth
- 1/2 ounce Pernod
- 2 dashes orange bitters
- Crushed ice

Combine ingredients in mixing glass. Add ice, stir to chill, and strain into glass filled with crushed ice.

THE CLOISTERS

A garden of delights

- 1 1/2 ounces gin
- 1/2 ounce sweet vermouth
- 1 ounce Campari
- 1 teaspoon Bénédictine
- 1 teaspoon Pernod
- 2 dashes bitters of choice
- Orange twist for garnish

Combine all ingredients except garnish in mixing glass. Add ice and stir to chill. Strain into glass and garnish.

COMMEDIA DELL'ARTE

Named for a style of Italian comedy dating from the 16th century

- 2 ounces gin
- 1 ounce Galliano
- 1/2 ounce black sambuca

Combine gin and liqueurs in mixing glass. Add ice, stir to chill, and strain into glass.

THE CRATER

A Four Seasons special that "flies you to the moon"

- 2 ounces gin
- 1 ounce dark crème de cacao
- 1/2 ounce Chambord
- 1/2 ounce heavy cream

Combine ingredients in mixing glass. Add ice, shake, and strain into glass.

CRUSADER

Spread the word

- 2 ounces gin
- 1 ounce white crème de cacao
- 1 ounce green Chartreuse

Pour ingredients into mixing glass. Add ice and stir to chill. Pour contents into glass or strain into martini glass.

DAMSEL

Gin with vodka and fruity flavors . . . a fair lady indeed

- 1 ounce Tanqueray gin
- 1 ounce vodka
- 1 ounce Cointreau
- 1 ounce orange juice
- 1 ounce cranberry juice
- Orange twist for garnish

Combine all ingredients except garnish in mixing glass. Add ice and shake. Pour contents into glass and garnish.

GIN

DELANCEY

*Olivey treat called after
the historic street on NYC's
Lower East Side*

- 2 ounces gin
- 1 ounce Absolut Peppar
- 1 ounce olive juice
- 3 olives for garnish

Combine gin, vodka, and
olive juice in mixing glass.
Add ice and stir to chill.
Strain into glass and garnish.

 DELMONICO

*Brandy-laced cocktail born
at the famous hotel*

- 1 1/2 ounces gin
- 1/2 ounce brandy
- 1/2 ounce
  sweet vermouth
- 2 dashes
  Angostura bitters

Pour ingredients into mixing
glass. Add ice, stir to chill,
and strain into glass.

DREAMY

Aptly named

- 1 ounce gin
- 1 ounce vodka
- 1 ounce Godiva
  White Chocolate Liqueur
- 1 ounce white
  crème de cacao

Combine all ingredients in
mixing glass. Add ice and
stir to chill. Pour contents
into glass or strain into
martini glass.

 **EAST END
AVENUE**

*Sherried gin named for the
silk-stocking district street*

- 1 1/2 ounces gin
- 1/2 ounce dry sherry
- 1 ounce Lillet Blanc
- Crushed ice
- Lemon twist for garnish

Combine liquid ingredients in
mixing glass. Add ice and
shake. Pour into glass filled
with crushed ice and garnish.

 ELVIRA

*The sultry vamp(ire)'s
martini of choice*

- 2 ounces gin
- 1/2 ounce
  dry vermouth
- 1 teaspoon blue curaçao
- 2 dashes orange bitters

Combine ingredients in mixing
glass. Add ice, stir to chill, and
strain into glass.

EQUESTRIAN

*A gin and tonic for
the horsey set*

- 2 ounces Bombay gin
- 2 ounces tonic water
- 1 dash Grand Marnier
- 2 dashes bitters of choice
- Lime wedge for garnish

Combine all ingredients except
garnish in glass filled with ice.
Stir and garnish.

FAIRY TALE

As enchanting as it sounds

- 2 ounces gin
- 1/2 ounce apricot brandy
- 1/2 ounce peach schnapps
- 1/2 ounce Lillet Rouge
- Crushed ice
- Orange twist for garnish

Combine liquid ingredients in glass filled with crushed ice. Stir and garnish.

FAUST

Hot as the devil

- 4 ounces gin
- 3 dashes Tabasco
- Chili pepper for garnish

Pour gin into glass and add Tabasco. Stir and garnish.

FLORENTINE

Best savored in a piazza in Florence

- 1 1/2 ounces gin
- 1 ounce Campari
- 1/2 ounce grapefruit juice
- 1/2 ounce Cynar

Combine ingredients in glass filled with ice and stir.

GENTLE PINK

Gin and tonic with bitters

- 2 ounces gin
- 4 ounces tonic water
- 3 dashes bitters of choice
- Lemon twist for garnish

Combine liquids in ice-filled glass. Stir and garnish.

CIN AND TONIC

A classic among classics

- 2 ounces Gordon's London dry gin
- 4 ounces tonic water
- Lime wedge for garnish

Pour gin and tonic into ice-filled glass. Stir and garnish.

CIN DAISY

In cocktail lingo, daisy means slightly sour

- 3 ounces gin
- 1 1/2 ounces fresh sour mix
- 3 dashes grenadine
- Orange slice for garnish
- Maraschino cherry for garnish

Combine gin, sour mix, and grenadine in mixing glass. Add ice and shake. Pour contents into glass and garnish.

CIN FIZZ

Bubbly and tart

- 2 1/2 ounces gin
- 1 ounce sour mix
- 4 ounces club soda

Combine gin and sour mix in mixing glass. Add ice and shake. Strain into glass, top with club soda, and stir gently.

GINGERLY

Gin plus ginger

- 3 ounces gin
- 5 ounces ginger ale
- Lemon wedge for garnish

Pour gin and ginger ale into glass filled with ice. Stir gently and garnish.

GIN GIBSON

The famous onion-pickler

- 3 ounces gin
- 1/2 ounce dry vermouth
- 3 cocktail onions
  for garnish

Pour gin and vermouth into mixing glass. Add ice and stir to chill. Strain into glass and garnish.

GIN GIMLET

An antique (in the good sense)

- 3 ounces gin
- 1/2 ounce Roses lime juice
- Lemon wedge for garnish

Pour gin and juice into mixing glass. Add ice and stir to chill. Strain into glass and garnish.

GIN MADRAS

Closer to the fruit stand than to India

- 3 ounces Bombay gin
- 2 ounces orange juice
- 2 ounces cranberry juice

Pour gin and juices into glass filled with ice and stir.

GIN PRESBYTERIAN

Respectably light on the gin

- 2 ounces gin
- 3 ounces club soda
- 3 ounces ginger ale

Pour gin, soda, and ginger ale into glass filled with ice. Stir gently.

GIN SOUR

A bracing draft

- 3 ounces gin
- 1 ounce fresh sour mix
- Orange slice for garnish
- Maraschino cherry
  for garnish

Combine gin and sour mix in mixing glass. Add ice and shake. Pour contents into glass and garnish.

GOLDEN DROP

With a touch of dry vermouth and Scotch

- 3 1/2 ounces
  Tanqueray 10 gin
- 1 teaspoon
  dry vermouth
- 3 drops Scotch
- Lemon twist or olive
  for garnish

Pour gin, vermouth, and Scotch into mixing glass. Add ice and stir to chill. Strain into glass and garnish.

GIN

GRAND TOUR

Flavorful equal-parts cocktail

- 2 ounces gin
- 2 ounces Campari
- 2 ounces orange juice

Combine ingredients in glass filled with ice and stir.

GREEN RIVER

"Green" meaning Chartreuse in this case. This herb- and spice-crammed liqueur was created by French Carthusian monks in the 16th century

- 2 1/2 ounces gin
- 1/2 ounce
  green Chartreuse
- 1/2 ounce
  yellow Chartreuse

Pour gin and liqueurs into mixing glass. Add ice, stir to chill, and strain into glass.

GREEN WIDOW

Gin and melon liqueur splashed with champagne

- 2 1/2 ounces gin
- 1 ounce Midori
- 1/2 ounce
  fresh sour mix
- 1 splash champagne

Combine gin, liqueur, and sour mix in mixing glass. Add ice and shake. Strain into glass and splash with champagne.

HAUNTED BRIDE

Named for bar patron second-guessing her engagement

- 1 1/2 ounces gin
- 1 ounce dry vermouth
- 1/2 ounce Bénédictine
- 1 teaspoon Pernod
- 2 dashes bitters of choice

Combine ingredients in mixing glass. Add ice, stir to chill, and strain into glass.

HOMER'S CHOICE

Did ouzo inspire the Greek poet?

- 2 1/2 ounces gin
- 1 ounce ouzo

Pour gin and ouzo into mixing glass. Add ice, stir to chill, and strain into glass.

KATE'S FAVE

Choice of a lady who lunches

- 2 ounces Boodles gin
- 1 ounce orange liqueur
- 1 ounce Roses lime juice

Combine ingredients in glass filled with ice and stir.

LATIN TWIST

Gin with tequila and rum

- 1 ounce gin
- 1 ounce tequila
- 1 ounce rum
- 1 ounce Cointreau
- 1/2 ounce blue curaçao
- Orange slice for garnish

Pour liquid ingredients into ice-filled glass. Stir and garnish.

GIN

THE MARTINI

Theories on the origin of this "cocktail of cocktails" could fill a small book, so we'd rather offer a tip: Fill your martini glass with crushed ice as you prepare the drink, then discard the ice before pouring. Water is often added to the glass to hasten the process, but unless you dry the glass before using it you'll end up with a less-than-perfect drink. For more martinis, see Vodka Martinis (page 90) and index.

GIN MARTINI

The classic

- 3 1/2 ounces Tanqueray dry gin
- 1 teaspoon dry vermouth
- Lemon twist or olive for garnish

Pour gin and vermouth into mixing glass. Add ice and shake. Strain into chilled glass and garnish.

CHATEAU MARTINI

With a touch of raspberry

- 3 ounces gin
- 1/2 ounce Chambord
- Orange twist for garnish

Pour gin and liqueur into mixing glass and proceed as in Gin Martini.

SOHO MARTINI

A little more complex

- 2 1/2 ounces gin
- 1/2 ounce Chambord
- 1 ounce sour mix
- Lemon twist for garnish

Combine gin, liqueur, and sour mix in mixing glass and proceed as in Gin Martini.

NOHO MARTINI

A lighter martini

- 2 ounces gin
- 2 ounces pineapple juice
- 1/2 ounce Chambord
- Pineapple spear for garnish

Pour gin, juice, and liqueur into mixing glass and proceed as in Gin Martini.

DIRTY GIN MARTINI

Extra olive flavor

- 3 ounces gin
- 1/2 ounce olive juice
- 1 dash dry vermouth
- 3 olives for garnish

Pour gin, juice, and vermouth into mixing glass and proceed as in Gin Martini.

LONG ISLAND ICED TEA

Not for the faint of heart

- 1/2 ounce gin
- 1/2 ounce rum
- 1/2 ounce vodka
- 1/2 ounce Cointreau
- 1/2 ounce tequila
- 1 ounce fresh sour mix
- 3 ounces Coca-Cola

Combine all ingredients except cola in mixing glass. Add ice and shake. Strain into glass filled with ice. Top with cola and stir gently.

THE MONK

A Bénédictine-laced drink on which to meditate

- 2 ounces gin
- 1 ounce Bénédictine
- 2 ounces orange juice

Combine ingredients in glass filled with ice and stir.

NAPOLEON

Très français

- 3 ounces gin
- 1/2 ounce Dubonnet Rouge
- 1/2 ounce Grand Marnier

Pour gin and liqueurs into mixing glass. Add ice, stir to chill, and strain into glass.

NATURE GIRL

Free-spirited and alluring

- 2 ounces gin
- 1 ounce triple sec
- 1 teaspoon blue curaçao
- 1 dash orange bitters

Combine ingredients in mixing glass. Add ice, stir to chill, and strain into glass.

NEGRONI

The Campari classic, served straight up or on the rocks

- 2 ounces gin
- 1 1/2 ounces Campari
- 1/2 ounce sweet vermouth
- Orange twist for garnish

Combine gin, Campari, and vermouth in mixing glass. Add ice and stir to chill. Strain into martini glass or ice-filled rocks glass and garnish.

ORANGE BLOSSOM

Grandmother of the beloved Screwdriver

- 2 ounces Gordons gin
- 2 ounces orange juice
- 1 teaspoon superfine sugar
- Orange twist for garnish

Combine all ingredients except garnish in mixing glass. Add ice and shake. Strain into glass and garnish.

PARIS OPERA

A taste of the Right Bank

- 2 ounces
  Tanqueray 10 gin
- 1 ounce
  Dubonnet Rouge
- 3 dashes orange bitters
- Orange twist for garnish

Combine gin, Dubonnet, and bitters in mixing glass. Add ice and stir to chill. Strain into glass and garnish.

PINK LADY I

Dates from the Art Deco era

- 2 ounces gin
- 1 ounce white
  crème de cacao
- 1 teaspoon grenadine
- 1/2 ounce heavy cream

Combine all ingredients in mixing glass. Add ice, shake, and strain into glass.

PINK LADY 2

A cherry-flavored variation on the classic

- 2 ounces gin
- 1 teaspoon
  cherry brandy
- 1 teaspoon grenadine
- 1/2 ounce heavy cream

Combine ingredients in mixing glass. Add ice, shake, and strain into glass.

PINK PANTHER

Splashed with champagne

- 2 ounces gin
- 1 ounce Campari
- 1/2 ounce
  grapefruit juice
- 1/2 ounce champagne

Combine gin, Campari, and juice in mixing glass. Add ice and shake. Strain into glass and top with champagne.

PINK PUSSYCAT

Almond-flavored indulgence

- 2 ounces gin
- 1 ounce
  crème de noyaux
- 3 ounces pineapple juice

Combine ingredients in mixing glass. Add ice and stir to chill. Pour contents into glass or strain into martini glass.

PINK ROSE

Served in a sugar-rimmed glass

- 1 teaspoon
  powdered sugar
- 1 lime wedge
- 2 ounces gin
- 1 ounce apricot brandy
- 1 ounce lime juice

Spread powdered sugar on a clean surface. Moisten rim of glass with lime wedge and dip into sugar. Combine gin, brandy, and juice into mixing glass. Add ice, stir to chill, and carefully strain into glass.

GIN

PINK SQUIRREL

The furry-tailed one's nut of choice: the almond

- 2 ounces gin
- 1 ounce crème de noyaux
- 1 teaspoon grenadine
- 1 ounce light cream

Pour ingredients into mixing glass. Add ice, shake, and strain into glass.

QUEEN'S RUBY

Tinted with cherry brandy

- 2 ounces Barton London extra dry gin
- 1/2 ounce cherry brandy
- 1 teaspoon sweet vermouth

Combine gin, brandy, and vermouth in mixing glass. Add ice, stir to chill, and strain into glass.

THE POOLSIDE

Two liqueurs share billing in this Pool Room favorite

- 2 ounces gin
- 1/2 ounce amaretto
- 1/2 teaspoon blue curaçao
- Orange twist for garnish

Pour gin and liqueurs into glass filled with ice. Stir and garnish.

ROOT BEER HIGHBALL

The soft drink dresses up

- 2 ounces gin
- 1 ounce fresh sour mix
- 1 teaspoon Galliano
- 3 ounces root beer
- Orange twist for garnish

Combine gin, sour mix, and Galliano in mixing glass. Add ice, shake, and pour contents into glass. Top with root beer, stir gently, and garnish.

QUEEN MUM

British to the core

- 2 ounces Boodles gin
- 3 ounces Pimm's No. 1
- 1 ounce orange juice
- 2 ounces ginger ale
- Maraschino cherry for garnish

Pour gin, Pimm's, and juice into glass filled with ice. Top with ginger ale, stir gently, and garnish.

SERAPHIM

Fit for an angel

- 2 ounces gin
- 1 ounce dry vermouth
- 1 ounce crème de cassis
- Lemon twist for garnish

Pour gin, vermouth, and cassis into glass filled with ice. Stir and garnish.

Paging Pablo Picasso

The Bronfman family, who built New York City's Seagram Building and actively participated in the development of its ambitious new restaurant, sought in the late 1950s to display the work of some of the world's finest modern artists, including Pablo Picasso. When contacted, Picasso declined to create a wished-for large painting for the Pool Room, pleading too little time. Instead, the artist offered a curtain designed for the Paris production of the ballet *The Three-Cornered Hat*—a prize that had been promised to New York's Museum of Modern Art but was found to be too large for the museum's walls.

The Bronfmans jumped at the chance, buying the curtain to hang in the Pool Room of The Four Seasons. But Restaurant Associates vice president Joe Baum had reservations about its placement. "It depicted a bullfight," he explained, "and I just didn't think that would go down well with customers dining on tournedos of beef." As a result, the Picasso curtain was hung on a 20-foot-high marble wall in the spacious corridor between the restaurant's Pool Room and Grill Room.

Nothing lasts forever—and should the Picasso curtain ever vacate the space, the work of another famous artist will take its place. Hanging fine art is a Four Seasons tradition, and in 1961 the restaurant was the scene of an important exhibition of works by modern masters. Still today, art welcomes guests entering on 52nd Street from the moment they step into the lobby.

SEXY MAIDEN

The head-turner with the citrusy perfume. Cointreau, while French, is made from the peels of oranges from Curaçao and Spain

- 2 1/2 ounces gin
- 1 ounce Cointreau
- 1 teaspoon blue curaçao
- 1 ounce fresh sour mix
- 1 ounce grapefruit juice

Combine all ingredients in mixing glass. Add ice, shake, and strain into glass.

SINGAPORE SLING

Created more than a century ago at the legendary Raffles Hotel in Singapore

- 2 1/2 ounces gin
- 1/2 ounce cherry brandy
- 1 ounce fresh sour mix
- 5 ounces club soda
- Maraschino cherry for garnish
- Orange slice for garnish

Combine gin, brandy, and sour mix in mixing glass. Add ice and shake. Strain into ice-filled glass and top with club soda. Stir gently and garnish.

SOUTH SIDE COCKTAIL

A minty vintage cocktail

- 3 mint leaves
- 1 teaspoon superfine sugar
- 2 ounces gin
- 1 1/2 ounces lemon juice
- Mint sprig for garnish

Muddle leaves and sugar in bottom of mixing glass. Pour in gin and juice. Add ice and stir to chill. Strain into glass and garnish.

TOM COLLINS

One for the ages

- 2 ounces gin
- 1 ounce fresh sour mix
- 3 ounces club soda
- Maraschino cherry for garnish
- Orange slice for garnish

Combine gin and sour mix in mixing glass. Add ice and shake. Strain into glass filled with ice and top with club soda. Stir gently and garnish.

TRITON

Three liqueurs put you over the moon: Neptune's!

- 2 ounces gin
- 1 ounce triple sec
- 1 ounce white crème de cacao
- 1/2 teaspoon blue curaçao

Combine ingredients in mixing glass. Add ice, stir to chill, and strain into glass.

GIN

VODKA

VODKA

Distilled from grains, fruits, or vegetables (potatoes and beets, for two), vodka has eclipsed gin in cocktail after cocktail. Its very purity —no aroma, little taste—makes it perfect for mixing with liqueurs and other tools of the bartender's trade. The spirit we think of as Russian is even more popular now that flavored vodkas are sold.

ABRA CADABRA

Works its magic sip by sip

- 2 ounces vodka
- 1/2 ounce peach schnapps
- 1/2 ounce apricot brandy
- 1 ounce pineapple juice

Combine ingredients in mixing glass. Add ice, stir to chill, and strain into glass.

ALPINE SUNSET

Orangy pink, thanks to Campari and peach

- 2 ounces vodka
- 2 ounces Campari
- 1 ounce peach schnapps
- 2 ounces orange juice
- Orange slice for garnish

Pour liquid ingredients into mixing glass. Add ice and shake. Pour contents into glass and garnish.

AMBROSIA

Fruity and rich

- 2 ounces vodka
- 1 ounce apricot schnapps
- 1 ounce peach juice
- 1/2 ounce light cream

Combine ingredients in mixing glass. Add ice, shake, and strain into glass.

ANNA KARENINA

Doomed heroine, sprightly drink

- 2 ounces vodka
- 2 ounces cranberry juice
- 4 ounces club soda
- Lime wedge for garnish

Pour vodka and juice into ice-filled glass. Top with club soda, stir gently, and garnish.

VODKA

AZTEC GOLD

With Cuervo Gold and rum

- 1 ounce Absolut
- 1 ounce José Cuervo
  Gold tequila
- 1 ounce Mount Gay rum
- 1 ounce pineapple juice

Combine ingredients in
mixing glass. Add ice, stir to
chill, and strain into glass.

BANANARAMA

Mellow yellow

- 2 ounces vodka
- 1 ounce
  crème de banane
- 1/2 ounce white
  crème de cacao
- 1/2 ounce light cream
- 2 drops yellow
  food coloring

Combine ingredients in
mixing glass. Add ice, shake,
and strain into glass.

BANANA SPLIT

Roll up sleeves and dig in

- 1 ounce vodka
- 1 ounce
  crème de banane
- 1 ounce Godiva
  White Chocolate Liqueur
- 1/2 ounce
  strawberry syrup
- 1/2 ounce heavy cream
- Strawberry for garnish

Combine liquid ingredients in
mixing glass. Add ice, shake,
strain into glass, and garnish.

BIRTH OF VENUS

*Sensual, like Botticelli's
painting of the same name*

- 2 ounces vodka
- 1 ounce Cointreau
- 1 teaspoon blue curaçao
- 1 ounce peach juice
- 1 ounce champagne

Combine vodka, liqueurs,
and juice in mixing glass.
Add ice and stir to chill.
Strain into glass, top with
champagne, and stir gently.

BLACK RUSSIAN

*Flavored with Kahlúa
or Tia Maria*

- 2 ounces vodka
- 1 ounce coffee liqueur
- 1 dash lemon juice

Combine vodka and liqueur in
glass filled with ice, add dash
of lemon juice, and stir.

BLOODY BULLSHOT

*Take one for a hangover
and call us in the morning*

- 2 ounces vodka
- 2 ounces beef broth
- 1 ounce tomato juice
- 1 teaspoon
  Worcestershire sauce
- 1/4 teaspoon lemon juice
- 3 dashes Tabasco

Combine ingredients in
mixing glass. Add ice, shake,
and pour contents in glass.

VODKA

BLOODY CAESAR

Avoid in the Ides of March

- 2 1/2 ounces vodka
- 3 ounces tomato juice
- 3 dashes Tabasco
- 4 dashes clam juice
- Salt and pepper to taste
- Lime slice for garnish
- Shelled clam for garnish

Combine all ingredients except lime juice and clam juice in glass filled with ice. Stir and garnish.

BLOODY MARY

Queen of the Brunch

- 2 ounces Smirnoff vodka
- 4 ounces tomato juice
- 1 tablespoon Worcestershire sauce
- 1 dash Tabasco
- Lime slice for garnish

Combine liquid ingredients in glass filled with ice. Stir and garnish.

BLUE ANGEL

Heavenly

- 2 ounces vodka
- 1 ounce blue curaçao
- 1 ounce white crème de cacao

Pour ingredients into mixing glass. Add ice, stir to chill, and strain into glass.

BLUE APE

A banana-flavored buzz

- 2 ounces vodka
- 1 ounce crème de banane
- 1 ounce white crème de cacao
- 1/2 teaspoon blue curaçao

Combine ingredients in mixing glass. Add ice, stir to chill, and strain into glass.

BLUEBIRD

Simple and pretty

- 3 ounces vodka
- 1 ounce blue curaçao

Pour vodka and liqueur into mixing glass. Add ice, stir to chill, and strain into glass.

BLUE INCA

Flavored with tequila

- 2 ounces vodka
- 1 ounce silver tequila
- 1 ounce light rum
- 1 ounce blue curaçao

Pour all ingredients into mixing glass. Add ice, stir to chill, and strain into glass.

BLUE ORANGE

With blue curaçao and Cointreau

- 2 ounces vodka
- 1 ounce blue curaçao
- 1 ounce Cointreau

Pour ingredients into mixing glass. Add ice, stir to chill, and strain into glass.

THE BLUE PERIOD

Bartender John's admiring salute to Picasso

- 2 ounces Ketel One vodka
- 1 ounce Southern Comfort
- 1/2 ounce Pernod
- 1/2 ounce blue curaçao
- 1/2 ounce Chambord

Pour all ingredients into mixing glass. Add ice, stir to chill, and strain into glass.

BULLSHOT

Hearty and spicy

- 2 ounces vodka
- 2 ounces beef broth
- 1 teaspoon Worcestershire sauce
- 1/4 teaspoon lemon juice
- 3 dashes Tabasco
- Lime slice for garnish

Combine liquid ingredients in mixing glass. Add ice and shake. Pour contents into glass and garnish.

CANDY CANE

For Christmas cheer

- 1/2 ounce vodka
- 1/2 ounce Absolut Peppar
- 1 ounce sambuca
- 1 ounce white crème de menthe
- 1 ounce white crème de cacao

Pour all ingredients into mixing glass. Add ice, stir to chill, and strain into glass.

CAPE COD

One of the classics, originally known as the Cape Codder

- 2 ounces vodka
- 3 ounces cranberry juice

Pour vodka and juice into glass filled with ice and stir.

CAPRI

As seductive as the isle

- 1 ounce vodka
- 2 ounces Campari
- 1 ounce grapefruit juice
- 1 ounce apricot brandy
- 3 ounces club soda

Pour all ingredients except club soda into mixing glass. Add ice and shake. Pour contents into glass, top with club soda, and stir gently.

CATHERINE THE GREAT

Russian Empress smitten with France and Italy. The latter is home to the apéritif Campari, named for the Milanese restaurateur who created it

- 2 ounces vodka
- 2 ounces Campari
- 1/2 ounce Pernod
- 3 ounces club soda

Pour vodka, Campari, and Pernod into ice-filled glass and stir. Top with club soda and stir gently.

CELLO'S DREAM

Heady concoction named for John's Yorkshire terrier

- 1 ounce vodka
- 1 ounce white crème de cacao
- 1 ounce Godiva White Chocolate Liqueur
- 1/2 ounce Chambord
- 1/2 ounce light cream

Combine ingredients in mixing glass. Add ice, shake, and strain into glass.

CHELSEA

As arty as the NYC nabe

- 2 ounces vodka
- 1 ounce apricot brandy
- 1 ounce peach juice
- 4 ounces club soda

Pour vodka, brandy, and juice into ice-filled glass. Top with club soda and stir gently.

CHERRY PIE

Yum-yum

- 2 ounces vodka
- 1 ounce brandy
- 1 ounce cherry brandy

Combine ingredients in mixing glass. Add ice, stir to chill, and strain into glass.

CHINATOWN

In Manhattan, Chinatown blurs into Little Italy

- 2 ounces vodka
- 1 ounce sambuca
- 1 ounce fresh peach juice
- 4 ounces club soda
- Lychee for garnish

Pour vodka, sambuca, and juice into ice-filled glass. Top with club soda, stir gently, and garnish.

CÎROC ROCKS

With Cîroc grape vodka

- 2 ounces Cîroc vodka
- 1/4 ounce Grand Marnier
- 1/4 ounce fresh sour mix
- 1 splash champagne
- 3 red grapes for garnish

Shake all ingredients but grapes and champagne. Pour, add champagne, and garnish.

COASTAL BREEZE

Rummy and refreshing

- 2 ounces vodka
- 2 ounces light rum
- 1 ounce blue curaçao
- 2 ounces pineapple juice

Pour ingredients into glass filled with ice and stir.

VODKA

THE COSMOPOLITAN

A decked-out cranberry cooler, the Cosmopolitan made a fashionably late entrance to the scene near the end of the 1980s. Within a decade it had elbowed its way past other newcomers to become one of the most-ordered mixed drinks in the U.S.A.—no small feat, given our country's status as hub of the cocktail universe.

COSMOPOLITAN

The trend-making original

- 2 ounces vodka
- 1 ounce Cointreau
- 1/2 ounce cranberry juice
- 1/2 ounce fresh sour mix
- Lemon twist for garnish

Combine all ingredients except garnish in mixing glass. Add ice and shake. Strain into glass and garnish.

LEMON COSMOPOLITAN

A sharper version

- 2 ounces lemon-flavored vodka
- 1 ounce Cointreau
- 1 ounce cranberry juice
- 1/2 ounce lemon juice
- Lemon twist for garnish

Combine liquid ingredients in mixing glass and proceed as in Cosmopolitan.

ORANGE COSMOPOLITAN

For orange lovers

- 2 ounces orange-flavored vodka
- 1 ounce Cointreau
- 1 ounce cranberry juice
- 1 ounce fresh sour mix
- Orange twist for garnish

Combine liquid ingredients in mixing glass and proceed as in Cosmopolitan.

RASMOPOLITAN

Jazzed up with raspberry

- 2 ounces raspberry-flavored vodka
- 1 ounce Cointreau
- 1 ounce cranberry juice
- 1 ounce fresh sour mix
- Lemon twist for garnish

Combine liquid ingredients in mixing glass and proceed as in Cosmopolitan.

VODKA

CREAMSICLE

Anything but childish

- 2 ounces vodka
- 1 ounce triple sec
- 1 ounce orange juice
- 1 ounce heavy cream

Pour all ingredients into mixing glass. Add ice, shake, and strain into glass.

 CREAMY DREAM

Visions of black currant and orange

- 2 ounces vodka
- 1 ounce Grand Marnier
- 1/2 ounce crème de cassis
- 1/2 ounce light cream

Combine ingredients in mixing glass. Add ice, shake, and strain into glass.

CUTER THAN

The fruit of a friendly bout of mixology one-upsmanship with a cute female customer who'd done a little bartending

- 1 1/2 ounces vodka
- 1 ounce Southern Comfort
- 1/2 ounce Galliano
- 1/2 ounce apricot liqueur
- 1/2 ounce cranberry juice
- Orange twist for garnish

Pour vodka, Southern Comfort, liqueurs, and juice into mixing glass. Add ice and stir to chill. Strain into glass and garnish.

 DELILAH

Colorful cocktail as tempting as its biblical namesake

- 2 ounces Stoli Ohranj
- 1 ounce Cointreau
- 1 ounce white crème de cacao
- 1/2 teaspoon grenadine

Combine ingredients in mixing glass. Add ice, stir to chill, and strain into glass.

 DIRTY BLONDE

But not exactly cheap

- 2 ounces vodka
- 1 ounce Johnnie Walker Gold Label
- 1 ounce Drambuie

Combine ingredients in mixing glass. Add ice, stir to chill, and strain into glass.

 DIRTY MARY

In cocktail lingo, dirty means "with olive juice"—so no maligning dear old Mary

- 2 1/2 ounces vodka
- 3 ounces tomato juice
- 1/2 ounce olive juice
- 4 dashes Worcestershire sauce
- 3 dashes Tabasco
- 3 olives for garnish

Combine liquid ingredients in glass filled with ice, stir, and garnish.

FLIRTINI

Not relegated to singles nights

- 1 1/2 ounces vodka
- 1/2 ounce triple sec
- 1/2 ounce cranberry juice
- 1/2 ounce lemon juice
- 1/2 teaspoon sugar
- 1 ounce champagne
- Orange twist for garnish

Combine vodka, liqueur, juices, and sugar in mixing glass. Add ice and shake. Strain into glass and top with champagne. Stir gently and garnish.

 FUDGESICLE

The grown-up version of a lasting favorite

- 2 ounces vodka
- 1/2 ounce dark crème de cacao
- 1 1/2 ounces chocolate syrup

Combine ingredients in mixing glass. Add ice, shake, and pour contents into glass.

THE GENIE

For those who wish for cassis

- 2 ounces vodka
- 1 ounce dry vermouth
- 1 ounce crème de cassis
- Lemon twist for garnish

Pour vodka, vermouth, and cassis into glass filled with ice. Stir and garnish.

 GODCHILD

A creamy delight

- 1 ounce vodka
- 1 ounce amaretto
- 1 ounce heavy cream

Combine ingredients in mixing glass. Add ice, shake, and strain into glass.

 GODMOTHER

Gentler than the Godfather

- 2 ounces vodka
- 2 ounces amaretto

Pour vodka and liqueur into ice-filled glass and stir.

 GOLDEN GONDOLA

Venice, vicariously

- 2 ounces vodka
- 1/2 ounce Strega
- 2 teaspoons crème de banane
- 1 ounce orange juice

Combine ingredients in mixing glass. Add ice, shake, and pour contents into glass.

 GREENE STREET

Liqueur-laced Soho special

- 2 ounces vodka
- 1 ounce Midori
- 1/2 ounce Cointreau
- 1/2 ounce lemon juice
- 1/4 teaspoon superfine sugar

Combine ingredients in mixing glass. Add ice, shake, and strain into glass.

VODKA

GREENSLEEVES

Perfect for St. Patrick's Day

- 2 ounces vodka
- 1 ounce Irish Mist
- 1 ounce green
  crème de menthe

Pour ingredients into mixing glass. Add ice, stir to chill, and strain into glass.

GREYHOUND

The grapefruit-flavored ancestor of the Salty Dog

- 2 ounces vodka
- 3 ounces grapefruit juice

Pour vodka and juice into glass filled with ice and stir.

HARVEY WALLBANGER

There's life in the old boy yet

- 2 ounces vodka
- 1 ounce Galliano
- 3 ounces orange juice

Pour ingredients into glass filled with ice and stir.

HEADLESS HORSEMAN

A favorite in Sleepy Hollow?

- 2 ounces vodka
- 1 dash bitters of choice
- Ginger ale

Pour bourbon into ice-filled glass and add bitters. Top with ginger ale to taste and stir gently.

ICE AGE

Très cool

- 2 ounces vodka
- 1 ounce white
  crème de menthe
- 1 ounce
  Jägermeister
- Crushed ice

Pour vodka and liqueurs into mixing glass. Add ice, stir to chill, and strain into glass filled with crushed ice.

THE ICON

Inspired by The Four Seasons's parade of renowned customers, from Marilyn Monroe to Elton John to Princess Diana

- 1 1/2 ounces vodka
- 1/2 ounce pineapple juice
- 1/2 ounce
  Southern Comfort
- 1/2 ounce Chambord
- 1/2 ounce blue curaçao

Pour ingredients into mixing glass. Add ice, stir to chill, and strain into glass.

ICY DOG

Another variation on the Greyhound

- 2 ounces vodka
- 1 ounce grapefruit juice
- 1 ounce peach schnapps
- Crushed ice

Combine liquid ingredients in mixing glass. Add ice, stir to chill, and strain into glass filled with crushed ice.

The Magic Draperies

Customers enjoying a drink at the bar in The Four Seasons may think they've had one too many when they notice the gentle undulations of the draperies covering the towering windows. But what they are witnessing is one of the bar's unique charms —a phenomenon that appeared as if by magic.

When the Grill Room was taking shape in the late 1950s, the enormity of the windows posed a serious problem. Fabric draperies wouldn't have stood up to the bright sunlight that streamed in from the street, so chain-mail-like curtains were seen as the answer.

Artisan Marie Nichols was commissioned to create the draperies, fitting millions of anodized aluminum beads into vertical channels. The finished curtains were extraordinary, but on the day they were installed the workmen noticed something odd— even disastrous, they feared. An urgent call was placed to Phillip Johnson, the architect in charge, who rushed down to find the bronze-hued draperies rippling from top to bottom.

Mystified at first, Johnson realized the motion must have been caused by air currents—or perhaps the rumble of the trains that travel beneath Park Avenue. But he was more than a little worried. A phone call to Joe Baum of Restaurant Associates would put his mind at ease. On seeing the spectacle, Baum declared it beautiful. Johnson, too, came to love the eerie rippling stirred by what he called "the shock of New York." Today, neither those who first saw the "magic draperies" nor the countless people who have since wined and dined in their shadow could imagine the venerable Grill Room without them.

THE IMPRESARIO

With Cynar (CHEE-nahr), the artichoke-flavored apéritif

- 1 ounce vodka
- 1 ounce Cynar
- 1 ounce Campari
- 1 ounce orange juice
- 3 ounces club soda

Pour all ingredients except soda into mixing glass. Add ice and shake. Pour contents into glass, top with club soda, and stir gently.

ISLAND DELIGHT

Don your flip-flops and enjoy

- 2 ounces vodka
- 1 ounce light rum
- 1 ounce triple sec
- 3 ounces orange juice
- 1/2 teaspoon grenadine
- Orange slice for garnish

Combine all ingredients except garnish in glass filled with ice. Stir and garnish.

ISLAND SUNSET

Warm and rosy, thanks to rum and grenadine

- 2 ounces vodka
- 2 ounces light rum
- 3 ounces pineapple juice
- 1/2 teaspoon grenadine

Combine ingredients in ice-filled glass and stir.

JUBILEE

A festival in a glass

- 2 ounces Grey Goose vodka
- 1/2 ounce Cointreau
- 1 ounce fresh sour mix
- 2 mint leaves, crushed
- Mint sprig for garnish

Combine vodka, liqueur, sour mix, and leaves in mixing glass. Add ice, shake, strain into glass, and garnish.

KAMIKAZE

So drinkable it's dangerous

- 2 ounces vodka
- 1 ounce triple sec
- 3 teaspoons Roses lime juice
- Lime wedge for garnish

Pour vodka, liqueur, and juice into glass filled with ice. Stir and garnish.

KARAMAZOV

A nod to Dostoevsky's Russian brothers

- 3 ounces vodka
- 1 ounce sambuca
- 4 ounces club soda

Pour vodka and liqueur into ice-filled glass. Top with club soda and stir gently.

LA GIOCONDA

*Would put a smile on
Mona Lisa's face*

- 1 ounce vodka
- 1 ounce Campari
- 1 ounce peach schnapps
- 1 1/2 ounces champagne
- Orange twist for garnish

Combine vodka, Campari,
liqueur, and schnapps in
mixing glass. Add ice, stir to
chill, and strain into glass.
Top with champagne, stir
gently, and garnish.

LA RUFA'S HONOR

*Named for a Four Seasons
customer known for his
impeccable character*

- 3 ounces vodka
- 1 splash orange juice
- 1 splash cranberry juice

Pour vodka into glass filled
with ice. Add juices and stir.

THE LATINO

*Spirited triple treat of
vodka, tequila, and rum*

- 1 ounce vodka
- 1 ounce tequila
- 1 ounce rum
- 4 ounces club soda
- Lime wedge for garnish

Pour vodka, tequila, and
rum into glass filled with ice.
Top with club soda,
stir gently, and garnish.

LIMEY

*Not quite as English
as it sounds*

- 2 ounces vodka
- 1 ounce Grand Marnier
- 2 ounces
  Roses lime juice
- 3 ounces club soda
- Lime wedge for garnish

Pour vodka, liqueur, and juice
into ice-filled glass. Top with
soda, stir gently, and garnish.

LINCOLN CENTER

Positively operatic

- 1 ounce vodka
- 1 ounce Campari
- 1 ounce peach juice
- 1/2 ounce peach schnapps
- 1 teaspoon Pernod

Combine ingredients in
glass filled with ice and stir.

LUCASTA

*A vanilla vodka drink for a
Four Seasons waitress named
Lucy—poetically, "Lucasta"*

- 2 ounces
  Stoli Vanil
- 1 ounce white
  crème de cacao
- 1/2 ounce Godiva
  White Chocolate Liqueur
- 1/2 ounce sambuca

Combine ingredients in
mixing glass. Add ice, stir to
chill, and strain into glass.

MARTINIS, VODKA

The true martini is all about minimalism, with purists holding that even a drop of vermouth compromises the clean bite of the gin. So it's hardly surprising that when "martinis" began to be mixed with everything save dishwater, versatile vodka was the starting point. By any other name, many vodka-based martinis would elicit unstinting praise, so don't let the "M word" keep you from enjoying them.

BASIC VODKA MARTINI

The Great Pretender?

- 3 ounces vodka
- 1 teaspoon dry vermouth
- Lemon twist or 3 olives for garnish

Pour vodka and vermouth into mixing glass. Add ice and stir to chill. Strain into glass and garnish.

APPLE MARTINI

With sour apple liqueur

- 2 ounces vodka
- 1 1/2 ounces Bols sour apple liqueur
- 1/2 ounce lemon juice
- Apple slice for garnish

Pour ingredients into mixing glass and proceed as in Basic Vodka Martini.

CHOCOLATE VODKA MARTINI

Heresy, or sheer decadence?

- 2 ounces vodka
- 1 ounce Godiva Liqueur
- 1 ounce white crème de cacao
- Chocolate stick for garnish (optional)

Pour liquid ingredients into mixing glass and proceed as in Basic Vodka Martini. Garnish with chocolate stick, if you like.

DRY SHERRY MARTINI

An interesting twist

- 2 ounces vodka
- 1/2 ounce dry vermouth
- 1/2 ounce dry sherry
- Lemon twist for garnish

Combine liquid ingredients in mixing glass and proceed as in Basic Vodka Martini.

FRENCH MARTINI

Ooh-la-la . . .

- 2 ounces vodka
- 1 ounce Chambord
- 1 1/2 ounces pineapple juice

Pour vodka, liqueur, and juice into mixing glass. Add ice, stir to chill, and strain into glass.

MARC'S MARTINI

"The regular" for a popular
Four Seasons customer

- 3 ounces Belvedere vodka
- Lemon twist for garnish
- Crushed ice

Pour vodka into mixing glass, add ice, and stir to chill. Pour into chilled glass filled with crushed ice and garnish.

 ## MELON BALL

And with some orange and
cranberry to boot

- 2 ounces vodka
- 1 ounce Midori
- 1 ounce orange juice
- 1 ounce cranberry juice

Pour vodka, liqueur, and juices into ice-filled glass and stir.

 ## MELON REFRESHER

The Japanese created
Midori, the bright green
honeydew melon liqueur

- 2 1/2 ounces vodka
- 1 ounce Midori
- Orange slice for garnish

Pour liquids into ice-filled glass. Stir and garnish.

 ## MERRY BERRY

The berry? Raspberry

- 2 ounces Stoli Razberi
- 1 ounce Chambord
- 1/2 ounce sloe gin
- 1/2 ounce lemon juice

Combine ingredients in a shaker. Add ice, stir to chill, and strain into glass.

 ## METROPOLITAN

Seriously sophisticated

- 1 1/2 ounces
  Absolut Kurant
- 1 ounce Cointreau
- 1/2 ounce Chambord
- 1 ounce fresh
  sour mix
- 1 ounce
  cranberry juice
- Lemon twist
  for garnish

Pour liquid ingredients into mixing glass. Add ice and stir to chill. Strain into glass and garnish.

VODKA

MONKEY

Banana-y and rich. For the sake of clarity, some makers of the banana liqueur called crème de banane change the French spelling of the last word and end it with "a"

- 1 1/2 ounces vodka
- 1 ounce crème de banane
- 1 ounce dark crème de cacao
- 1/2 ounce light cream

Pour ingredients into mixing glass. Add ice, shake, and strain into glass.

MOSCOW MULE

The 1940s cocktail that introduced vodka to America

- 2 ounces vodka
- Juice of half a lime
- Ginger beer
- Lime wedge for garnish

Pour vodka, juice, and ginger beer into glass filled with ice. Stir and garnish.

MOUNT ETNA

Ready to erupt

- 2 ounces Absolut Peppar
- 1 ounce tomato juice
- 1 ounce sambuca
- 2 dashes Tabasco

Combine ingredients in mixing glass. Add ice, stir to chill, and strain into glass.

MUDSLIDE

Dangerously delicious

- 1 ounce vodka
- 1 ounce Baileys Irish Cream
- 1 ounce dark crème de cacao

Combine vodka and liqueur in mixing glass. Add ice, stir to chill, and strain into glass. Slowly drizzle crème de cacao down inside of glass.

NEON LIGHT

"Are we all lit?" (Auntie Mame)

- 1 1/2 ounces vodka
- 1/2 ounce yellow Chartreuse
- 2 teaspoons Galliano
- 2 teaspoons blue curaçao
- 1/2 teaspoon lemon juice
- Maraschino cherry for garnish

Pour liquid ingredients into mixing glass. Add ice and stir to chill. Strain into glass and garnish.

NUTS AND BERRIES

A favorite in California

- 2 ounces Absolut Kurant
- 1 ounce Frangelico
- 1/2 ounce Chambord
- 1/2 ounce dark crème de cacao
- 1/2 ounce light cream

Combine ingredients in mixing glass. Add ice, shake, and strain into glass.

OPHELIA

Drives you mad with delight

- 2 ounces Stoli Ohranj
- 1 ounce white crème de cacao
- 4 ounces club soda
- Orange twist for garnish

Pour vodka and liqueur into ice-filled glass. Top with club soda, stir gently, and garnish.

POLITICIAN

Even-steven amounts of vodka, tonic, and soda

- 2 ounces vodka
- 2 ounces tonic water
- 2 ounces club soda
- Lime wedge for garnish

Pour vodka and tonic into ice-filled glass. Top with club soda, stir gently, and garnish.

ORANGE DELIGHT

As orangy as can be

- Orange twist
- 1/2 teaspoon powdered sugar
- 2 ounces orange-flavored vodka
- 1 ounce Cointreau
- 1 ounce orange juice

Moisten glass rim with twist, then dip rim into sugar. Pour liquid ingredients into mixing glass. Add ice and stir to chill. Strain into glass and garnish with twist.

THE POTION

A sweet temptation for all. Chambord is the black raspberry liqueur of intense flavor and French origin

- 2 ounces vodka
- 1 ounce Chambord
- 1 ounce lemon juice
- 1/2 teaspoon superfine sugar

Combine ingredients in mixing glass. Add ice, shake, and strain into glass.

PERCOLATOR

A cognac-infused energizer

- 1 ounce vodka
- 1 ounce cognac
- 1 ounce Grand Marnier
- 1 ounce white crème de cacao

Pour ingredients into mixing glass. Add ice, stir to chill, and strain into glass.

PURPLE PASSION

An oldie but goodie

- 2 ounces vodka
- 3 ounces red grape juice
- 3 ounces grapefruit juice
- 1/2 teaspoon superfine sugar

Combine ingredients in mixing glass. Add ice, stir to chill, and strain into glass.

THE RASPUTIN

*Named for the hypnotic
Russian monk*

- 2 ounces vodka
- 1 ounce Frangelico
- 1/2 ounce dark
  crème de cacao
- 1/2 ounce light cream

Combine ingredients in
mixing glass. Add ice, shake,
and strain into glass.

THE REAL MAN

*A Four Seasons managing
partner's tribute to
his counterpart*

- 2 ounces Cîroc grape vodka
- 2 ounces Campari
- 1/2 ounce pineapple juice
- Orange twist for garnish

Combine vodka, Campari,
and juice in ice-filled glass.
Stir, then garnish.

RENDEZVOUS

Meeting of four kindred spirits

- 1 ounce vodka
- 1 ounce brandy
- 1 ounce Grand Marnier
- 1 ounce crème de cassis

Combine ingredients in
mixing glass. Add ice, stir to
chill, and strain into glass.

RUSSIAN
ALEXANDER

*A sumptuous taste worthy
of the Romanovs*

- 2 ounces vodka
- 1 ounce dark
  crème de cacao
- 1 ounce light cream
- Nutmeg for sprinkling

Pour liquid ingredients into
mixing glass. Add ice and
shake. Strain into glass and
sprinkle with nutmeg.

RUSSIAN
MONK

A Rasputin cousin?

- 2 ounces vodka
- 1 ounce Frangelico
- 1 ounce heavy cream

Pour ingredients into mixing
glass. Add ice, shake, and
strain into glass.

RUSSICANO

*Vodka is added to the
Americano, one of the
earliest Campari cocktails*

- 2 ounces vodka
- 2 ounces Campari
- 1 ounce Cinzano
  Rosso vermouth
- 3 ounces club soda
- Orange wedge for garnish

Pour vodka, Campari, and
vermouth into ice-filled glass.
Top with club soda, stir gently,
and garnish.

SALTY DOG

*Gradually overtook its
Greyhound grandfather*

- Lime wedge
- 2 teaspoons salt
- 2 ounces vodka
- 5 ounces grapefruit juice

Moisten rim of glass with
lime wedge, then dip rim into
salt to coat. Fill glass with ice,
pour in vodka, salt, and juice.
Stir, then garnish with lime.

 ## SCREWDRIVER

The unadorned classic

- 2 ounces vodka
- 4 ounces orange juice

Pour vodka and juice into glass
filled with ice and stir.

 ## SEA BREEZE

*An old favorite,
wafting your way*

- 2 ounces vodka
- 2 ounces grapefruit juice
- 2 ounces cranberry juice

Pour vodka and juices into
glass filled with ice and stir.

SECTION EIGHT

*Inspired by a drive-you-crazy
night at The Four Seasons bar*

- 1 1/2 ounces vodka
- 1 ounce Hennessy cognac

Pour vodka and cognac into
glass filled with ice and stir.

 ## SEX IN THE POOL

*Jokey reference to the high-
octane flirting occasionally
seen in our Pool Room*

- 2 ounces vodka
- 1 ounce white
  crème de cacao
- 1/2 teaspoon blue curaçao
- 1/2 teaspoon
  Grand Marnier
- Fig half for garnish

Pour liquid ingredients into
mixing glass. Fill with ice and
stir to chill. Strain into glass
and garnish.

 ## SEX ON THE BEACH

*The naughtily named cocktail
from the oh-so-cool 1970s*

- 2 ounces vodka
- 1 ounce peach schnapps
- 2 ounces orange juice
- 2 ounces cranberry juice

Combine all ingredients in
glass filled with ice.

 ## SHE WALKS
IN BEAUTY

A taste of Byron's poetry

- 3 ounces Cîroc
  grape vodka
- 1/2 ounce Chambord
- 1/2 ounce apricot brandy
- Maraschino cherry
  for garnish

Combine liquid ingredients
in mixing glass. Add ice and
stir to chill. Strain into glass
and garnish.

VODKA

SILVER LINING MARTINI

The favorite potable of the designer of this guide

- 2 ounces Chopin Polish vodka, chilled
- 2 large Spanish olives with pimientos, marinated in aquavit or dry white sherry

Pour small amount of aquavit or sherry into well-chilled glass; swirl once and discard. Add chilled vodka and garnish with olives on toothpick.

 ## SLOW COMFORTABLE SCREW

Relax—it's a Screwdriver with sloe gin and Southern Comfort

- 2 ounces vodka
- 1 ounce sloe gin
- 1 ounce Southern Comfort
- 3 ounces orange juice

Combine all ingredients in glass filled with ice.

 ## SNOW STORM

Sparkly white

- 2 ounces vodka
- 1 ounce Godiva White Chocolate Liqueur
- 1 ounce white crème de cacao
- Crushed ice

Combine all ingredients in mixing glass. Add ice, stir to chill, and strain into glass filled with crushed ice.

 ## SOUTHERN ANGEL

With a touch o' Georgia peach

- 2 ounces vodka
- 1 ounce Southern Comfort
- 1 ounce peach juice
- 2 mint leaves, crushed
- 1/2 teaspoon superfine sugar
- Mint sprig for garnish

Combine vodka, Southern Comfort, juice, leaves, and sugar in mixing glass. Add ice and shake. Strain into glass and garnish.

 ## SOUTHERN SKIES

Romance takes flight

- 1 ounce vodka
- 1 ounce light rum
- 1 ounce blue curaçao
- 1 ounce pineapple juice

Pour ingredients into mixing glass. Add ice, stir to chill, and strain into glass.

 ## SPICY MARY

She's so hot!

- 2 1/2 ounces Absolut Peppar
- 3 ounces tomato juice
- 4 dashes Worcestershire sauce
- 3 dashes Tabasco
- Salt and pepper to taste
- Lime slice for garnish

Combine liquid ingredients and condiments in glass filled with ice. Stir and garnish.

VODKA

SUBURBAN

A tribute to our valiant "bridge-and-tunnel" customers

- 2 ounces vodka
- 1 ounce peach schnapps
- 1 ounce apricot brandy
- 2 ounces orange juice
- 2 ounces club soda
- Orange slice for garnish

Pour vodka, schnapps, brandy, and juice into ice-filled glass. Top with club soda, stir gently, and garnish.

SUMMER COOLER

Refreshingly minty

- 3 mint sprigs
- 1 teaspoon superfine sugar
- 1 ounce lemon juice
- 2 1/2 ounces vodka
- Mint sprig for garnish

Muddle mint, sugar, and juice in bottom of mixing glass. Add ice and shake. Strain into glass and garnish.

SUMMER SNAP

Two snaps up

- 2 ounces vodka
- 1/2 ounce white crème de menthe
- 1 ounce apricot brandy
- 1/2 ounce lemon juice
- Mint sprig for garnish

Combine liquid ingredients in mixing glass. Add ice and stir to chill. Strain into glass and garnish.

SWISS ALPS

Think snow and chocolate

- 1 ounce vodka
- 1 ounce Godiva White Chocolate Liqueur
- 1 ounce white crème de cacao
- 1 ounce light cream
- Chocolate shavings for garnish

Combine liquid ingredients in mixing glass. Add ice, shake, strain into glass, and garnish.

TANNHAUSER

Wagnerian in its richness. Jägermeister (first syllable pronounced YAY) is a German liqueur with a bitter but interesting herbal flavor

- 2 ounces vodka
- 1 ounce dark crème de cacao
- 1/2 ounce light cream
- 1/2 ounce Jägermeister

Combine ingredients in mixing glass. Add ice, shake, and strain into glass.

THUNDERCLOUD

A dark but delectable Four Seasons special

- 2 ounces vodka
- 1/2 ounce Chambord
- 1/2 ounce blue curaçao
- 1/2 ounce heavy cream

Combine ingredients in mixing glass. Add ice, shake, and strain into glass.

VODKA

TOPAZ

Shimmeringly orange

- 2 ounces vodka
- 1 ounce orange juice
- 1 ounce apricot brandy

Combine ingredients in mixing glass. Add ice, stir to chill, and strain into glass.

 ## TOP BANANA

In competition here with an orange

- 2 ounces vodka
- 2 ounces crème de banane
- 4 ounces orange juice
- Orange slice for garnish

Combine vodka, liqueur, and juice in mixing glass. Add ice and stir to chill. Strain into ice-filled glass and garnish.

 ## TRIXIE'S TROPICAL DREAM

Best enjoyed under a palm— preferably when clinking glasses with Trixie

- 2 ounces vodka
- 2 ounces light rum
- 1 ounce blue curaçao

Combine ingredients in mixing glass. Add ice, stir to chill, and strain into glass.

 ## TRUFFLE

Velvety treat for the holidays

- 2 ounces vodka
- 1 ounce dark crème de cacao
- 1/2 teaspoon Chambord
- 1 ounce heavy cream

Pour ingredients into mixing glass. Add ice, shake, and strain into glass.

 ## TUTTI FRUTTI

Three fruits in one

- 1 ounce Grey Goose orange vodka
- 1 ounce Stoli Razberi
- 1 ounce Chambord
- 1 ounce orange juice
- 1 ounce cranberry juice

Combine ingredients in mixing glass. Add ice, stir to chill, and strain into glass.

 ## VELVET HAMMER

Sneaks up on you

- 2 ounces vodka
- 1 ounce white crème de cacao
- 1 ounce light cream

Combine ingredients in mixing glass. Add ice, shake, and strain into glass.

VIVA EUROPA

*A toast to the glories of
Italy and Provence*

- 1 1/2 ounces vodka
- 1/2 ounce amaretto
- 1/2 ounce Cointreau
- 1/2 ounce Galliano
- 1 ounce orange juice
- 1 ounce pineapple juice
- 2 dashes bitters

Combine ingredients in mixing
glass. Add ice, stir to chill,
and strain into glass.

VODKA AND TONIC

*Overtaking Gin and Tonic
in the stretch*

- 2 ounces vodka
- Tonic water
- Lime wedge for garnish

Pour vodka into ice-filled glass.
Fill with tonic water to taste.
Stir and garnish.

VODKA COLLINS

*Russian slant on a
British classic*

- 2 ounces vodka
- 1 ounce fresh sour mix
- 3 ounces club soda
- Maraschino cherry
  for garnish
- Orange slice for garnish

Combine vodka and sour mix in
mixing glass. Add ice, shake,
and strain into glass. Top with
soda, stir gently, and garnish.

VODKA DAMSEL

Delightfully fruity

- 1 ounce vodka
- 1 ounce Stoli Razberi
- 1 ounce grapefruit juice
- 1 ounce peach schnapps

Combine ingredients in
mixing glass. Add ice, stir to
chill, and strain into glass.

VODKA GIBSON

*A martini garnished
with onions*

- 3 ounces vodka
- 1 teaspoon
  dry vermouth
- 3 cocktail onions
  for garnish

Pour vodka and vermouth
into mixing glass. Add ice
and stir to chill. Strain into
glass and garnish.

VODKA

VODKA GIMLET

For lime lovers

- 2 1/2 ounces vodka
- 1 1/2 ounces
  Roses lime juice
- Lime wedge for garnish

Pour vodka and juice into ice-filled glass. Stir and garnish.

VODKA GINGERLY

With ginger ale and crème de menthe

- 2 ounces vodka
- 1/2 ounce white
  crème de menthe
- 1 ounce fresh sour mix
- 4 ounces ginger ale
- Orange slice for garnish

Combine vodka, liqueur, and sour mix in mixing glass. Add ice and shake. Strain into ice-filled glass, top with ginger ale, stir gently, and garnish.

VODKA GRASSHOPPER

Springier than the original, made with liqueurs only

- 1 ounce vodka
- 1 ounce green
  crème de menthe
- 1 ounce white
  crème de cacao

Combine vodka and liqueurs in mixing glass. Add ice, stir to chill, and strain into glass.

VODKA HOPPER

Yet another vodka variation on the Grasshopper

- 2 ounces vodka
- 1 ounce green
  crème de menthe
- 1/2 ounce light cream
- Mint sprig for garnish

Pour liquid ingredients into mixing glass. Add ice, shake, strain into glass, and garnish.

VODKA MADRAS

Equal parts vodka, cranberry, and orange

- 2 ounces vodka
- 2 ounces cranberry juice
- 2 ounces orange juice

Pour vodka and juices into glass filled with ice and stir.

VODKA NEGRONI

Vodka stands in for gin in the classic Campari cocktail

- 2 1/2 ounces vodka
- 1 1/2 ounces Campari
- 1/2 ounce
  sweet vermouth

Pour ingredients into mixing glass. Add ice, stir to chill, and strain into glass.

VODKA ORANGE BLOSSOM

The classic cocktail, updated with orange-flavored vodka

- 2 ounces Stoli Ohranj
- 1 ounce Cointreau
- 1 ounce orange juice
- 2 dashes orange bitters

Combine ingredients in mixing glass. Add ice, stir to chill, and strain into glass.

VODKA REFRESHER

Tart and summery

- 2 ounces Absolut Citron
- 1 ounce fresh sour mix
- 4 ounces tonic water
- Lime wedge for garnish

Combine vodka and sour mix in mixing glass. Add ice and shake. Strain into glass, add tonic water, and garnish.

VODKA SOUR

Serve straight up or on the rocks

- 2 1/2 ounces vodka
- 1 1/2 ounces fresh sour mix
- Orange slice for garnish
- Maraschino cherry for garnish

Combine vodka and sour mix in mixing glass. Add ice and shake. Strain into sour glass or ice-filled rocks glass and garnish.

VODKA STINGER

Stinger = crème de menthe

- 2 1/2 ounces vodka
- 1 1/2 ounces white crème de menthe

Pour vodka and liqueur into mixing glass. Add ice, stir to chill, and strain into glass.

THE WARSAW

Elegant cocktail made with potato vodka from Poland

- 2 ounces Lukusowa potato vodka
- 1 ounce Hiram Walker blackberry brandy
- 1 ounce dry vermouth
- 1 teaspoon lemon juice

Combine all ingredients in mixing glass. Add ice, shake, and strain into glass.

WATERMELON

Melon liqueur tinged with cranberry juice

- 2 1/2 ounces vodka
- 1 ounce Midori
- 1 1/2 ounces cranberry juice

Pour vodka, liqueur, and juice into ice-filled glass and stir.

VODKA

WHITE LICORICE

Sumptuous is the word

- 2 ounces vodka
- 1 ounce white crème de cacao
- 1/2 ounce sambuca
- 1/2 ounce light cream

Combine ingredients in mixing glass. Add ice, shake, and strain into glass.

WHITE RUSSIAN

Defiant survivor of the cocktail wars

- 2 ounces vodka
- 1 ounce white crème de cacao
- 1 ounce light cream

Combine ingredients in mixing glass. Add ice, shake, and pour contents into glass.

WICKED MONK

Wickedly good, that is

- 1 1/2 ounces vodka
- 1 ounce Frangelico
- 1/2 ounce blue curaçao
- 1/2 ounce Southern Comfort

Combine ingredients in mixing glass. Add ice, stir to chill, and strain into glass.

WOO WOO

Vintage cocktail, saucy name

- 2 ounces vodka
- 1 ounce peach schnapps
- 4 ounces cranberry juice

Pour ingredients into glass filled with ice and stir.

YORKVILLE

A nod to the neighborhood on Manhattan's Upper East Side

- 2 ounces vodka
- 1 ounce Cointreau
- 1 ounce peach juice
- 4 ounces club soda

Pour vodka, liqueur, and juice into ice-filled glass. Top with club soda and stir gently.

RUM

RUM

Rum conjures up all things Caribbean, and cocktails made from this sugar-cane spirit needn't be decked out with a tiny umbrella to seem exotic. Light rums are made in Puerto Rico, Barbados, and a few other subtropical isles, while dark rums (heavier and richer from longer aging) hail from the tropics: Jamaica, Haiti, and Martinique.

 ## ALMOND JOY

For your sweet tooth

- 2 ounces light rum
- 1/2 ounce
  cream of coconut
- 1/2 ounce amaretto
- 1/2 ounce Godiva Liqueur
- Crushed ice

Pour all ingredients into glass filled with crushed ice and stir.

 ## APPLE FIZZ

With sour apple liqueur

- 2 ounces Myers's rum
- 1/2 ounce
  sour apple liqueur
- Club soda

Pour rum and liqueur into ice-filled glass. Top with club soda to taste and stir gently.

 ## APPLE PIE

A good choice for Mom

- 2 ounces light rum
- 1/2 ounce calvados
  apple brandy
- 1/2 teaspoon cinnamon
- Apple slice for garnish

Combine rum, brandy, and cinnamon in mixing glass. Add ice, shake, pour contents into glass, and garnish.

 ## APPLESAUCE

An autumn cocktail. Applejack is a potent apple brandy of American origin

- 2 ounces gold rum
- 1 ounce applejack
- 1 teaspoon cinnamon
- Apple slice for garnish

Combine rum, apple puree, and cinnamon in mixing glass. Add ice and stir to chill. Strain into glass and garnish.

BANANA CREAM PIE

As yummy as it sounds

- 2 ounces light rum
- 1/2 ounce crème de banane
- 1/2 ounce Godiva Liqueur
- 1/2 ounce white crème de cacao

Pour rum and liqueurs into mixing glass. Add ice, stir to chill, and strain into glass.

BASTARD CHILD

Named for the offspring of Spanish sailors, c. 1492?

- 1 ounce light rum
- 1 ounce sambuca
- 1 ounce Frangelico

Pour rum and liqueurs into glass filled with ice and stir.

BLIND KAMIKAZE

More formidable than its vodka counterpart

- 2 ounces light rum
- 1/2 ounce peach schnapps
- 1/2 ounce Midori
- 1/2 ounce Chambord
- Lemon twist for garnish

Pour rum, schnapps, and liqueurs into mixing glass. Add ice and stir to chill. Strain into martini glass or ice-filled rocks glass, then garnish.

BLUE HAWAIIAN

Calling Don Ho

- 1 ounce light rum
- 1 ounce blue curaçao
- 2 ounces pineapple juice
- 1 ounce cream of coconut
- Pineapple wedge for garnish

Combine liquids in glass filled with ice. Stir and garnish.

BROOKLYN BRIDGE

A bow to the bodega-studded neighborhoods over the bridge

- 2 ounces light rum
- 1/4 ounce white crème de menthe
- 1/4 ounce white crème de cacao
- Lemon twist for garnish

Combine liquid ingredients in mixing glass. Add ice and stir to chill. Pour contents into rocks glass or strain into martini glass.

CANDY APPLE

A sour apple sweetened with cherry

- 2 ounces dark rum
- 1/2 ounce sour apple liqueur
- 1/2 ounce Cherry Heering
- 1/2 ounce lemon juice

Pour rum, liqueurs, and juice into mixing glass. Add ice and stir to chill. Strain into glass and garnish.

RUM

CARIBBEAN COCKTAIL

A fruity subtropical treat

- 2 ounces light rum
- 1/2 ounce Malibu rum
- 1/2 ounce orange liqueur
- 1/2 ounce crème de banane
- 1/2 ounce pineapple juice
- Coconut wedge for garnish

Pour liquids into ice-filled glass. Stir and garnish.

 ## CARIBBEAN SUNSET

Think "rosy glow"

- 2 ounces light rum
- 1/2 ounce triple sec
- 1/2 ounce lemon juice
- Lemon twist for garnish

Combine rum, liqueur, and juice in mixing glass. Add ice and stir to chill. Strain into glass and garnish.

 ## CARIBBEAN TWILIGHT

With dark rum. Peychaud's bitters were formulated in New Orleans in 1793

- 2 ounces dark rum
- 1/2 ounce orange liqueur of choice
- 1/2 ounce lemon juice
- 1 dash Peychaud's bitters
- Orange twist for garnish

Combine rum, liqueur, and juice in mixing glass. Add ice and stir to chill. Strain into glass and garnish.

CARLITO'S WAY

"Carlito" is none other than Four Seasons barkeep Charles

- 2 1/2 ounces light rum
- 1/2 ounce triple sec
- 1/2 ounce lemon juice
- 1/2 ounce lime juice
- Lemon twist for garnish

Pour liquid ingredients into ice-filled glass. Stir and garnish.

 ## CARTHUSIAN MONK

Carthusian monks gave the world Chartreuse, France's aromatic liqueur

- 2 ounces light rum
- 1/2 ounce yellow Chartreuse
- Club soda
- Lemon twist for garnish

Pour rum and liqueur in ice-filled glass. Top with club soda to taste, stir gently, and garnish.

 ## CHOCOLATE-COVERED ORANGE

Peel off some pleasure

- 2 ounces gold rum
- 1/2 ounce Cointreau
- 1/2 ounce Godiva Liqueur
- Orange twist for garnish

Combine rum and liqueurs in mixing glass. Add ice and stir to chill. Strain into glass and garnish.

RUM

CHOCOLATE MINT COCKTAIL

With the dark chocolate Godiva Liqueur, which also comes in white chocolate and cappuccino flavors

- 2 ounces light rum
- 1/2 ounce white crème de menthe
- 1/2 ounce Godiva Liqueur
- Mint sprig for garnish

Combine rum and liqueurs in mixing glass. Add ice and stir to chill. Strain into glass and garnish.

 ## CHOCOLATE TWISTER

Spinning your way

- 2 ounces dark rum
- 1/2 ounce black sambuca
- 1/2 ounce Godiva Liqueur

Combine ingredients in glass filled with ice and stir.

 ## THE COLISEUM

Let the games begin

- 2 ounces light rum
- 1/2 ounce Campari
- 1/2 ounce Cointreau
- 1/2 ounce fresh sour mix
- Lemon twist for garnish

Combine liquid ingredients in mixing glass. Add ice and shake. Pour contents into glass and garnish.

 ## THE CORPION CONNECTION

Charles's idea and namesake

- 2 ounces Bacardi 151
- 1/2 ounce Cointreau
- 1/2 ounce fresh sour mix
- Lemon twist for garnish

Pour liquids into mixing glass. Add ice and shake. Strain into glass and garnish.

 ## CUBA LIBRE

Also known as Rum and Coke

- 2 1/2 ounces Bacardi
- 1 1/2 ounces Coca-Cola
- Lime wedge for garnish

Pour rum and cola into glass filled with ice and garnish.

 ## DAIQUIRI

The nonfrozen original. For frozen daiquiris, see page 110

- 2 1/2 ounces Bacardi Light
- 2 ounces fresh lime juice
- 1 teaspoon superfine sugar

Combine ingredients in mixing glass. Add ice, shake, and strain into glass.

 ## DAN'S DESERT INN

A Vegas barman's special

- 2 1/2 ounces light rum
- 1/2 ounce orange liqueur of choice
- 1/2 ounce dry Dubonnet

Combine ingredients in mixing glass. Add ice, shake, and strain into glass.

RUM

DON DIEGO

Named for a Spanish monk

- 2 ounces light rum
- 1 1/2 ounces Bénédictine
- Lemon twist for garnish

Pour rum and liqueur into ice-filled glass. Stir and garnish.

DONKEY EXPRESS

With a little sloe gin

- 2 ounces light rum
- 1/2 ounce sloe gin
- 1/2 ounce triple sec
- Lime wedge for garnish

Pour liquids into ice-filled glass. Stir and garnish.

EASTERN EXPRESS

Gingery fizz

- 2 ounces light rum
- 1/2 ounce orange liqueur of choice
- Ginger ale
- Orange twist for garnish

Pour rum and liqueur into ice-filled glass. Add ginger ale to taste, stir gently, and garnish.

THE 1812

Man the torpedoes

- 2 ounces Bacardi Silver
- 1/2 ounce peach schnapps
- 1/2 ounce Southern Comfort
- Orange twist for garnish

Combine liquids in mixing glass. Add ice, stir to chill, strain into glass, and garnish.

EXTREME SOUR APPLE

Tarter than the Sour Apple Cocktail

- 2 ounces dark rum
- 1/2 ounce sour apple liqueur
- 1/2 ounce lemon juice
- Green apple slice for garnish

Pour rum, liqueur, and juice into glass filled with ice. Stir and garnish.

F-16 TOMCAT

For the fighting spirit in you

- 2 ounces light rum
- 1/2 ounce Baileys Irish Cream
- 1/2 ounce Grand Marnier

Pour rum and liqueurs into glass filled with ice and stir.

THE FIDEL

No cigar required

- 2 ounces light rum
- 1/2 ounce Midori
- 1/2 ounce Cointreau
- 1/2 ounce orange juice
- 1/2 ounce pineapple juice
- 1/2 ounce grapefruit juice
- 1 splash cranberry juice
- Pineapple spear for garnish

Combine liquid ingredients in ice-filled glass and stir. Add splash of cranberry juice and garnish with pineapple.

FOREIGN LEGION

For a nicely textured drink, use O. J. with pulp

- 2 ounces Mount Gay rum
- 1/2 ounce Dubonnet Rouge
- 1/2 ounce orange juice

Combine rum, liqueur, and juice in mixing glass. Add ice, shake, and strain into glass.

FOUR SEASONS HURRICANE

Pineapple stands in for the passion fruit of the New Orleans original

- 2 ounces light rum
- 1/2 ounce blue curaçao
- 1/2 ounce pineapple juice
- 1/2 ounce lemon juice
- Crushed ice
- Club soda
- Pineapple wedge for garnish

Pour rum, liqueur, and juices into glass filled with crushed ice. Top with club soda, stir gently, and garnish.

FOUR SEASONS PARADISE COCKTAIL

The original Paradise Cocktail calls for brandy

- 2 ounces gold rum
- 1/2 ounce Cointreau
- 1/2 ounce Pernod

Pour rum and liqueurs into glass filled with ice and stir.

FOXY SQUIRREL

An almond-crazy heister?

- 2 ounces light rum
- 1/2 ounce amaretto
- 1/2 ounce crème de noyaux
- 1/2 ounce Chambord

Combine rum and liqueurs in mixing glass. Add ice and stir to chill. Strain into martini glass or ice-filled rocks glass.

FRANGELICO RUM FIZZ

For hazelnut lovers. Frangelico is traced to Fra. Angelico, a 17th-century monk who lived as a hermit in the hills of Italy's Piedmont region

- 2 ounces dark rum
- 1 ounce Frangelico
- Crushed ice
- Club soda

Pour rum and liqueur into glass filled with crushed ice. Top with club soda to taste and stir gently.

FRENCH ISLAND

Martinique, peut-être?

- 2 ounces dark rum
- 1 ounce Pernod
- Club soda

Pour rum and liqueur into ice-filled glass. Top with club soda to taste and stir gently.

FROZEN DAIQUIRIS

Frozen daiquiris were all the rage in the 1950s, and the tongue-chillers have hung on despite inroads made by a Mexican relative, the frozen Margarita. Legend holds that an American engineer invented the daiquiri in 1896 in the Cuban town of the same name.

WATERMELON DAIQUIRI

Pretty and pink

- 2 ounces light rum
- 1/2 ounce watermelon liqueur
- 1 1/2 ounces fresh sour mix
- 1 cup crushed ice

Combine ingredients and crushed ice in blender, blend until smooth, and pour into glass.

KIWI SURPRISE

Pleasantly tart

- 2 ounces light rum
- 1/2 ounce kiwi liqueur
- 1 1/2 ounces fresh sour mix
- 1 cup crushed ice
- Kiwi slice for garnish

Combine liquid ingredients and crushed ice in blender and blend until smooth. Pour into glass and garnish.

BANANA DAIQUIRI

With banana-flavored liqueur

- 2 ounces light rum
- 1 ounce fresh sour mix
- 1/2 ounce crème de banane
- 1 cup crushed ice

Combine and prepare as in Watermelon Daiquiri.

SEÑOR ZEUS

A Greco-Latin treat

- 2 ounces light rum
- 1/2 ounce ouzo
- 1 ounce fresh sour mix
- 1 cup crushed ice

Combine and prepare as in Watermelon Daiquiri.

MANGO DAIQUIRI

Starring what's been called "the king of fruits"

- 2 ounces light rum
- 1 ounce fresh sour mix
- 1 ounce mango puree
- 1 cup crushed ice

Combine and prepare as in Watermelon Daiquiri.

APRICOT-GUAVA DAIQUIRI

A happy marriage of apricot brandy and guava nectar

- 2 ounces light rum
- 1 ounce fresh sour mix
- 1/2 ounce apricot brandy
- 1/2 ounce guava nectar
- 1 cup crushed ice
- Apricot half for garnish

Combine and prepare as in Kiwi Surprise.

SHARMA DAIQUIRI

Peachy karma

- 2 ounces light rum
- 1/2 ounce peach liqueur
- 1 ounce fresh sour mix
- 1 cup crushed ice

Combine and prepare as in Watermelon Daiquiri.

STRAWBERRY DAIQUIRI

An old favorite

- 2 ounces light rum
- 1/2 ounce strawberry liqueur
- 1 ounce fresh sour mix
- 1 cup crushed ice
- Strawberry half for garnish

Combine and prepare as in Kiwi Surprise.

SAN JUAN DAIQUIRI

Perfect for a lazy day in the sun

- 2 ounces light rum
- 1/2 ounce Grand Marnier
- 1 ounce fresh sour mix
- 1 cup crushed ice
- Orange twist for garnish

Combine and prepare as in Kiwi Surprise.

THE MARY LOU

She came, she saw, she drank

- 2 ounces light rum
- 1/2 ounce crème de cassis
- 1 ounce fresh sour mix
- 1 cup crushed ice

Combine and prepare as in Watermelon Daiquiri.

SWEET START

A raspberry tempter

- 2 ounces light rum
- 1/2 ounce Chambord
- 1 ounce fresh sour mix
- 1 cup crushed ice
- Raspberry for garnish

Combine and prepare as in Kiwi Surprise.

RUM

FRUITY MIST

*Apricot and grapefruit
with lots of ice*

- 2 ounces light rum
- 1/2 ounce apricot liqueur
- 1/2 ounce grapefruit juice
- Crushed ice

Combine ingredients in glass
filled with ice and stir.

GEORGIA
SPRITZER

Peach and lemon-lime

- 2 ounces light rum
- 1/2 ounce peach schnapps
- 7-Up or Sprite
- Lime slice for garnish

Pour rum and schnapps into
ice-filled glass. Top with
soft drink to taste, stir
gently, and garnish.

GOLDEN
ISLAND

An inviting place to relax

- 2 ounces gold rum
- 1/2 ounce Cointreau
- Tonic water
- Lime wedge for garnish

Pour rum and liqueur into ice-
filled glass. Top with tonic to
taste, stir gently, and garnish.

THE GRAPSTA

Rap on, bro

- 2 ounces light rum
- 1/2 ounce grape liqueur
- 1/2 ounce lemon juice
- 1/2 teaspoon
  superfine sugar
- Lemon twist for garnish

Combine all ingredients except
garnish in mixing glass. Add
ice and shake. Strain into
glass and garnish.

HAITIAN
KAMIKAZE

*With Barbancourt rum
from Haiti*

- 2 ounces Barbancourt rum
- 1/2 ounce orange
  liqueur of choice
- 1/2 ounce lime juice

Pour ingredients into glass
filled with ice and stir.

HAWAIIAN
SOUR

For pineapple lovers

- 2 ounces light rum
- 1/2 ounce
  pineapple liqueur
- 1/2 ounce fresh sour mix
- Pineapple wedge
  for garnish

Combine liquid ingredients
in mixing glass. Add ice and
shake. Strain into sour glass
or pour contents into rocks
glass, then garnish.

RUM

ITALIAN COOLER

Rum and an herby liqueur

- 2 ounces light rum
- 1/2 ounce Strega

Pour rum and liqueur into ice-filled glass and stir.

JOLLY GREEN GIGANTE

Rum with crème de menthe

- 1 1/2 ounces dark rum
- 1/2 ounce green crème de menthe
- 1 dash Angostura bitters

Combine ingredients in glass filled with ice and stir.

JUBILEE COOLER

Mint, lemon, lime

- 2 ounces light rum
- 1/2 ounce lemon juice
- 3 sprigs mint, crushed
- 1/2 ounce club soda
- 1/2 ounce Sprite
- Mint sprig for garnish

Combine rum, juice, and mint in mixing glass. Add ice and stir. Strain into ice-filled glass and top with soda and soft drink. Stir gently and garnish.

LEMON MERINGUE

As delish as the pie

- 2 ounces light rum
- 1/2 ounce limoncello
- 1/2 ounce orange liqueur of choice
- 1/2 ounce lemon juice

Combine rum, liqueurs, and juice in mixing glass. Add ice, shake, and strain into glass.

LIBERTY FIZZ

Freedom from boredom

- 2 ounces light rum
- 1/2 ounce Galliano
- Club soda

Pour rum and liqueur into ice-filled glass. Top with club soda to taste and stir gently.

LIME IN THE SUN

Imbibe while working on your tan

- 2 ounces light rum
- 1/2 ounce Cointreau
- 7-Up or Sprite
- Orange slice for garnish

Pour rum and liqueur into ice-filled glass. Top with soft drink to taste, stir gently, and garnish.

RUM

BARTENDER'S TIP Know what you're buying when you pick a rum from the shelf. **Light** rums (also called silver or white) are clear and are best used for fruit-based cocktails. **Gold**, or *oro*, rums are aged longer and can be enjoyed neat or on the rocks. **Dark** rums (also labeled as black or añejo) are the aristocrats of the bunch and, like brandy, are often drunk from a snifter.

MAI TAI

Tiki-party time!

- 1 1/2 ounces Myers's rum
- 1/2 ounce triple sec
- 1/2 ounce amaretto
- 1/2 ounce grenadine
- 1/2 ounce lime juice
- Pineapple spear
  for garnish

Combine ingredients in ice-filled glass. Stir and garnish.

MIAMI COCKTAIL

With a touch of orange

- 2 ounces dark rum
- 1/2 ounce
  Southern Comfort
- 1/2 ounce Cointreau
- Club soda
- Orange twist for garnish

Pour rum, Southern Comfort, and liqueur into ice-filled glass. Top with club soda to taste, stir gently, and garnish.

MINT CHOCOLATE CUP

A drinkable candy bar

- 2 ounces light rum
- 1/2 ounce white
  crème de menthe
- 1/2 ounce Cointreau
- 1/2 ounce Godiva Liqueur
- Mint sprig for garnish

Combine rum and liqueurs in mixing glass. Add ice and stir to chill. Strain into glass and garnish.

MOJITO

The classic from Havana

- 1 teaspoon superfine sugar
- 1 ounce lime juice
- 2 mint sprigs
- 2 ounces light rum
- Crushed ice
- Sparkling water

Muddle sugar, juice, and mint in bottom of glass. Pour in rum, add crushed ice, and top with sparkling water.

MOONLIGHT SOOTHER

Especially good after a heavy meal. Unicum bitters were formulated in Hungary in the 18th century, and the 40-plus herbs the mix contains are still a closely guarded secret

- 2 ounces light rum
- 1/2 ounce Unicum bitters
- Club soda
- Lemon twist for garnish

Pour rum and bitters into ice-filled glass and top with club soda to taste, stir gently, and garnish.

NEGRUMMI

A Four Seasons take on the Negroni, with two apéritifs

2 ounces light rum
2 ounces Campari
2 ounces Punt e Mes
Orange twist for garnish

Combine liquid ingredients in mixing glass. Add ice and stir to chill. Strain into glass and garnish.

NUT COCKTAIL

Hazelnut and almond in one

- 2 ounces light rum
- 1 ounce Frangelico
- 1 ounce amaretto
- 1 ounce club soda

Pour rum and liqueurs into ice-filled glass. Top with club soda and stir gently.

NUT CREAM PIE

Enriched with Baileys

- 2 ounces dark rum
- 1 ounce Frangelico
- 1 ounce
  Baileys Irish Cream
- 1 ounce club soda
- Chocolate stick
  for garnish

Pour rum and liqueurs into ice-filled glass. Top with club soda and stir gently.

NUTTY HISPANIC

Crazy about hazelnuts

- 2 ounces light rum
- 1/2 ounce Frangelico

Pour ingredients into glass filled with ice and stir.

NUTTY ISLANDER

With crème de noyaux, a sweet pink liqueur tasting of almond

- 2 ounces rum
- 1/2 ounce
  crème de noyaux

Pour rum and liqueur into ice-filled glass and stir.

OLD SAN JUAN

An homage to P. R.'s capital

- 2 ounces Bacardi Limón
- 1/2 ounce lemon juice
- 1/2 ounce Cointreau
- 1/2 ounce blue curaçao
- 2 ounces Bacardi 151

Combine all ingredients except Bacardi 151 in mixing glass. Add ice and shake. Pour contents into glass and top with Bacardi 151.

PAGO PAGO

Named after the capital of American Samoa. How to say it? PAHN-go PAHN-go

- 2 ounces light rum
- 1 teaspoon white
  crème de cacao
- 1 teaspoon
  green Chartreuse
- 1/2 ounce
  pineapple juice
- 1 teaspoon
  fresh lime juice
- Crushed ice

Combine ingredients in mixing glass. Add ice, shake, and strain into glass filled with crushed ice.

PARADISE LOST

A rum variation on the Fallen Angel gin cocktail

- 2 ounces gold rum
- 1/2 ounces Tuaca

Pour rum and liqueur into glass filled with ice and stir.

PEACH FIXER

A fruity hangover soother

- 2 ounces light rum
- 1/2 ounce peach schnapps
- 1/2 ounce
  Southern Comfort
- Club soda

Pour all ingredients except soda into glass filled with ice. Top with club soda to taste and stir gently.

 ## PIÑA COLADA

The Puerto Rican classic, enjoyed since the 1950s

- 2 ounces light rum
- 4 ounces pineapple juice (unsweetened)
- 2 ounces cream of coconut
- 4 ounces crushed ice
- Pineapple spear for garnish

Combine all ingredients except garnish in a shaker. Blend until smooth, pour into chilled glass, and garnish.

  ## POLLY'S CHOICE

Named for a witty customer who hails from Australia

- 2 ounces light rum
- 1/2 ounce apricot brandy
- 1/2 ounce fresh sour mix
- Lemon twist for garnish

Combine ingredients in mixing glass. Add ice, shake, strain into glass, and garnish.

 ## RAVEL'S BOLERO

Thumpingly good

- 2 ounces light rum
- 1 ounce peach schnapps
- 1/2 ounce apple brandy
- 1/4 ounce dry vermouth
- 1/4 ounce sweet vermouth

Combine ingredients in mixing glass. Add ice, stir to chill, and strain into glass.

 ## RAVISHING HAZEL

Rich with hazelnut liqueur and heavy cream

- 2 1/2 ounces gold rum
- 1/2 ounce Frangelico
- 1/2 ounce heavy cream

Combine ingredients in mixing glass. Add ice, shake, and strain into glass.

REFRESHING BREEZE

Wafting your way

- 2 ounces Mount Gay rum
- 1/2 ounce Cointreau
- 1/2 ounce lemon juice
- 3 sprigs mint, crushed
- Mint sprig for garnish

Combine all ingredients except garnish in mixing glass. Add ice and stir. Strain into glass and garnish.

RICKEY'S RUM

Yes, that Rickey . . . the limey

- 1 1/2 ounces light rum
- Juice of half a lime
- Club soda
- Lime slice for garnish

Pour rum and juice into ice-filled glass. Top with soda to taste, stir gently, and garnish.

 ROYAL SOUR

Fit for a king

- 2 ounces Barton Gold rum
- 1/2 ounce Chambord
- 1/2 ounce fresh sour mix
- Lemon twist for garnish

Combine liquid ingredients in mixing glass. Add ice, shake, strain into glass, and garnish.

 RUM AND H2O

Plain but good

- 2 1/2 ounces Bacardi 151
- 1 1/2 ounces still water

Pour rum and water into glass filled with ice and stir.

RUM AND SODA

For a bit of fizz

- 2 1/2 ounces gold rum
- 1 1/2 ounces club soda
- Lime wedge for garnish

Pour rum into glass filled with ice. Top with club soda, stir gently, and garnish.

 RUM AND SPRITE

With a little lemon-lime fizz

- 2 1/2 ounces dark rum
- 1 1/2 ounces Sprite
- Lime wedge for garnish

Pour liquids into ice-filled glass. Stir gently and garnish.

 RUM AND TONIC

Tonic = touch of sweetness

- 2 1/2 ounces gold rum
- 1 1/2 ounces tonic
- Lime wedge for garnish

Pour rum and tonic into ice-filled glass. Stir and garnish.

 RUM BLUEBIRD

With blueberry liqueur

- 2 ounces light rum
- 1/2 ounce blueberry liqueur
- 1/2 ounce fresh sour mix

Combine ingredients in mixing glass. Add ice, shake, and strain into glass.

 RUM DAISY

Light 'n' lemony

- 2 ounces light rum
- Juice of half a lemon
- 1 teaspoon grenadine
- 1/2 teaspoon powdered sugar
- Lemon slice for garnish

Combine all ingredients except garnish in glass filled with ice. Stir and garnish.

RUM

RUM FIZZES

Many rum cocktails are a riot of flavors, but some rum lovers like to keep it simple. The flavor of rum goes particularly well with fruit juices, especially those squeezed from tropical fruits.

RUM AND ORANGE

Pulpy O. J. or smooth? Your call

- 2 1/2 ounces light rum
- 1 1/2 ounces orange juice
- 1/2 teaspoon grenadine
- Club soda
- Orange slice for garnish

Pour rum and juice into glass filled with ice. Top with club soda to taste, stir gently, and garnish.

RUM AND LEMON

Use only freshly squeezed juice, of course

- 2 1/2 ounces light rum
- 1 1/2 ounces lemon juice
- Club soda
- Lemon slice for garnish

Prepare as in Rum and Orange.

RUM AND LIME

Fresh-from-the-fruit only!

- 2 1/2 ounces light rum
- 1 1/2 ounces lime juice
- 1 dash bitters of choice
- Club soda
- Lime slice for garnish

Prepare as in Rum and Orange.

RUM AND GRAPEFRUIT

Try Ruby Red grapefruit

- 2 1/2 ounces light rum
- 1 1/2 ounces grapefruit juice of choice
- 1 dash Angostura bitters
- Club soda
- Grapefruit wedge for garnish

Prepare as in Rum and Orange.

RUM AND PINEAPPLE

Take your pick of sweetened or unsweetened juice

- 2 1/2 ounces light rum
- 1 1/2 ounces pineapple juice
- Club soda
- Pineapple spear for garnish

Prepare as in Rum and Orange.

RUM JUBILEE

A celebration of Mentha piperita, or peppermint

- 3 sprigs peppermint
- 1/2 ounce fresh sour mix
- 2 ounces light rum
- Peppermint sprig for garnish

Muddle peppermint and sour mix in bottom of mixing glass. Add rum, ice, and shake. Strain into glass and garnish.

RUM LEMON DROP

A tongue-tingling treat

- 2 ounces light rum
- 1 ounce fresh sour mix
- Crushed ice
- Lemon twist for garnish

Combine rum and sour mix in mixing glass. Add ice and shake. Pour contents into glass filled with crushed ice and garnish.

RUM LOVER'S FRUIT CUP

Strong Bacardi with three tart juices

- 2 ounces Bacardi 151
- 1/2 ounce orange juice
- 1/2 ounce cranberry juice
- 1/2 ounce lemon juice

Combine ingredients in mixing glass. Add ice, shake, and strain into glass.

RUM MARTINI

And why not?

- 2 ounces gold or dark rum
- 1 ounce dry vermouth
- 3 olives for garnish

Pour rum and vermouth into mixing glass. Add ice and stir to chill. Strain into chilled glass and garnish.

RUMMY MEDITATION

With Bénédictine D.O.M., a cognac infused with aromatic herbs. The Bénédictine monks of a Normandy abbey began making the liqueur in 1510

- 2 ounces light rum
- 1 ounce Bénédictine
- Lemon twist for garnish

Pour rum and liqueur into mixing glass. Add ice and stir to chill. Strain into glass and garnish.

RUMMY MINT FIZZ

Oh, so good

- 2 ounces light rum
- 1/2 ounce white crème de menthe
- Club soda

Pour rum and liqueur into ice-filled glass. Top with club soda to taste and stir gently.

RUMMY SOUTHERN BELLE

Rum cuts in on a winsome drink that's usually made with bourbon

- 2 ounces light rum
- 1 1/2 ounces peach schnapps
- 1 1/2 ounces Southern Comfort
- Peach slice for garnish

Combine all ingredients except garnish in mixing glass. Add ice and stir to chill. Strain into martini glass or pour contents into rocks glass, then garnish.

RUM MUDSLIDE

Rum subs for the usual vodka

- 2 ounces light rum
- 2 ounces Baileys Irish Cream
- 1 ounce Kahlúa

Combine rum and Baileys in mixing glass. Add ice, shake, and strain into glass. Drizzle Kahlúa down inside of glass.

RUM NEGRONI

The gin of the true Negroni is here replaced with rum

- 2 ounces light rum
- 2 ounces Campari
- 2 ounces sweet vermouth
- Orange twist for garnish

Combine liquid ingredients in mixing glass. Add ice and stir to chill. Strain into martini glass or pour contents into rocks glass, then garnish.

RUM NUTSHAKER

The nuts in play: coconut and almond. Malibu is a rum-based, intensely flavored coconut liqueur often called Malibu rum

- 2 ounces Malibu rum
- 1 ounce crème de noyaux
- 1/2 ounce Kahlúa

Combine rum and liqueurs in glass filled with ice.

RUM OLD-FASHIONED

Who needs whiskey?

- 1 maraschino cherry
- 1 orange slice
- 1 teaspoon superfine sugar
- 2 ounces gold rum
- 4 dashes bitters of choice
- Club soda

Muddle fruit and sugar in bottom of glass, then add ice. Add rum and bitters, top with club soda to taste, and garnish.

RUM PRESBYTERIAN

For those who like it light

- 2 1/2 ounces Mount Gay rum
- 1/2 ounce club soda
- 1/2 ounce ginger ale

Pour rum into glass filled with ice. Top with club soda and ginger ale and stir gently.

RUM
PURPLE PASSION

With red grape juice

- 2 ounces light rum
- 1/2 ounces red grape juice
- 1/2 ounce raspberry liqueur
- White grape for garnish

Pour liquids into mixing glass. Add ice and stir to chill. Strain into glass and garnish.

RUM RICO

Rich served either way—straight up or on ice

- 2 ounces light rum
- 1 ounce Malibu rum
- 1 ounce cranberry juice
- 1 ounce crème de banane
- Orange twist for garnish

Combine liquid ingredients in mixing glass. Add ice and stir to chill. Strain into martini glass and garnish.

RUM SANGRIA

Rum subs for the usual red wine

- 2 ounces light rum
- 1/2 ounce ruby port
- 1/2 ounce dark crème de menthe
- 1/2 ounce club soda
- Citrus slices of choice for garnish

Combine rum, port, and liqueur in ice-filled glass. Top with soda, stir gently, and garnish.

RUM
SCREWDRIVER

Simplicity itself

- 1 1/2 ounces light rum
- 5 ounces orange juice

Pour rum and juice into glass filled with ice and stir.

RUM
SHAKER

Hold on tight

- 2 ounces dark rum
- 1/2 ounce Cointreau
- 1 ounce fresh sour mix
- 3 dashes orange bitters
- Crushed ice

Combine rum, liqueur, sour mix, and bitters in mixing glass. Add ice and stir to chill. Strain into glass filled with crushed ice.

RUM
STABILIZER

Sip after a big meal. Fernet-Branca is an herby digestif from Italy. The potent liqueur may take some getting used to but has legions of fans

- 2 ounces dark rum
- 2 ounces Fernet-Branca
- Lemon twist for garnish

Pour rum and bitters in ice-filled glass. Stir and garnish.

Quality Goods

Nobody could call the drinks that come from behind the bar of The Four Seasons stuffy (to the contrary, the house-originated cocktails are free-spirited and fun), but there is no mistaking the quality that goes into them. The bartenders choose cognac over brandy, Cointreau over triple sec. Each drink with soda gets a freshly opened bottle, not water from a bar gun. And all citrus juice is freshly squeezed, so that most customers who order, say, vodka with grapefruit juice state that it's the best they ever had. Even the citrus peel twists (see page 26) are different: not as pretty, perhaps, but superior to a regular twist as a flavoring.

Are we saying that you have to buy only the best to make the perfect drink? Of course not. The reliance of John, Charles, and Greg on expensive ingredients is understandable, given their commitment to Four Seasons customers. You might want to buy and keep to a bottle or two of the better stuff for parties, but even home bartenders on the tightest budget can mix knock-out drinks so long as they choose the right recipe, pay attention to what they're doing, and remember that "fresh is best."

 RUM STINGER

A minty refresher

- 2 ounces light rum
- 1/2 ounce white crème de menthe
- Mint sprig for garnish

Pour rum into ice-filled glass, top with liqueur, and garnish.

 RUM TWISTER

With two liqueurs

- 2 ounces light rum
- 1/4 ounce white crème de menthe
- 1/4 ounce crème de cacao
- Lemon twist for garnish

Pour liquids into mixing glass. Add ice and stir to chill. Strain into glass and garnish.

 ST. BARTS

A toast to the chic isle

- 2 ounces gold rum
- 1/2 ounce Cointreau
- Club soda
- Orange twist for garnish

Pour rum and liqueur into ice-filled glass. Top with club soda to taste, stir gently, and garnish.

 SELENA

In remembrance of the late singing star from Mexico

- 2 ounces light rum
- 1/2 ounce Cointreau
- 1/2 ounce orange juice
- 1/2 ounce grapefruit juice

Combine ingredients in glass filled with ice and stir.

SEÑOR MARIPOSA

With brandy and citrus juices

- 2 ounces gold rum
- 1/2 ounce brandy
- 1 tablespoon orange juice
- 1 tablespoon lemon juice
- 1 dash grenadine

Combine ingredients in mixing glass. Add ice, stir to chill, and strain into glass.

SEÑORA CAESAR

An Italian beauty. Galliano, introduced to most Americans by the Harvey Wallbanger cocktail, is yellow, sweet, and intriguingly complex

- 2 ounces light rum
- 1/2 ounce Galliano
- 1/2 ounce fresh sour mix
- Lemon twist for garnish

Combine rum, liqueur, and sour mix in mixing glass. Add ice and shake. Strain into glass and garnish.

SEÑORA McGILLICUDDY

With an Irish brogue

- 2 ounces light rum
- 1/2 ounce Irish Mist
- 1/2 ounce fresh sour mix
- Lemon twist for garnish

Combine rum, liqueur, and sour mix in mixing glass. Add ice and shake. Strain into glass and garnish.

SHIPWRECK

Malibu coconut rum (really a liqueur) to the rescue!

- 1 ounce light rum
- 1 ounce Malibu rum
- Pineapple juice
- 1 ounce Bacardi 151
- Pineapple spear for garnish

Pour light rum and Malibu rum into ice-filled glass. Fill with pineapple juice to taste. Stir, top with Bacardi, and garnish.

SOUR APPLE COCKTAIL

Pucker up

- 1 ounce light rum
- 1/2 ounce sour apple liqueur
- Apple slice for garnish

Pour rum and liqueur into glass filled with ice. Stir and garnish.

SOUR EMPEROR

Green with envy, perhaps? Midori is the green honeydew melon liqueur from Japan

- 2 ounces gold rum
- 1/2 ounce Midori
- 1/2 ounce fresh sour mix

Combine ingredients in mixing glass. Add ice, shake, and strain into glass.

RUM

SOUR GENERAL LEE

Imbibed at Appomattox?

- 2 ounces gold rum
- 1/2 ounce
  Southern Comfort
- 1/2 ounce fresh sour mix
- Orange twist for garnish

Combine ingredients in mixing glass. Add ice and shake. Strain into glass and garnish.

SOUR GORILLA

Better sour than irate . . .

- 2 ounces light rum
- 1/2 ounce
  crème de banane
- 1/2 ounce fresh sour mix

Combine ingredients in mixing glass. Add ice, shake, and strain into glass.

SOUR MONK

We all have bad days

- 2 ounces gold rum
- 1/2 ounce Bénédictine
- 1/2 ounce fresh sour mix

Combine ingredients in mixing glass. Add ice, shake, and strain into martini glass or pour contents into rocks glass.

SOUR THORN

Named for the blackthorn tree, the sloe plums of which are the source of sloe gin

- 2 ounces light rum
- 1/2 ounce sloe gin
- 1/2 ounce fresh sour mix
- Maraschino cherry
  for garnish

Combine rum, sloe gin, and sour mix in mixing glass. Add ice and shake. Strain into glass and garnish.

SQUIRREL'S NEST

An almondy treat, straight up or on ice

2 ounces dark rum
1/2 ounce amaretto
1/2 ounce
crème de noyaux

Combine ingredients in mixing glass. Add ice, shake, and strain into glass.

STARBURST

Three-fruit explosion

- 2 ounces light rum
- 1/2 ounce apricot brandy
- 1/2 ounce orange juice
- 1/2 ounce cranberry juice

Combine ingredients in glass filled with ice and stir.

BARTENDER'S TIP If you like playing bartender at parties—complete with taking charge of the shaker—take heed: As you shake a drink, turn away from other people. It's easier than you think for the top to come off a shaker and a bystander to have her nice new frock splattered with droplets of Piña Colada.

SUCCULENT MELON

Shares the glass with pineapple

- 2 ounces light rum
- 1/2 ounce Midori
- 1/2 ounce pineapple juice
- Club soda
- Lemon twist for garnish

Pour rum, liqueur, and juice into glass filled with ice. Top with club soda to taste, stir gently, and garnish.

 ## TIJUANA EXPRESS

For rum lovers partial to chocolate sundaes

- 1 1/2 ounces light rum
- 1/2 ounce dark crème de cacao
- Whipped cream for topping

Pour rum and liqueur into mixing glass. Add ice and shake. Strain into glass and top with whipped cream.

 ## TROPICAL BREEZE I

One drink, four fruit juices

- 1 1/2 ounces Mount Gay rum
- 1/2 ounce orange juice
- 1/2 ounce pineapple juice
- 1/2 ounce cranberry juice
- 2 drops lemon juice

Combine ingredients in glass filled with ice and stir.

 ## TROPICAL BREEZE 2

Less floral, more melony

- 2 ounces light rum
- 1/2 ounce pineapple juice
- 1/2 ounce Midori
- 1/2 ounce lemon juice
- Pineapple spear for garnish

Pour liquids into ice-filled glass. Stir and garnish.

 ## TWO-FOR-ONE

With light and dark rums

- 2 ounces light rum
- 2 ounces dark rum
- 1/2 ounce crème de menthe
- 1/2 ounce Cointreau
- 1/2 ounce Godiva Liqueur
- Chocolate stick for garnish

Combine ingredients in mixing glass. Add ice and shake. Strain into martini glass or pour contents into rocks glass, then garnish.

 ## VERY BERRY BERRY

Black currant + raspberry

- 2 ounces rum
- 1/4 ounce crème de cassis
- 1/4 ounce Chambord
- 1/4 ounce Absolut Kurant
- Raspberry for garnish

Pour rum and liqueurs into mixing glass. Add ice and stir to chill. Strain into glass and garnish.

VIRGIN SKIES

*Made with a rum from the
U.S. Virgin Islands*

- 2 ounces Cruzan Single
  Barrel Estate rum
- 1/2 ounce Midori
- 1/2 ounce pineapple juice
- 1/2 ounce grapefruit juice
- Splash of cranberry juice
- Pineapple spear
  for garnish

Combine liquid ingredients in
ice-filled glass, ending with
splash of cranberry. Stir
and garnish.

WHITE ISLAND

With Kahlúa and cream

- 2 ounces gold rum
- 1/2 ounce heavy cream
- 1/2 ounce Kahlúa

Combine ingredients in mixing
glass. Add ice, shake, and
strain into ice-filled glass.

ZOMBIE

In a word, BEWARE

- 1 1/2 ounces light rum
- 1 ounce Jamaica rum
- 1 ounce apricot brandy
- 2 ounces orange juice
- 1 ounce pineapple juice
  (unsweetened)
- 1 teaspoon
  superfine sugar
- 1/2 cup crushed ice
- 1 ounce Bacardi 151
- Pineapple spear
  for garnish
- Maraschino cherry
  for garnish

Combine light rum, Jamaica
rum, brandy, juices, sugar, and
ice in blender. Blend at low
speed for one minute, then
strain into frosted glass. Float
Bacardi on top and garnish.

TEQUILA

TEQUILA

This Mexican spirit is the gift of the blue agave, the huge succulent that grows in the country's desert reaches. The most popular types are silver tequila and gold tequila—the latter simply silver tequila with caramel or another flavoring. The crown jewel of tequilas is añejo, aged for one to three years and often likened to fine cognac.

ACAPULCO FIZZ

A toast to the scenic resort

- 2 ounces tequila
- 1 ounce lemon juice
- Sprite or 7-Up

Pour tequila and juice into ice-filled glass. Top with soft drink to taste and stir gently.

AFTER THE RAIN

Silver droplets, great taste

- 2 ounces silver tequila
- 1 ounce anisette

Pour tequila and liqueur into glass filled with ice and stir.

THE ALAMO

A drink to remember

- 1 1/2 ounces tequila
- 1/2 ounce amaretto
- 1 splash orange juice
- Lime twist for garnish

Combine tequila, liqueur, and juice in ice-filled glass. Stir and garnish.

ALOHA

Flavored with coconut rum

- 2 ounces tequila
- 1 ounce Malibu rum
- Pineapple spear for garnish

Pour tequila and rum into glass filled with ice. Stir and garnish.

APRICOT MARGARITA

With apricot brandy and Cointreau

- 1 1/2 ounces tequila
- 1/2 ounce apricot brandy
- 1/2 ounce Cointreau
- 1 splash Roses lime juice
- Lime wedge for garnish

Combine tequila, brandy, liqueur, and juice in mixing glass. Add ice, shake, and strain into glass. Garnish and serve with a straw.

ARTICHOKE HIGH

An artichoke-flavored apéritif

- 2 ounces tequila
- 1 ounce Cynar

Pour tequila and Cynar into glass filled with ice and stir.

BLOODY MARIA

Mary's Mexican cousin

- 2 ounces tequila
- 4 ounces tomato juice
- 1 tablespoon Worcestershire sauce
- 1 dash Tabasco
- Lime slice for garnish

Combine liquids in ice-filled glass. Stir and garnish.

BORDER CROSSING

Across the Rio Grande

- 1 1/2 ounces tequila
- 1/2 ounce orange juice
- 1/2 ounce pineapple juice
- 1/2 ounce Chambord
- Club soda
- Orange slice for garnish

Pour tequila, juices, and liqueur into glass filled with ice. Stir gently and garnish.

BRAVE BULL

Simple but classic

- 2 ounces tequila
- 1 ounce Kahlúa
- Lemon twist for garnish

Pour liquid ingredients in glass filled with ice and garnish.

CACTUS

Soothing, not prickly. The Mexican coffee-flavored liqueur Kahlúa has a roasted coffee taste with a hint of chocolate

- 2 ounces gold tequila
- 1 ounce Kahlúa
- Club soda
- Lemon twist for garnish

Pour tequila and liqueur into ice-filled glass. Top with club soda to taste, stir gently, and garnish.

CALIFORNIA SKY

Down Tijuana way

- 1 1/2 ounces silver tequila
- 1/2 ounce light rum
- 1/2 ounce blue curaçao
- 1/2 ounce fresh sour mix
- Maraschino cherry for garnish
- Orange slice for garnish

Combine tequila, rum liqueur, and sour mix in mixing glass. Add ice and shake. Strain into glass and garnish.

COCONUT CREAM

As rich as it gets

- 1 1/2 ounces tequila
- 1/2 ounce Malibu rum
- 1/2 ounce white crème de cacao
- 1/2 ounce heavy cream
- Coconut slice for garnish

Combine tequila, rum, liqueur, and cream in mixing glass. Add ice and shake. Strain into glass and garnish.

COSTA MESA

The recipe of a Texan transplanted to Paris

- 2 ounces tequila
- 4 ounces cranberry juice
- Club soda
- Lime wedge for garnish

Pour tequila and juice into ice-filled glass. Top with club soda to taste, stir gently, and garnish.

CRESCENT MOON

A drink for romantics

- 2 ounces tequila
- 1 ounce Pernod
- Lemon twist for garnish

Pour tequila and liqueur into glass filled with ice. Stir and garnish.

CRYSTAL PALACE

A shimmering beauty

- 1 ounce silver tequila
- 1 ounce Crown Royal whiskey
- 1 ounce Galliano
- Crushed ice

Pour tequila, whiskey, and liqueur into glass filled with crushed ice and stir.

DIVINE PLEASURE

Equal parts tequila and vodka

- 1 ounce Patrón silver tequila
- 1 ounce vodka
- 1 ounce fresh sour mix
- Lemon twist for garnish

Combine tequila, vodka, and sour mix in mixing glass. Add ice and shake. Strain into glass and garnish.

THE EXPLORER

In search of El Dorado

- 2 ounces José Cuervo Gold
- 1 ounce peach schnapps
- 1/2 ounce crème de cassis

Pour tequila and liqueurs into ice-filled glass and stir.

FOUR SEASONS MARGARITA

Our take on a classic

- 2 ounces tequila
- 1 ounce Cointreau
- 1 ounce fresh sour mix
- 1 splash Roses lime juice
- Lime wedge for garnish

Pour liquid ingredients into mixing glass. Add ice and shake. Strain into glass and garnish.

FROZEN MARGARITAS

Some folks—especially those who live in warmer climes—prefer their margaritas frozen. As you no doubt know, any margarita can be enjoyed frozen or nonfrozen, and that includes those shown here and on pages 128, 130, 134, 136, and 138.

BLUE MARGARITA

More liqueur than tequila

- 1 ounce silver tequila
- 1/2 ounce blue curaçao
- 1/2 ounce Cointreau
- 1/2 ounce Roses lime juice
- 10 ounces crushed ice
- Lime wedge for garnish

Combine liquids and ice in blender. Blend well at high speed, pour into glass, and garnish. Serve with a straw.

CHOCORITA

The inevitable chocolate one

- 1 1/2 ounces tequila
- 1/2 ounce Godiva Liqueur
- 1/2 ounce Cointreau
- 1 splash Roses lime juice
- 10 ounces crushed ice
- Chocolate stick for garnish

Combine liquids and ice and proceed as in Blue Margarita.

COFFEE MARGARITA

Muy Mexicano

- 1 1/2 ounces gold tequila
- 1/2 ounce Kahlúa
- 1/2 ounce Cointreau
- 1 splash Roses lime juice
- 10 ounces crushed ice
- Lime slice for garnish

Combine liquids and ice and proceed as in Blue Margarita.

MANGO MARGARITA

Tropical yet frosty

- 1 1/2 ounces tequila
- 1/2 ounce mango puree
- 1/2 ounce Cointreau
- 1 splash Roses lime juice
- 10 ounces crushed ice
- Mango slice for garnish

Combine liquids and ice and proceed as in Blue Margarita.

VANILLARITA

Anything but plain

- 1 1/2 ounces tequila
- 1/2 ounce Absolut Vanilia
- 1/2 ounce Cointreau
- 1 splash Roses lime juice
- 10 ounces crushed ice
- Lime wedge for garnish

Combine liquids and ice and proceed as in Blue Margarita.

TEQUILA

FROSTED ROSE

Named for its rosy color

- 2 1/2 ounces tequila
- 1 ounce grenadine
- Lemon twist for garnish

Pour liquids into ice-filled glass. Stir and garnish.

FROSTY WITCH

Casts a spell

- 1 1/2 ounces silver tequila
- 1/2 ounce amaretto
- 1/2 ounce pineapple juice

Pour tequila, liqueur, and juice into ice-filled glass. Stir and garnish.

GENTLE JUAN

This Juan prefers Tia Maria over nerve-jangling coffee

- 2 ounces tequila
- 1 ounce Tia Maria
- Lemon twist for garnish

Pour liquids into ice-filled glass. Stir and garnish.

GOLD LEAF

The leaf? Mint

- 2 ounces José Cuervo Gold
- 1 ounce white crème de menthe
- Mint sprig for garnish

Combine liquid ingredients in mixing glass. Add ice and stir to chill. Strain into glass and garnish.

THE GUADALUPE

Tequila, rum, and ginger

- 1 1/2 ounces tequila
- 1 ounce rum
- Ginger ale

Pour tequila and rum into ice-filled glass. Add ginger ale to taste, stir gently, and garnish.

GULF OF MEXICO

With blue curaçao liqueur

- 2 ounces gold tequila
- 1 ounce blue curaçao
- 1/2 ounce fresh sour mix

Combine ingredients in mixing glass. Add ice, shake, and strain into glass.

HOT SOUR

Pepper-flavored vodka gives it the heat

- 1 1/2 ounces tequila
- 1 1/2 ounces
- Absolute Peppar
- 1/2 ounce fresh sour mix
- Lemon twist for garnish

Combine liquid ingredients in mixing glass. Add ice, shake, strain into glass, and garnish.

ICE PICK

Spiked iced tea

- 2 ounces tequila
- 6 ounces tea of choice, sweetened to taste
- Lemon wedge for garnish

Pour liquids into ice-filled glass. Stir and garnish.

ICICLE

Straight tequila on ice

- Crushed ice
- 2 1/2 ounces
  silver tequila
- Lime slice for garnish

Fill glass with crushed ice.
Pour in tequila and garnish.

IRISH ECHO

Erin go bueno

- 1 1/2 ounces tequila
- 1 1/2 ounces Irish Mist
- Lemon twist for garnish

Pour liquids into ice-filled
glass. Stir and garnish.

LA BOMBA

*Traditionally served in
a sugar-rimmed glass*

- 1 1/2 ounces gold tequila
- 3/4 ounce Cointreau
- 1 1/2 ounces
  pineapple juice
- 1 1/2 ounces
  orange juice
- 2 dashes grenadine
- Lime slice for garnish

Combine liquid ingredients
in mixing glass. Add ice and
shake. Pour contents into
glass and garnish.

LANDSCAPER

Drink at a slow clip

- 2 ounces tequila
- 1 ounce green
  crème de menthe

Combine ingredients in glass
filled with ice and stir.

THE LIZARBE

*Named for a Four Seasons
cook from Mexico*

- 2 ounces tequila
- 1/2 ounce
  Absolut Vanilia
- 1/2 ounce heavy cream

Combine ingredients in
mixing glass. Add ice, shake,
and pour contents into glass.

LONG ISLAND SOUND

*A silver twist on the Gulf
of Mexico cocktail*

- 2 ounces
  Sauza silver tequila
- 1/2 ounce blue curaçao
- 1/2 ounce fresh sour mix
- Lemon twist for garnish

Combine tequila, liqueur,
and sour mix in mixing glass.
Add ice and shake. Strain
into glass and garnish.

THE FOUR SEASONS

TEQUILA

**MELON
MARGARITA**

Made green by Midori

- 1 1/2 ounces tequila
- 1/2 ounce Midori
- 1/2 ounce Cointreau
- 1 splash Roses lime juice
- Lime wedge for garnish

Combine liquid ingredients in
mixing glass. Add ice and
shake. Strain into glass and
garnish. Serve with a straw.

 MEXICANA I

An old favorite

- 2 ounces tequila
- 1 ounce pineapple juice
- 1 ounce fresh sour mix
- 1 teaspoon grenadine
- Maraschino cherry
  for garnish

Combine liquid ingredients in
mixing glass. Add ice and
shake. Strain into glass
and garnish.

 MEXICANA 2

*A tarter variation on
the original*

- 2 ounces tequila
- 1 ounce pineapple juice
- 1 tablespoon lemon juice
- Lemon twist for garnish

Combine liquid ingredients in
mixing glass. Add ice, shake,
strain into glass, and garnish.

 **MEXICAN
BANDIT**

May steal your heart

- 1 ounce tequila
- 1 ounce Myers's rum
- 1 ounce sambuca
- Lime twist for garnish

Combine tequila, rum, and
sambuca in mixing glass. Add
ice and shake. Strain into
glass, then garnish.

 **MEXICAN
DOCTOR**

Will fix you right up

- 2 ounces gold tequila
- 1 teaspoon grenadine
- 2 dashes bitters of choice
- Maraschino cherry
  for garnish

Pour tequila and grenadine
into ice-filled glass. Add
bitters, stir, and garnish.

**MEXICAN
EGG CREAM**

*Close your eyes and think
of Brooklyn*

- 2 ounces tequila
- 1 ounce white
  crème de cacao
- Club soda

Pour tequila and liqueur into
ice-filled glass. Top with club
soda to taste and stir gently.

MEXICAN HOLIDAY

Drink on Cinco de Mayo

- 2 ounces tequila
- 1 ounce Harveys Bristol Cream sherry

Pour tequila and sherry into glass filled with ice and stir.

MEXICAN KING

Tequila and Crown Royal

- 1 1/2 ounces tequila
- 1 1/2 ounces Crown Royal whiskey

Pour tequila and whiskey into ice-filled glass and stir.

MEXICAN MADRAS

Tequila with two juices

- 2 ounces tequila
- 2 ounces orange juice
- 1/2 ounce cranberry juice

Pour tequila and juices into glass filled with ice and stir.

MEXICAN STINGER

With cognac and mint

- 2 ounces Patrón silver tequila
- 1/2 ounce Rémy Martin V.S.O.P.
- 1 splash white crème de menthe
- Lemon twist for garnish

Combine liquid ingredients in glass filled with ice. Stir and garnish.

MEZCAL MARTINI

For your next chili cookoff

- 3 ounces mezcal
- 1 ounce sweet vermouth
- 3 jalapeño-stuffed olives for garnish

Pour mezcal and vermouth into mixing glass. Add ice, shake, strain into glass, and garnish.

MONTEREY SUNSET

Beautiful scene, beautiful drink

- 2 ounces tequila
- 1/2 ounce crème de cassis
- Club soda
- Lemon twist for garnish

Pour tequila and liqueur into glass filled with ice. Top with club soda to taste, stir gently, and garnish.

MUSIC TREE

You could break out in song

- 2 ounces gold tequila
- 1 ounce blue curaçao
- Pineapple juice
- Lemon twist for garnish

Combine tequila and liqueur in ice-filled glass. Top with juice to taste, stir, and garnish.

NAFTA

An across-the-border handshake

- 1 1/2 ounces tequila
- 1 1/2 ounce bourbon

Pour tequila and bourbon into glass filled with ice and stir.

NEW YORK SKYLINE

South-of-the-border salute to Gotham

- 2 ounces silver tequila
- 1 ounce cranberry juice
- 1/2 ounce lime juice
- 1 ounce club soda
- Lime twist for garnish

Pour tequila and juices into glass filled with ice. Top with club soda, stir gently, and garnish.

PEACH MARGARITA

Peachy keen

- 1 1/2 ounces tequila
- 1/2 ounce peach schnapps
- 1/2 ounce Cointreau
- 1 splash Roses lime juice
- Peach wedge for garnish

Combine liquid ingredients in mixing glass. Add ice, shake, and strain into glass. Garnish, then serve with a straw.

RAINDROP

Flavored with sambuca

- 2 ounces Sauza silver tequila
- 1 ounce sambuca
- 3 coffee beans for garnish

Pour tequila and liqueur into glass filled with ice. Stir and garnish.

RASPBERRY MARGARITA

Nice and red

- 1 1/2 ounces tequila
- 1/2 ounce framboise
- 1/2 ounce Cointreau
- 1 splash Roses lime juice
- Raspberry for garnish

Combine liquid ingredients in mixing glass. Add ice, shake, and strain into glass. Garnish and serve with a straw.

RED APPLE

With sour apple liqueur

- 1 ounce tequila
- 1 ounce sour apple liqueur
- 1/2 ounce Chambord
- Slice of apple for garnish

Combine liquids in ice-filled glass. Stir and garnish.

ROSITA

Pretty as a red rose

- 2 ounces tequila
- 1 ounce Campari
- 1/2 ounce Cointreau

Combine ingredients in ice-filled glass. Stir and garnish.

RUSTY STAKE

Nail, schmail

- 1 1/2 ounces gold tequila
- 1 1/2 ounces Drambuie
- Lemon twist for garnish

Combine tequila and liqueur in glass filled with ice. Stir and garnish.

SLOE TEQUILA

Follow with a siesta?

- 2 ounces tequila
- 1 ounce sloe gin
- 1/2 ounce fresh sour mix

Combine ingredients in mixing glass. Add ice, shake, and strain into glass.

SOUTH OF THE BORDER

Tequila with coffee liqueur and a kick of lemon

- 2 ounces gold tequila
- 3/4 ounce Kahlúa
- 1/2 ounce fresh sour mix

Combine ingredients in mixing glass. Add ice, shake, and strain into glass.

SPANISH IMPRESSIONIST

On this particular palette, tequila and sherry stand out

- 2 ounces tequila
- 1/2 ounce
  Tio Pepe sherry

Pour tequila and sherry into glass filled with ice and stir.

SPICED APPLE

With sour apple liqueur

- 2 ounces tequila
- 1 ounce sour apple liqueur
- Apple slice for garnish

Pour tequila and liqueur into glass filled with ice. Stir and garnish.

THE SPICY ENGLISHMAN

A jolly good cup. . .
but packing a mighty punch

- 2 ounces tequila
- 1 ounce Pimm's
- Lemon wedge for garnish

Pour liquid ingredients into glass filled with ice. Stir and garnish.

THE SPICY ITALIAN

Tequila with an Italian eau-de-vie (see Spicy Pear, page 138)

- 2 ounces tequila
- 1 ounce grappa

Pour tequila and grappa into glass filled with ice and stir.

TEQUILA

SPICY MELON

Tequila with a touch of honeydew liqueur

- 2 ounces tequila
- 1 ounce Midori

Pour tequila and liqueur into ice-filled glass and stir.

SPICY PEAR

Flavored with Poire William, the pear-flavored eau-de-vie (a clear, potent spirit distilled from fruit juice) made in Switzerland and France

- 2 ounces tequila
- 1 ounce Poire William

Pour tequila and liqueur into ice-filled glass and stir.

SPRING BREAK

In honor of generations of Acapulco-bound college students from Texas

- 2 ounces tequila
- 1 ounce pineapple juice
- 1 ounce orange juice

Pour ingredients into glass filled with ice and stir.

STRAWBERRY MARGARITA

To freeze or not to freeze?

- 1 1/2 ounces tequila
- 1/2 ounce strawberry schnapps
- 1/2 ounce Cointreau
- 1 splash Roses lime juice
- Strawberry for garnish

Combine liquid ingredients in mixing glass. Add ice, shake, and strain into glass. Garnish, then serve with a straw.

STRAWBERRY WHIP

The secret's in the schnapps

- 2 ounces tequila
- 1 ounce triple sec
- 1 ounce strawberry schnapps
- Strawberry for garnish

Pour ingredients into ice-filled glass. Stir and garnish.

TEN HIGH

Sparks a double high-five

- 2 ounces gold tequila
- 1 ounce Tuaca
- Lime twist for garnish

Pour liquids into ice-filled glass. Stir and garnish.

TEQUILA

TEQUILA AND TONIC

A no-nonsense draft for tequila lovers

- 2 ounces tequila
- Tonic water
- Lime slice for garnish

Pour tequila into ice-filled glass. Top with tonic to taste, stir gently, and garnish.

TEQUILA ANGEL

Light as a cloud

- 2 ounces Patrón silver tequila
- 1 ounce white crème de cacao
- Lemon twist for garnish

Combine tequila and liqueur in glass filled with ice. Stir and garnish.

TEQUILA APRICOT COOLER

Fizzy refreshment

- 2 ounces tequila
- 1 ounce apricot brandy
- Club soda
- Lemon twist for garnish

Combine tequila and liqueur in glass filled with ice. Top with club soda to taste, stir gently, and garnish.

TEQUILA CANYON

Carved out by the cranberry juice?

- 1 1/2 ounces tequila
- 1/4 ounce triple sec
- 4 ounces cranberry juice
- 1/2 ounce orange juice
- 1/2 ounce pineapple juice
- Lime slice for garnish

Pour tequila, liqueur, and cranberry juice into ice-filled glass. Top with orange and pineapple juices. Stir, garnish, and serve with a straw.

TEQUILA CLOUDS

With a silver lining, of course

- 1 1/2 ounces silver tequila
- 1/2 ounce white crème de menthe
- Sprite
- Lemon twist for garnish

Pour tequila and liqueur into ice-filled glass. Top with Sprite to taste, stir gently, and garnish.

TEQUILA COLLINS

Tom heads southwest

- 2 ounces tequila
- 1 ounce fresh sour mix
- Club soda
- Maraschino cherry for garnish
- Orange slice for garnish

Combine tequila and sour mix in mixing glass. Add ice, shake, and strain into ice-filled glass. Top with club soda to taste, stir gently, and garnish.

TEQUILA FIZZES

Carbonate tequila with club soda only if you're a purist. The spirit also blends nicely with soft drinks, making tequila fizzes good drinks for picnics. Serve these deceptively benign drinks on ice, and don't let their potency sneak up on you.

TEQUILA AND SODA

For those who like it unsweetened

- 2 ounces silver tequila
- Club soda
- Lime slice for garnish

Pour tequila into ice-filled glass. Top with club soda to taste, then garnish.

TEQUILA AND COKE

You'll be tempted to gulp. . . but take it easy

- 2 ounces tequila
- Coca-Cola
- Lime twist for garnish

Proceed as in Tequila and Soda.

TEQUILA AND GINGER

Ginger ale, of course

- 2 ounces tequila
- Ginger ale
- Lime slice for garnish

Proceed as in Tequila and Soda.

TEQUILA AND CREAM SODA

Silver tequila spikes a mellow old-timer

- 2 ounces silver tequila
- Cream soda
- Lime slice for garnish

Proceed as in Tequila and Soda.

TEQUILA AND CEL-RAY

With the piquant celery-flavored soft drink

- 2 ounces tequila
- Dr. Brown's Cel-Ray Soda
- Thin celery slice for garnish

Proceed as in Tequila and Soda.

TEQUILA AND ROOT BEER

A Latin bubbler

- 2 ounces gold tequila
- Root beer
- Lemon slice for garnish

Proceed as in Tequila and Soda.

TEQUILA GIMLET

With a touch of lime

- 1 1/2 ounces tequila
- 1/2 ounce Roses lime juice
- Lime slice for garnish

Pour liquids into ice-filled glass. Stir and garnish.

TEQUILA GREYHOUND

Tequila subs for vodka in this Latin version of a classic

- 2 ounces tequila
- Grapefruit juice

Pour tequila into glass filled with ice. Top with juice to taste and stir.

TEQUILA MANHATTAN

Tequila stands in for rye

- 2 1/2 ounces gold tequila
- 1 ounce sweet vermouth
- Lime slice for garnish

Combine tequila and vermouth in mixing glass. Add ice and shake. Pour contents into glass and garnish.

TEQUILA MOCKINGBIRD

Sings with a Latin beat

- 2 ounces tequila
- 1/2 ounce green crème de menthe
- Juice of one lime
- Lime slice for garnish

Combine tequila, liqueur, and juice in mixing glass. Add ice and shake. Pour contents into glass and garnish.

TEQUILA OLD-FASHIONED

A classic cocktail redefined

- 1 orange slice
- 1 maraschino cherry
- 1/2 teaspoon superfine sugar
- 2 ounces tequila
- 1 dash bitters of choice
- Still water

Muddle orange, cherry, and sugar in bottom of glass, then add ice. Pour in tequila and add bitters, stir, and top up with water.

TEQUILA PRES

Short for Presbyterian

- 2 ounces tequila
- Ginger ale
- Club soda
- Lime twist for garnish

Pour tequila into ice-filled glass. Top with equal parts ginger ale and club soda to taste, stir gently, and garnish.

TEQUILA SCREWDRIVER

Stronger than its vodka counterpart

- 2 ounces tequila
- 4 ounces orange juice

Combine tequila and juice in glass filled with ice and stir.

TEQUILA SOUR

Straightforward and tasty

- 2 ounces tequila
- 3 ounces fresh sour mix
- Lime slice for garnish

Combine tequila and sour mix in mixing glass. Add ice and shake. Strain into glass or pour contents into rocks glass before garnishing.

TEQUILA SUNRISE

Immortalized in song by Mr. Jimmy Buffett

- 2 ounces tequila
- 1/2 ounce grenadine
- 3 ounces orange juice

Combine ingredients in glass filled with ice and stir.

TEQUILA SUNSET

A pleasurable end to the day

- 2 1/2 ounces silver tequila
- 1/2 ounce Roses lime juice
- 1/2 ounce Chambord
- Lime slice for garnish

Combine liquids in ice-filled glass. Stir and garnish.

TIJUANA SUNSHINE

Catch some rays

- 2 ounces Sauza gold tequila
- 1 ounce orange juice
- 1/2 ounce Chambord
- Orange slice for garnish

Combine liquids in glass filled with ice. Stir and garnish.

THE VERA CRUZ

For a taste of Cancún

- 2 ounces tequila
- 1 ounce white crème de menthe
- 1 splash club soda
- Mint sprig for garnish

Pour tequila and liqueur into glass filled with ice. Splash with club soda and garnish.

WONKEY DONKEY

Steady there, boy

- 1 1/2 ounces tequila
- 1 1/2 ounces Mount Gay rum
- Lime slice for garnish

Pour liquids into ice-filled glass. Stir and garnish.

BRANDY

BRANDY

Regular brandy is distilled from wine, while fruit-flavored brandies are the fermented juice of the apple or other fruit. The finest wine brandy is cognac, distilled in and around the eponymous French town. While some cognacs are more affordable than others, a few hit the stratosphere. Should you win the lottery, you might want to consider a bottle of Rémy Martin Louis XIII—if you have around $1400 to spare.

APPLE BRANDY RICKEY

With a little lime. Calvados, from Normandy, is the king of apple brandies

- 1 1/2 ounces Calvados
- 1 splash
  Roses lime juice
- Club soda
- Lime wedge for garnish

Pour brandy into ice-filled glass. Add juice, then soda to taste. Stir gently and garnish.

APRICOT FIZZ

Apricot-flavored brandy is one of The Four Seasons bartenders' favorite mixers

- 2 ounces apricot brandy
- 1 ounce fresh sour mix
- 4 ounces club soda

Combine brandy, juice, and sugar in mixing glass. Add ice, shake, and pour contents into glass. Top with club soda and stir gently.

APRICOT KISS

For Scotch lovers

- 2 ounces apricot brandy
- 1 ounce Scotch
- 1/2 ounce
  sweet vermouth

Pour brandy, Scotch, and vermouth into glass filled with ice and stir.

APRICOT SOUR

Tart and refreshing

- 3 ounces apricot brandy
- 1 ounce fresh sour mix
- Orange slice for garnish
- Maraschino cherry
  for garnish

Combine liquid ingredients in mixing glass. Add ice and shake. Strain into glass and garnish.

ARMAGNAC COOLER

Gascony's gift to the world, Armagnac is slightly fuller in flavor than cognac

- 2 ounces Armagnac
- 1 ounce Absolut Vanilia
- Lemon-lime soda
- Lemon wedge for garnish

Pour brandy and vodka into glass filled with ice. Add soft drink to taste, stir gently, and garnish.

BARCELONA BABY

Flavored with orange and apricot . . . fruits that thrive in the fair Castilian capital

- 2 ounces apricot brandy
- 1 ounce gin
- 1 ounce orange juice
- 1/2 teaspoon sweet vermouth

Combine ingredients in mixing glass. Add ice, shake, and strain into glass.

BLACKBERRY BLAST

With a touch of chocolate

- 2 ounces Hiram Walker blackberry brandy
- 1 ounce Godiva Liqueur
- 1 ounce Baileys Irish Cream

Combine brandy and liqueurs in ice-filled glass and stir.

BLACKJACK

Two brandies plus cream

- 1 1/2 ounces brandy
- 1 ounce blackberry brandy
- 1 ounce heavy cream

Combine brandies and cream in mixing glass. Add ice, shake, and strain into glass.

BLISSFUL BANANA

Cognac teams up with a dreamy banana liqueur

- 2 ounces cognac
- 1 ounce crème de banane

Combine ingredients in mixing glass. Add ice, stir to chill, and pour contents into glass.

BRANDY ALEXANDER

Classic and ultrarich

- 1 1/2 ounces brandy
- 1 ounce white crème de cacao
- 1 ounce heavy cream
- Nutmeg for sprinkling

Combine brandy, liqueur, and cream in mixing glass. Add ice and shake. Strain into glass and sprinkle with nutmeg.

BRANDY AND SODA

See also Harmony, page 149

- 2 ounces brandy
- 5 ounces club soda
- Orange slice for garnish

Pour brandy into ice-filled glass. Top with club soda, stir gently, and garnish.

BRANDY CANDY CANE

No Santa cap required

- 2 ounces brandy
- 1/2 ounce green crème de menthe
- 1/2 ounce grenadine
- Maraschino cherry for garnish

Pour brandy, liqueur, and grenadine into glass filled with ice. Stir and garnish.

BRANDY MELON

An intriguing pairing

- 2 ounces brandy
- 1 ounce Midori
- Lime wedge for garnish

Pour brandy and liqueur into glass filled with ice. Stir and garnish.

BRANDY RUNNER

More polished than the typical rumrunner

- 1 1/2 ounces brandy
- 1 ounce pineapple juice
- 1 splash grenadine
- Maraschino cherry for garnish

Pour brandy and juice into ice-filled glass. Add splash of grenadine, stir, and garnish.

BRANDY STINGER

Fashionable in British literary circles of the 1930s

- 2 ounces brandy
- 1 ounce white crème de menthe
- Ice water

Pour brandy into glass filled with ice. Top with liqueur and stir. Serve with a glass of ice water as a chaser.

BRONZE BULLET

Fortified with B & B, a mix of brandy and Bénédictine liqueur

- 2 ounces brandy
- 1 ounce B & B
- Maraschino cherry for garnish

Pour brandy and B & B into glass filled with ice. Stir and garnish.

BULL MARKET

Affordable only at bonus time

- 2 1/2 ounces
  Rémy Martin
  Louis XIII cognac
- Club soda
- Lemon twist for garnish

Pour brandy into ice-filled glass. Add club soda to taste, stir gently, and garnish.

BURNT CHERRY

A cherry double whammy

- 2 ounces cherry brandy
- 1/2 ounce maraschino
- 1/2 ounce Cointreau
- 1/2 ounce lemon juice
- 1 tablespoon
  powdered sugar
- Maraschino cherry
  for garnish

Combine all ingredients except cherry in mixing glass. Add ice and shake. Strain into glass and garnish.

CAFÉ MYSTIQUE

With coffee-flavored brandy

- 2 ounces DeKuyper
  coffee-flavored brandy
- 1 1/2 ounces tawny port
- 1/2 teaspoon Cointreau
- 3 coffee beans for garnish

Combine brandy, port, and liqueur in mixing glass. Add ice and stir to chill. Strain into glass and garnish.

CENTRIFUGE

Whirling with flavor

- 2 ounces brandy
- 1 ounce black sambuca
- 1/4 ounce fresh sour mix

Combine ingredients in mixing glass. Add ice, shake, and strain into glass.

CHARMED

The flatterer is Madeira

- 2 ounces brandy
- 1 ounce Madeira
- 1/2 ounce Cointreau

Combine ingredients in mixing glass. Add ice, stir to chill, and strain into glass.

BRANDY

CHOCOLATE - COVERED CHERRY

As tempting as it sounds

- 1 1/2 ounces cherry brandy
- 1 1/2 ounces dark crème de cacao
- 1/2 ounce Kahlúa
- 1/2 ounce heavy cream

Combine ingredients in mixing glass. Add ice, shake, and strain into glass.

THE CLUB BOUNCER

A licorice-flavored drink that doesn't mess around

- 1 1/2 ounces brandy
- 1/2 ounce anisette
- 1 dash bitters of choice

Pour brandy and liqueur into glass filled with ice. Add bitters and stir.

CREAMY NUT

Embellished with nutmeg. Dark crème de cacao is a chocolate-flavored liqueur with a hint of vanilla. White crème de cacao is the liqueur's clear form

- 2 ounces brandy
- 1 ounce dark crème de cacao
- 1 ounce half-and-half
- 1/4 teaspoon grated nutmeg
- Nutmeg for sprinkling

Combine first four ingredients in mixing glass. Add ice and shake. Strain into glass and sprinkle with nutmeg.

ELIXIR OF LOVE

Inspired by Donizetti's opera

- 1 ounce apricot brandy
- 1 ounce cherry brandy
- 1 ounce sweet vermouth
- 1 ounce peach juice

Combine ingredients in mixing glass. Add ice, shake, and strain into glass.

FIFTH AVENUE

Old-guard and pricey

- 1 1/2 ounces brandy
- 1 ounce 25-year-old Macallan Scotch

Pour brandy and whiskey into glass filled with ice and stir.

FIGHTING IRISH

A toast to the footballers of Notre Dame

- 2 ounces brandy
- I ounce Irish whiskey
- Lemon twist for garnish

Pour liquids into ice-filled glass. Stir and garnish.

FREDO'S FAVE

The choice of a bookish regular

- 1 1/2 ounces Armagnac
- 1 1/2 ounces Grand Marnier
- Orange slice for garnish

Pour brandy and liqueur into glass filled with ice. Stir and garnish.

FRESH MELON

A great cognac casts its spell on a honeydew liqueur

- 1 1/2 ounces Martell Cordon Bleu
- 1/2 ounce Midori

Pour cognac and liqueur into glass filled with ice.

 GINICOT

Apricot brandy with gin

- 2 ounces apricot brandy
- 1 ounce gin
- 1 ounce fresh sour mix
- Club soda

Combine brandy, gin, and sour mix in mixing glass. Add ice and shake. Pour contents into glass. Top with club soda to taste and stir gently.

 HARMONY

Brandy in tune with soda

- 2 ounces brandy
- 1 ounce fresh sour mix
- 3 ounces club soda
- Orange slice for garnish

Pour brandy and sour mix into mixing glass. Add ice, shake, and pour contents into glass. Add club soda, then garnish.

IRISH BEAUTY

With a French background

- 2 ounces cognac
- 1 ounce Irish Mist

Pour cognac and liqueur into snifter and swirl to mix.

 JACK ROSE

A sturdy old-timer

- 1 1/2 ounces applejack
- Juice of half a lime
- 1 teaspoon grenadine

Combine ingredients in mixing glass. Add ice, shake, and strain into glass.

 KENTUCKY FINISHER

After-dinner drink for country gentlemen of means

- 1 1/2 ounces Hennessy X.O. cognac
- 1 ounce Wild Turkey bourbon

Pour cognac and bourbon into glass filled with ice and stir.

 KISSING COUSINS

They hail from France

- 2 ounces cognac
- 1 ounce anisette

Pour brandy and liqueur into mixing glass. Add ice, shake, and strain into glass.

 LEMON FROST

A tart pleasure

- 2 ounces brandy
- 1 ounce fresh sour mix
- Lemon twist for garnish

Combine brandy and sour mix in mixing glass. Add ice and shake. Strain into glass and garnish.

BRANDY

LIGHTNING FLASH

With lashings of vermouth

- 2 ounces brandy
- 1/2 ounce sweet vermouth
- 1/2 ounce dry vermouth
- 2 teaspoons Cointreau

Combine ingredients in mixing glass. Add ice, stir to chill, and strain into glass.

MINT LEAF

An eclectic mix

- 2 ounces brandy
- 1/2 ounce dry vermouth
- 1/2 ounce tawny port
- 1 splash white crème de menthe
- 1 ounce orange juice
- 1 teaspoon grenadine
- Mint sprig for garnish

Combine liquid ingredients in mixing glass. Add ice, shake, strain into glass, and garnish.

MUSIC NOTE

Tinkle, tinkle, little cubes . . .

- 2 ounces brandy
- 1 ounce fresh sour mix
- 1/2 teaspoon grenadine
- Orange slice for garnish
- Maraschino cherry for garnish

Combine brandy, sour mix, and grenadine in mixing glass. Add ice and shake. Strain into glass and garnish.

NATURE'S ESSENCE

With three fruit flavors

- 2 ounces brandy
- 1 1/2 ounces maraschino
- 1/2 ounce Cointreau
- 1 ounce pineapple juice
- 2 dashes Angostura bitters

Combine all ingredients in mixing glass. Add ice, shake, and strain into glass.

THE RUMSFELD

A resolute draft

- 2 ounces brandy
- 1 ounce light rum
- 1 ounce Cointreau
- 1 ounce fresh sour mix

Combine all ingredients in mixing glass. Add ice, shake, and strain into glass.

SHADOW OF YOUR SMILE

Sing it 'n' sip, Tony B.

- 2 ounces brandy
- 1 ounce amaretto
- 1 ounce peach schnapps
- Crushed ice

Combine ingredients in glass filled with crushed ice and stir.

THE SIDECAR

Most cocktail historians credit a bartender at Harry's New York Bar in Paris with the invention of this classic. It was named, they say, for a World War I army captain who was ferried to and from the bar in the sidecar of a motorcycle.

SIDECAR

A favorite in Prohibition days

- 2 ounces brandy
- 1 ounce fresh sour mix
- 1 splash Cointreau

Combine ingredients in mixing glass. Add ice, shake, and strain into glass.

FOUR SEASONS SIDECAR

Spares no expense

- 2 ounces Hennessy Paradis Cognac
- 1 ounce fresh sour mix
- 1 splash sweet vermouth

Combine ingredients in mixing glass and proceed as in Sidecar.

SWEET SIDECAR

With sweet vermouth

- 2 ounces brandy
- 1 ounce sweet vermouth
- 1 ounce fresh sour mix
- 1 splash Cointreau
- Maraschino cherry for garnish

Combine liquid ingredients in mixing glass. Add ice and shake. Strain into glass and garnish.

HOERDEMANN'S HOWL

A Sidecar variation said to make a reserved regular "howl with delight."

- 2 ounces Rémy Martin X.O. cognac
- 1 ounce Cointreau
- 1 ounce lemon juice
- 1/2 ounce sweet vermouth
- 1/2 ounce peach schnapps
- Lemon twist for garnish

Combine liquid ingredients in mixing glass and proceed as in Sweet Sidecar.

BRANDY

An American Landmark

One reason for the worldwide renown of The Four Seasons is its architectural provenance. How many restaurants occupy space designed by two of architecture's leading lights?

It was Phyllis Bronfman Lambert, daughter of Seagram Corporation founder Samuel Bronfman, who enlisted the team of Mies van der Rohe and Phillip Johnson to take on the task of designing a new Seagram headquarters in Manhattan. Having studied architecture at New York University, Lambert took great interest in her father's plans. She sought to explain, she recalled, "what the business's responsibility could mean in terms of architecture, and to convince [my father] of the validity of the new architectural thinking."

The German-born American architect Mies van der Rohe was a driving force behind the International Style, with its unornamented, seemingly weightless glass-and-steel buildings of cantilever construction. His design of the Seagram Building (van der Rohe's only building in New York) stands as one of his crowning achievements. Phillip Johnson, then architecture director at New York's Museum of Modern Art and an acolyte of van der Rohe's, designed the spare and elegant interiors.

The fruit of their labors opened in 1958: a dramatic black, "floating" skyscraper set 100 feet back from Park Avenue on a grand open plaza. And, to the good fortune of food lovers everywhere, an expansive space on the Seagram Building's south side was set aside for a restaurant—The Four Seasons, a landmark for the past 44 years and, like the Seagram Building, officially designated as such.

SILVER STREAK

For those with a taste for gin

- 1 1/2 ounces brandy
- 1/2 ounce gin
- 1 splash Roses lime juice
- Lime wedge for garnish

Pour brandy and gin into glass filled with ice. Add splash of juice, stir, and garnish.

THE SIT-DOWN

The drink you can't refuse

- 2 ounces Rémy Martin Louis XIII cognac
- 1 fine cigar

Pour brandy into steamed glass and light cigar. Sip, puff, and hope for the best.

SONNY'S LIMBO

A steel-drum dance of a drink

- 2 ounces peach brandy
- 2 ounces pineapple juice
- Pineapple spear for garnish

Combine liquids in ice-filled glass. Stir and garnish.

SOUR CHERRY

Tart and refreshing

- 2 ounces cherry brandy
- 1/2 ounce lemon juice
- 4 ounces club soda
- Lime wedge for garnish

Combine brandy and juice in mixing glass. Add ice, shake, and pour contents in glass. Add soda, stir gently, and garnish.

SOUR GRAPES

Brandy soured by apple . . . but happily so

- 1 1/2 ounces brandy
- 1/2 ounce sour apple liqueur
- 1/2 ounce fresh sour mix

Pour ingredients into mixing glass. Add ice, shake, and strain into glass.

SOUTHERN NAIL

Rémy meets Jack

- 1 1/2 ounces Rémy Martin V.S.O.P.
- 1 ounce Jack Daniels Tennessee whiskey

Pour liquids into ice-filled glass and stir.

SUPREMO

The name speaks for itself

- 2 ounces cognac
- 1 ounce Spanish brandy

Pour brandies into glass filled with ice and stir.

SWEET APPLE

Applejack (a strong American apple brandy) with vermouth

- 2 1/2 ounces applejack
- 1 1/2 ounces sweet vermouth
- Apple slice for garnish

Combine ingredients in mixing glass. Add ice and stir to chill. Strain into glass and garnish.

SWEET IVORY

Fizzy and toothsome

- 2 ounces brandy
- 1 teaspoon superfine sugar
- 3 ounces club soda
- Maraschino cherry for garnish

Combine brandy and sugar in mixing glass. Add ice, stir to chill, and strain into glass. Top with club soda, stir gently, and garnish.

TERMINATOR COCKTAIL

Based on a popular shot recipe

- 2 ounces blackberry brandy
- 2 ounces dark rum
- 2 ounces cranberry juice
- Lemon wedge for garnish

Combine brandy, rum, and juice in ice-filled glass and garnish. Serve with a straw.

THEO'S CADIZ

A slight variation on the Cadiz, a creamy classic

- 1 ounce Hiram Walker blackberry brandy
- 1/2 ounce dry sherry
- 1/2 ounce triple sec
- 1 tablespoon light cream

Combine ingredients in mixing glass. Add ice, shake, and strain into glass.

TREETOP

Lemon tree very pretty . . .

- 2 ounces brandy
- 1/2 ounce Stoli Limonnaya vodka
- 1 ounce fresh sour mix

Pour brandy, vodka, and sour mix into mixing glass. Add ice, shake, and strain into glass.

VANILLA DREAM

Featuring a vanilla-scented liqueur from Tuscany

- 2 ounces brandy
- 1 ounce Tuaca
- 1 ounce heavy cream
- 1/4 teaspoon grated nutmeg
- Nutmeg for sprinkling

Combine first four ingredients in mixing glass. Add ice and shake. Strain into glass and sprinkle with nutmeg.

WILLIAM TELL

Apple brandy shot through with lemon-lime

- 2 ounces apple brandy
- 4 ounces Sprite or 7-Up
- Lemon wedge for garnish

Pour brandy into ice-filled glass, top with soft drink, stir gently, and garnish.

LIQUEURS

LIQUEURS

Liqueurs date back to the monasteries and apothecaries of the Middle Ages, when herbs were added to medicinal potions to improve the taste. Today these sweet mixtures are essential to the art of mixology, adding a grace note to a cocktail or, as here, serving as the starting point for pleasant after-dinner drinks.

ALABAMMY DELIGHT

Bring out the banjo

- 2 ounces Southern Comfort
- 1 ounce amaretto
- 1/2 ounce sloe gin
- 1/2 ounce lemon juice

Combine ingredients in mixing glass. Add ice, shake, and pour contents into glass.

AMALFI COAST

Home of Italy's lemony liqueur

- 2 ounces limoncello
- 1 ounce Cointreau
- 1 ounce lime juice
- Lemon twist for garnish

Combine liqueurs and juice in mixing glass. Add ice and shake. Strain into glass and garnish.

AMARETTO SOUR

Almonds on the rocks

- 3 ounces amaretto
- 1 ounce fresh sour mix
- Orange slice for garnish
- Maraschino cherry for garnish

Combine amaretto and sour mix in mixing glass. Add ice and shake. Pour contents into glass and garnish.

THE ARISTOCRAT

Class in a glass. Cognac-based Grand Marnier is the queen of the orange liqueurs—rich but not excessively sweet

- 2 ounces Grand Marnier Cuvée du Cinquantenaire
- 1 ounce Rémy Martin V.S.O.P. cognac

Pour liqueur and Cognac into glass and stir.

B & B STINGER

Mint makes a prized liqueur sing. A mix of Bénédictine and brandy, topaz-colored B & B is relatively dry

- 2 ounces B & B
- 1 ounce white crème de menthe

Combine ingredients in mixing glass. Add ice, stir to chill, and strain into glass.

BANSHEE

Wild for bananas

- 2 ounces crème de banane
- 1 ounce white crème de cacao
- 1 ounce light cream

Combine ingredients in mixing glass. Add ice, shake, and strain into glass.

BLUE CRUSH

A variation on the Blue Wave

- 1 ounce blue curaçao
- 1 ounce Cointreau
- 1 ounce vodka
- 1 ounce Malibu rum
- Crushed ice
- Orange twist for garnish

Combine liqueurs, vodka, and rum in mixing glass. Add ice and stir to chill. Strain into glass filled with crushed ice and garnish.

BLUE WAVE

Catch it, dude

- 1 ounce blue curaçao
- 1 ounce Cointreau
- 1 ounce white crème de cacao
- 1 ounce vodka

Combine liquids in mixing glass. Add ice, stir to chill, and strain into glass.

BOCCIE BALL

Classic named for the Italian game of bowls

- 3 ounces amaretto
- 4 ounces fresh orange juice

Pour liqueur and juice into ice-filled glass and stir.

BREAKFAST AT TIFFANY'S

Scenes in the 1960 movie were shot on the plaza of the Seagram Building, home of The Four Seasons

- 1 ounce Southern Comfort
- 1 ounce orange juice
- 1/2 teaspoon grenadine
- 3 ounces champagne

Combine Southern Comfort, juice, and grenadine in mixing glass. Add ice and shake. Strain into glass, top with champagne, and stir gently.

THE CELIBATE

A monkish drink almost light enough for abstainers

- 1/2 ounce Frangelico
- 3 1/2 ounces club soda

Pour liqueur into glass filled with ice. Top with club soda and stir gently.

CHARLES'S RELAXER

A soothing mix

- 2 ounces amaretto
- 1 1/2 ounces dry vermouth

Combine ingredients in glass and stir.

CHATEAU KISS

Chambord: the Loire Valley chateau that gave the black raspberry liqueur its name

- 2 ounces Baileys Irish Cream
- 1 ounce Chambord
- 1/2 ounce Grand Marnier

Combine ingredients in glass filled with ice, then stir.

CHATEAU MONK

Chambord and Fra. Angelico's hazelnut concoction team up with a creamy Irish liqueur

- 2 ounces Baileys Irish Cream
- 1 ounce Chambord
- 1 ounce Frangelico

Combine ingredients in glass filled with ice and stir.

COASTAL DREAM

The coast? The Amalfi, on the Gulf of Salerno

- 1 ounce limoncello
- 1 ounce cherry brandy
- 1 ounce lemon juice
- 1 ounce lime juice
- Lime twist for garnish

Combine liqueur, brandy, and juices in mixing glass. Add ice and shake. Strain into glass and garnish.

THE COMFORTER

For when you've had what's been called "an elegant sufficiency"—i.e., you stuffed yourself

- 1 1/2 ounces white crème de menthe
- 1 1/2 ounces port

Combine liqueur and port in glass, then stir.

COOL KISS

Mucho minty

- 2 ounces peppermint schnapps
- 1/2 ounce blue curaçao
- 1 ounce lemon juice
- 4 ounces club soda

Combine schnapps, liqueur, and juice in mixing glass. Add ice, shake, and pour contents into glass. Top with club soda and stir gently.

CORDIALS

The word "cordial" is synonymous with "liqueur," but time was when it meant a dainty liqueur-based drink with a good percentage of fruit juice. Call the drinks what you may, these hearty cordials—like many of the other fruity drinks in this chapter—will make you smile.

HEAT WAVE

A welcome cooler-offer

- 1 1/2 ounces Malibu rum
- 1/2 ounce peach schnapps
- 3 ounces orange juice
- 3 ounces pineapple juice
- 1/2 ounce grenadine

Combine ingredients in glass filled with ice and stir.

MELON BALL CORDIAL

With pineapple and orange

- 1/2 ounce Midori
- 1/2 ounce vodka
- 2 ounces pineapple juice
- 1 ounce orange juice

Combine ingredients in glass filled with ice and stir.

ORANGE BLAST

Blowing up from the south

- 1 ounce Southern Comfort
- 1 ounce Cointreau
- 2 ounces fresh orange juice

Combine ingredients in ice-filled glass and stir.

PLANTATION

The crops? Honeydew melon and orange

- 2 ounces Southern Comfort
- 2 ounces Midori
- 4 ounces fresh orange juice

Combine ingredients in glass filled with ice, then stir.

TEQUILA DELIGHT

With Agavero tequila liqueur

- 2 ounces Agavero
- 4 ounces cranberry juice
- Orange slice for garnish

Combine liqueur and juice in glass filled with ice. Stir, then garnish.

COURT JESTER

"Oh, that's rich!" Black-cherry-flavored Cherry Heering is also called Peter Heering, after the Dane who created it c. 1835

- 1 ounce
  Cherry Heering
- 1 ounce white
  crème de cacao
- 1 ounce heavy cream
- Maraschino cherry
  for garnish

Combine liquid ingredients in mixing glass. Add ice, shake, strain into glass, and garnish.

CREAMSICLE CLOSER

An after-dinner indulgence

- 2 ounces Cointreau
- 1 ounce white
  crème de cacao
- 1 ounce heavy cream

Combine ingredients in mixing glass. Add ice, shake, and strain into glass.

THE DEAL-CLOSER

Equal shares all around

- 1 ounce B & B
- 1 ounce white
  crème de cacao
- 1 ounce white
  crème de menthe

Pour liqueurs into glass filled with ice and stir.

DE CHIRICO'S DELIGHT

Green, like the artist's favored color

- 2 ounces sambuca
- 1 ounce green Chartreuse
- 1 ounce Southern Comfort

Combine ingredients in glass filled with ice, then stir.

DOW-WOW

For those whose fortunes have suddenly taken a turn for the better

- 1 ounce Southern Comfort
- 2 ounces Drambuie
- 1 ounce scotch

Pour ingredients into glass and stir.

THE EROICA

Named for Beethoven's symphonic tribute to Napoleon I of France

- 2 ounces
  Jägermeister bitters
- 1 ounce Pernod
- 1 ounce orange juice
- 4 ounces soda
- Orange twist for garnish

Combine bitters, liqueur, and juice in ice-filled glass. Top with club soda, stir gently, and garnish.

FRUIT BASKET

Fruit flavor times three

- 1 ounce peach schnapps
- 1 ounce
  sour apple schnapps
- 1 ounce apricot brandy

Combine ingredients in mixing glass. Add ice, stir to chill, and strain into glass.

FUZZY NAVEL

Navel as in navel orange, thank goodness!

- 1 1/2 ounces
  peach schnapps
- 4 ounces orange juice

Pour schnapps into glass filled with ice. Top with juice and stir.

GRASSHOPPER

Still a favorite after all these years

- 1 ounce green
  crème de menthe
- 1 ounce white
  crème de cacao
- 1 ounce light cream

Combine ingredients in mixing glass. Add ice, shake, and strain into glass.

GREEN IRISH TWEED

Try it on for size

- Crushed ice
- 2 ounces
  Baileys Irish Cream
- 1 ounce green crème
  de menthe
- 1 ounce white
  crème de cacao

Combine ingredients in glass filled with crushed ice and stir.

HARVEST CORDIAL

Fall flavors laced with lemon

- 1 ounce Midori
- 1 ounce
  sour apple schnapps
- 1 ounce limoncello
- 1 ounce lemon juice

Combine ingredients in mixing glass. Add ice, shake, and strain into glass.

HELGA IN LOVE

She adores schnapps

- 1 ounce peach schnapps
- 1 ounce Southern Comfort
- 1 ounce apricot brandy
- 1 ounce limoncello

Combine ingredients in mixing glass. Add ice, stir to chill, and strain into glass.

HER EYES

*Inspired by the beautiful eyes
of a regular customer*

- 1 ounce Chambord
- 1 ounce Grand Marnier
- 1 ounce B & B

Pour liqueurs into
glass and stir.

THE HORSE'S MOUTH

For straight-shooters

- 1 ounce
  Southern Comfort
- 1 ounce Grand Marnier
- 1 ounce cognac

Pour ingredients into glass,
then stir.

IRISH MONK

A blessed winter warmer

- 2 ounces Frangelico
- 2 ounces Jameson
  Irish whiskey

Pour whiskey and liqueur into
glass filled with ice, then stir.

ITALIAN ROOT BEER

*Tastes just like the old
American favorite. For a
fancier version, see Pretend
Root Beer, page 164*

- 2 ounces Galliano
- 4 ounces Coca-Cola

Pour liqueur into glass, top
with soft drink, and stir gently.

JADE DREAM

Green flavor-conjurer

- 1 ounce Midori
- 1 ounce vodka
- 1 ounce apricot brandy
- 1 ounce light cream

Combine ingredients in
mixing glass. Add ice, shake,
and strain into glass.

JOHNNIE SPRITELY

*Mr. Walker introduces
himself to a soft drink*

- 2 ounces Midori
- 1 ounce
  Johnnie Walker Scotch
- 4 ounces Sprite
- 1 ounce lemon juice
- Club soda
- Lime wedge for garnish

Combine first four ingredients
in mixing glass. Add ice, shake,
and pour contents into glass.
Top with club soda to taste,
stir gently, and garnish.

LA BOHÈME

To die for

- 2 ounces limoncello
- 1 ounce Pernod
- 1 ounce orange juice
- 4 ounces club soda

Pour liqueurs and juice into
ice-filled glass. Top with club
soda and stir gently.

LICORICE DELIGHT

The name says it all

- 2 ounces sambuca
- 1 ounce white crème de cacao
- 1 ounce light cream

Combine ingredients in mixing glass. Add ice, shake, and strain into glass.

MANDOLIN

Inspired by the songs of the gondoliers

- 1 ounce Frangelico
- 1 ounce Grand Marnier Cuvée du Centenaire
- 1 ounce Punt e Mes

Pour liqueurs into glass and stir.

MELLOW ORANGE

With vanilla vodka

- 2 ounces Grand Marnier
- 1 ounce Stoli Vanil
- 1 ounce orange juice

Combine liqueur, vodka, and juice in glass filled with ice.

MELON KISS

One smooth smooch

- 2 ounces Midori
- 1 ounce vodka
- 1 ounce light cream

Combine ingredients in mixing glass. Add ice, shake, and strain into glass.

NASDAQ JITTERS

Hits the spot when you need a lift

- 1 ounce Drambuie
- 1 ounce B & B
- 1 ounce Scotch

Pour ingredients into glass filled with ice and stir.

NEWTON'S APPLE

A bubbly inspiration

- 2 ounces Pimm's No. 1
- 1 ounce Bombay gin
- 1 ounce sour apple liqueur
- 3 ounces club soda

Pour Pimm's, gin, and liqueur into ice-filled glass. Top with club soda and stir gently.

ORANGE CREAM

Lick your lips and enjoy

- 2 ounces Grand Marnier
- 1 ounce white crème de cacao
- 1 ounce light cream

Combine ingredients in mixing glass. Add ice, shake, and strain into glass.

THE O'REILLY

Irish with a touch of Italian

- 2 ounces Baileys Irish Cream
- 1 ounce Irish Mist
- 1 ounce amaretto

Combine ingredients in glass filled with ice and stir.

PEACHY-KEEN

With a touch of coffee

- 1 ounce peach schnapps
- 1/2 ounce coffee liqueur
- 1/2 ounce bourbon
- 1 ounce vodka
- 1 ounce light cream

Combine ingredients in mixing glass. Add ice, shake, and strain into glass.

PEPPERMINT PATTY

Sweet as candy

- 1 ounce white crème de menthe
- 1 ounce dark crème de cacao
- 1 ounce Godiva Liqueur
- 1 ounce Absolut Vanilia
- Chocolate stick for garnish

Combine liquid ingredients in mixing glass. Add ice and stir to chill. Strain into glass and garnish.

PEPPERMINT SWIRL

Minty and cooling. The word schnapps ("mouthful") is German, but most of these sweet-to-dry alcohols are produced in Denmark

- 1 ounce peppermint schnapps
- 1 ounce Kahlúa
- 1/2 ounce Godiva Liqueur
- 1 ounce light cream

Combine ingredients in mixing glass. Add ice, shake, and strain into glass.

THE PIAZZA

Transports you to sunny Italy

- 2 ounces Tuaca
- 1 ounce vodka
- 1 ounce fresh sour mix

Pour ingredients into mixing glass. Add ice, shake, and strain into glass.

PINK SQUIRREL MEAL-ENDER

A postprandial smoothie

- 2 ounces crème de noyaux
- 1 ounce white crème de cacao
- 1 ounce light cream

Combine ingredients in mixing glass. Add ice, shake, and strain into glass.

PRETEND ROOT BEER

Made with another soft drink

- 2 ounces Kahlúa
- 2 ounces Galliano
- 2 ounces Coca-Cola
- 2 ounces club soda

Pour liqueurs into ice-filled glass. Top with cola and club soda and stir gently.

PURPLE BLISS

With black raspberry

- 1 1/2 ounces Chambord
- 1 ounce apricot brandy
- 1/2 ounce pineapple juice

Combine liquid ingredients in mixing glass. Add ice, shake, and strain into glass.

RIVERSIDE DRIVE

As respectable as the address

- 1 ounce limoncello
- 1 ounce Grand Marnier
- 1 ounce vodka
- 1 ounce cranberry juice
- Orange twist for garnish

Combine liqueurs, vodka, and juice in mixing glass. Add ice and shake. Strain into glass and garnish.

SLOE AND EASY

A drink for a lazy afternoon

- 1 ounce sloe gin
- 1/2 ounce gin
- 1/2 ounce vodka
- 2 ounces fresh orange juice
- Orange slice for garnish

Combine liquid ingredients in glass filled with ice. Stir, then garnish.

SOUTHERN PLEASURE

Sip under gnarled oak hung with Spanish moss

- 2 ounces Southern Comfort
- 1 ounce peach schnapps
- 1 ounce apricot schnapps
- 2 ounces fresh orange juice
- 2 ounces cranberry juice
- Orange slice for garnish

Combine liquid ingredients in mixing glass. Add ice, shake, and pour contents into glass. Garnish, then serve with a straw, if desired.

THE SPARTAN

Stoic, like its namesake

- 1 ounce ouzo
- 7 ounces club soda

Pour ouzo into ice-filled glass. Top with club soda and stir gently.

STARRY SKIES

A flavorful constellation

- 1 ounce amaretto
- 1 ounce Chambord
- 1 ounce Drambuie

Pour liqueurs into glass and stir.

STRAIGHT SAMBUCA

In Italian tradition, the three coffee beans represent health, wealth, and prosperity

- 3 ounces sambuca
- 3 coffee beans

Pour into glass and garnish.

SWEET LASS

And a pretty colleen she is

- 1 ounce Baileys Irish Cream
- 1 ounce Jameson Irish whiskey
- 1 ounce Chambord
- 1/2 ounce grenadine

Combine ingredients in mixing glass. Add ice, shake, and strain into glass.

TOASTED ALMOND

With coffee and cream

- 1 1/2 ounces amaretto
- 1 1/2 ounces Kahlúa
- 1 ounce heavy cream

Combine liqueurs and
cream in mixing glass.
Add ice, shake, and
pour contents into glass.

THE TREE HUGGER

*A Four Seasons managing
partner's tribute to his
counterpart*

- 1 ounce Jägermeister
- 1/2 ounce sour apple
  schnapps

Combine liquid ingredients in
mixing glass. Add ice, stir to
chill, and strain into glass.

VANILLA KISS

With a little vanilla vodka

- 2 ounces Godiva
  White Chocolate Liqueur
- 1 ounce white
  crème de cacao
- 1 ounce Absolut Vanilia

Combine liquid ingredients in
mixing glass. Add ice, shake,
and strain into glass.

VELVET ALMOND

*Not just any nut. Amaretto di
Sarrono, from Italy, is the best
known of the almond-flavored
amaretto liqueurs*

- 1 ounce Amaretto
  di Sarrono
- 1 ounce Grand Marnier
- 1 ounce heavy cream
- Maraschino cherry
  for garnish

Combine liqueurs and cream
in mixing glass. Add ice and
shake. Strain into glass
and garnish.

VOLTAIRE'S SMILE

Quaff it and grin

- 1 ounce Pernod
- 1 ounce Chambord
- 2 ounces champagne

Pour liqueurs into mixing
glass. Add ice and shake.
Strain into glass. Top with
champagne and stir gently.

APÉRITIFS

APÉRITIFS

Some apéritifs live up to their name in a big way, noticeably stimulating the appetite. Not that you'll dash to the fridge every time you try one of the drinks in this chapter, but you'll probably come to realize why they are best enjoyed before a meal.

THE AMBASSADOR

The nickname conferred upon a polite European regular

- 3 ounces Campari
- 2 ounces grapefruit juice
- 3 ounces club soda
- Lime slice for garnish

Pour Campari and juice into glass filled with ice. Top with club soda, stir gently, and garnish.

ANGEL OF CORSICA

In honor of a saintly woman from the Mediterranean isle

- 1 ounce Dubonnet Blanc
- 1 ounce gin
- 1 ounce apricot brandy
- 1 ounce peach schnapps
- Orange twist for garnish

Combine liquid ingredients in mixing glass. Add ice, shake, strain into glass, and garnish.

AMERICANO

If you like, use dry vermouth for this classic cocktail

- 2 ounces Campari
- 2 ounces sweet vermouth
- 4 ounces club soda
- Lemon twist for garnish

Pour Campari and vermouth in glass. Top with club soda, stir gently, and garnish.

ANOTHER SPLENDOR

Inspired by a line from a poem by Shelley

- 2 ounces dry vermouth
- 1 ounce apricot brandy
- 1 ounce Chambord
- Rose petal for garnish

Combine all ingredients except garnish in mixing glass. Add ice and stir to chill. Strain into glass and garnish.

BELLA LIGURIA

A nod to the resort-studded Ligurian Sea off Italy's coast

- 2 ounces Campari
- 2 ounces Dubonnet Rouge
- 1 ounce orange juice
- 3 ounces club soda
- Orange slice for garnish

Pour Campari, Dubonnet, and juice into ice-filled glass. Top with club soda, stir gently, and garnish.

BON AMI

Your good French friend

- 1 ounce sweet vermouth
- 1 ounce dry vermouth
- 1 ounce cognac
- 1/2 ounce Cointreau

Combine vermouths and cognac in mixing glass. Add ice and stir to chill. Strain into glass and garnish.

CAMPARI BUON GIORNO

An Italian mimosa (translation: "Good day"). Restaurateur Gaspare Campari formulated his bittersweet mixture of herbs and fruit more than a century ago in Milan

- 1 ounce Campari
- 1 ounce orange juice
- 3 ounces champagne

Pour Campari and juice into glass filled with ice. Top with champagne and stir gently.

CAMPARI MADRAS

With orange and cranberry

- 3 ounces Campari
- 1 ounce vodka
- 2 ounces orange juice
- 2 ounces cranberry juice
- Orange slice for garnish

Combine liquid ingredients in mixing glass. Add ice and shake. Strain into glass and garnish.

CIAO BELLA

"Hello" to an Italian of the female persuasion

- 1 ounce Punt e Mes
- 1 ounce Cynar
- 1 ounce dry vermouth
- Orange twist for garnish

Combine liqueur, Cynar, and vermouth in mixing glass. Add ice and stir to chill. Strain into glass and garnish.

CORSICAN

The islander in mind: Emperor Napoleon I

- 2 ounces Campari
- 1 ounce cognac
- 2 ounces orange juice
- Orange twist for garnish

Combine Campari, cognac, and juice in mixing glass. Add ice and shake. Pour contents into glass and garnish.

DUBONNET FIZZ

*Flavored with cherry
and lemon*

- 2 ounces Dubonnet Rouge
- 1 ounce cherry brandy
- 1 ounce lemon juice
- 4 ounces club soda
- Orange slice for garnish

Combine Dubonnet, brandy,
and juice in mixing glass.
Add ice and shake. Strain
into glass and add soda.
Stir gently and garnish.

EIFFEL TOWER

With grape-flavored vodka

- 2 ounces dry vermouth
- 1 ounce gin
- 1 ounce
  Cîroc grape vodka
- 1/2 teaspoon Pernod

Combine ingredients in
mixing glass. Add ice, stir to
chill, and strain into glass.

EINE KLEINE
NACHTMUSIK

*Inspired by Mozart's
symphony—translated,
"A Little Night Music"*

- 2 ounces Jägermeister
- 2 ounces Punt e Mes
- Orange twist for garnish

Combine liqueurs in mixing
glass. Add ice and stir to chill.
Strain into glass and garnish.

FOUR SEASONS
BLUSHING ANGEL

An airy predinner pleaser

- 2 ounces Dubonnet Rouge
- 1 ounce cranberry juice
- 4 ounces champagne
- Orange twist for garnish

Pour Dubonnet and juice
into glass. Top with
champagne, stir gently,
and garnish.

FOUR SEASONS
DUBONNET COSMO

*A predinner variation
on the Cosmopolitan*

- 1 ounce Dubonnet Rouge
- 1 ounce orange
  liqueur of choice
- 1 ounce vodka
- 1 ounce cranberry juice
- 1 splash lime juice
- Orange twist for garnish

Combine Dubonnet, liqueur,
vodka, and juices in mixing
glass. Add ice, shake, strain
into glass, and garnish.

FRENCH COMFORT

*With Lillet, a venerable French
apéritif made from brandy,
wine, herbs, and fruit*

- 3 ounces Lillet Blanc
- 1 ounce
  Southern Comfort
- Crushed ice
- Orange twist for garnish

Combine Lillet and Southern
Comfort in glass filled with
crushed ice. Stir and garnish.

APÉRITIFS

HAPPY HOUR

At a continental bistro?
Punt e Mes is a vermouthlike
liqueur with the bittersweet
taste of herbs and orange

- 2 ounces Punt e Mes
- 1/2 ounce Cointreau
- 1/2 teaspoon Pernod
- 1/2 ounce cognac
- Orange twist for garnish

Combine liqueurs and cognac
in mixing glass. Add ice and
stir to chill. Strain into glass
and garnish.

KIND HEARTS AND CORONETS

Named for the film in which
Alec Guinness played an
Anglo-Italian. Pimm's No. 1
is an herby liqueur created by
London restaurateur James
Pimm in the 1880s

- 2 ounces Pimm's No. 1
- 2 ounces Campari
- 4 ounces club soda
- Orange twist for garnish

Pour Campari and Pimm's
into glass filled with ice. Top
with club soda and stir gently.

KNIGHT OF SPAIN

An on-the-rocks apéritif

- 2 ounces
  amontillado sherry
- 2 ounces Campari
- Juice of 1/2 lime
- 1 teaspoon raspberry syrup

Combine ingredients in
mixing glass. Add ice, shake,
and pour contents into glass.

LA DOLCE VITA

Bittersweet, like Fellini's film

- 3 ounces Campari
- 1 ounce sambuca

Pour ingredients into glass
filled with ice and stir.

LA DONNA VELATA

"The veiled woman"

- 4 ounces Campari
- 1/2 ounce dry vermouth
- 1/2 ounce Pernod

Combine ingredients in
mixing glass. Add ice, stir to
chill, and strain into glass.

LORD ELGIN

Inspired by the British
diplomat and art collector

- 1 ounce dry vermouth
- 1 ounce sweet vermouth
- 2 ounces Pimm's No. 1
- 4 ounces ginger ale
- Orange twist for garnish

Pour vermouths and
Pimm's into ice-filled glass.
Top with ginger ale,
stir gently, and garnish.

MEDITERRANEAN KISS

With artichoke bitters

- 2 ounces Cynar
- 1 ounce peach schnapps
- 3 ounces club soda
- Orange twist for garnish

Pour Cynar and schnapps into
ice-filled glass. Top with club
soda, stir gently, and garnish.

MEDITERRANEAN SUNDANCE

Feel the beat

- 2 ounces Dubonnet Blanc
- 1 ounce peach schnapps

Pour Dubonnet and schnapps into glass filled with ice and stir.

OCTOPUS

Inky and intriguing

- 3 ounces Campari
- 1 ounce blue curaçao

Pour Campari and liqueur into glass filled with ice and stir.

THE PARISIAN

With that elusive je ne sais quoi . . .

- 2 ounces dry vermouth
- 1 ounce Cointreau
- 1 ounce apricot brandy
- 1/2 teaspoon Pernod

Combine ingredients in glass filled with ice and stir.

PHANTOM OF DELIGHT

Name those herbs . . .

- 2 ounces Jägermeister
- 1 ounce Chambord
- Orange twist for garnish

Combine liqueurs in mixing glass. Add ice, stir to chill, and strain into glass.

PINK ANGEL

Campari with crème de cacao

- 3 ounces Campari
- 1 ounce white crème de cacao
- 4 ounces club soda
- Orange twist for garnish

Pour Campari and liqueur into glass filled with ice. Top with club soda, stir gently, and garnish.

ST. TROPEZ

A taste of the French Riviera. Dubonnet is a wine-based apéritif that comes in red (rouge) or white (blanc)

- 4 ounces Dubonnet Rouge
- 4 ounces orange juice
- Orange slice for garnish

Pour Dubonnet and juice into mixing glass. Add ice and shake. Pour contents into glass and garnish.

SENORE FRANCESE

Of Franco-Italian ancestry

- 2 ounces Campari
- 1 ounce dry vermouth
- 1/2 ounce Pernod
- 3 1/2 ounces club soda

Combine Campari, vermouth, and Pernod in glass filled with ice. Top with club soda and stir gently.

SHERRY

This fortified wine from the Andalusia region of Spain is a popular predinner drink. Types, in order of quality, include fino amontillado, manzanilla, and oloroso. Cream sherries, typically drunk *after* dinner, are heavily sweetened olorosos.

ALMOND DELUXE

Almond-flavored amaretto teams with manzanilla, the most delicate of sherries

- 1 1/2 ounces manzanilla sherry
- 1/2 ounce dry vermouth
- 1 ounce amaretto

Combine ingredients in mixing glass and proceed as in Coronation.

ANDALUSIA

Long venerated as an apéritif

- 2 ounces dry sherry
- 1/2 ounce brandy
- 1/2 ounce light rum

Combine ingredients in mixing glass. Add ice and stir to chill. Strain into glass and garnish.

CORONATION

Topped with a dash of maraschino liqueur

- 1/2 ounce fino amontillado sherry
- 1/2 ounce dry vermouth
- 2 dashes orange bitters
- 1 dash maraschino

Combine ingredients in mixing glass. Add ice, stir to chill, and strain into glass.

GEORGIA ON MY MIND

With—what else?—peach

- 2 ounces dry sherry
- 1 ounce DeKuyper Peachtree schnapps
- 1 dash bitters of choice

Combine ingredients in mixing glass and proceed as in Coronation.

MAC'S APÉRITIF

The favorite of a Scot from Manhattan's Upper East Side

- 1 ounce dry sherry
- 1/2 ounce Scotch
- 2 dashes Cointreau
- 1 ounce orange juice
- Orange twist for garnish

Combine liquid ingredients in mixing glass. Add ice, shake, strain into glass, and garnish.

TUSCAN SIPPER

For those fond of Tuaca, the vanilla-flavored liqueur

- 1 ounce dry sherry
- 1 ounce Tuaca
- Maraschino cherry for garnish

Combine liquid ingredients in mixing glass and proceed as in Mac's Apéritif.

SUNSET COCKTAIL

A rosy prelude to dinner

- 2 ounces Dubonnet Blanc
- 1 ounce cherry brandy
- 2 ounces orange juice
- 3 ounces club soda
- Orange slice for garnish
- Maraschino cherry for garnish

Pour first three ingredients into ice-filled glass. Top with club soda and garnish.

TE AMO

"I love you" in Italy

- 1 ounce Punt e Mes
- 1 ounce Arrow peach schnapps
- 1 ounce dry vermouth
- Orange twist for garnish

Combine all ingredients except garnish in mixing glass. Add ice and stir to chill. Strain into glass and garnish.

TESTA ROSSA

Named after the Ferrari "redhead" auto

- 1 ounce dry vermouth
- 1 ounce Dubonnet Rouge
- 1 ounce amaretto
- Lemon twist for garnish

Pour vermouth, Dubonnet, and amaretto into mixing glass. Add ice and stir to chill. Strain into glass and garnish.

VERMOUTH WITH CASSIS

A traditional apéritif. Cassis is the French name for the black currant

- 2 ounces dry vermouth
- 2 ounces crème de cassis
- Crushed ice
- Lemon twist for garnish

Pour vermouth and liqueur into glass filled with crushed ice and garnish.

VERMOUTH COCKTAIL

Two vermouths plus fizz

- 2 ounces sweet vermouth
- 2 ounces dry vermouth
- 2 dashes Peychaud's bitters
- 4 ounces club soda
- Orange twist for garnish

Pour vermouths into ice-filled glass, add bitters, and top with club soda.

YOURS TRULY

Sincerely good

- 1 ounce Punt e Mes
- 1 ounce apricot brandy
- 1/2 ounce Cointreau
- 1 ounce dry vermouth
- Orange twist for garnish

Combine all ingredients except garnish in mixing glass. Add ice and stir to chill. Strain into glass and garnish.

CHAMPAGNE
& WINE

CHAMPAGNE & WINE

Champagne is often embellished with a few drops of this or that, but red and white wines can also benefit from the mixer's art. While champagne-based drinks are served without ice, the other drinks in this chapter can be enjoyed either straight up or on the rocks.

ACADIAN COOLER

A toast to our French-Canadian neighbors

- 1/2 ounce Cointreau
- 1/2 ounce sweet vermouth
- 5 ounces champagne
- Orange twist for garnish

Combine liqueur and vermouth in glass. Top with champagne and garnish.

ADONIS

Not just for the handsome

- 2 ounces dry sherry
- 1/2 ounce sweet vermouth
- 1 dash orange bitters

Combine ingredients in mixing glass. Add ice, stir to chill, and strain into glass.

THE ANGLOPHILE

Beefed-up bubbly

- 3 drops Beefeater dry gin
- 6 ounces champagne

Drop gin into glass and top with champagne.

ATLANTA COOLER

Made with The Big Peach's most famous product: Coke

- 5 ounces red wine
- 1 ounce Coca-Cola
- Orange slice for garnish
- Lemon slice for garnish

Pour wine into glass filled with ice. Top with soft drink, stir gently, and garnish.

AUBRIETTA

*Named for the
pretty purple plant*

- 7 ounces sweet white wine
- 1/2 ounce framboise
- 1/2 ounce
  Bols grape liqueur

Combine ingredients in
mixing glass. Add ice, stir to
chill, and strain into glass.

BELLE OF THE BALL

Red wine waltzes with O. J.

- 3 ounces red wine
- 2 ounces orange juice
- 1 ounce fresh sour mix
- Orange slice for garnish

Pour wine, juice, and sour mix
into mixing glass. Add ice and
shake. Pour contents into
glass and garnish.

BELLINI

*The first Bellinis, from Harry's
Bar in Venice, used white
peach puree, not schnapps*

- 4 drops peach schnapps
- 6 ounces champagne

Pour schnapps into glass and
top with champagne.

BERRY COOLER

*For raspberry lovers . . .
and no seeds!*

- 6 ounces sweet white wine
- 2 ounces Absolut Kurant
- 1/2 ounce Chambord
- Crushed ice

Pour ingredients into glass
filled with crushed ice and stir.

BRANDIED PORT

An elegant pairing

- 4 ounces port
- 1/2 ounce brandy

Combine port and brandy
in glass and stir.

CHAMPAGNE BLEU

With a touch of Beaujolais

- 1/2 ounce Beaujolais
- 1/2 ounce blueberry syrup
- 4 ounces champagne

Pour wine and syrup into
glass, stir, and top with
champagne.

CHAMPAGNE COCKTAIL

One of the classics

- 1 sugar cube
- 2 dashes
  Angostura bitters
- 1 ounce cognac
- 5 ounces champagne
- Orange slice for garnish
- Maraschino cherry
  for garnish

Place sugar cube in bottom
of glass and soak with bitters.
Add cognac and top with
champagne. Stir gently
and garnish.

CHAMPAGNE WITH SCHNAPPS

Flavor bubbly as you like

- 2 to 4 drops
  schnapps of choice
- 6 ounces champagne

Drop schnapps into glass and top with champagne.

CRANBERRY COCKTAIL

Tart and very red

- 6 ounces red wine
- 3 ounces cranberry juice
- 2 splashes red vermouth
- Crushed ice

Combine all ingredients in mixing glass. Stir to chill and pour contents into glass.

DANISH RUBY

With the black cherry-flavored Danish liqueur

- 1/2 ounce Cherry Heering
- 5 1/2 ounces champagne

Pour liqueur into glass and top with champagne.

> **BARTENDER'S TIP** When buying champagne, look on the label for the following words to learn how sweet or dry it is. From sweetest to driest, the categories are **demi-sec** (sweet), **sec** (medium-sweet), **extra sec** (dry), and **brut** (drier).

EUROPEAN SWINGER

À votre santé, babe

- 4 ounces sauterne
- 1 ounce dry vermouth
- 1/2 ounce Chambord
- 3 ounces club soda
- 3 blueberries for garnish

Pour wine, vermouth, and liqueur into mixing glass. Add ice, stir to chill, and strain into glass. Top with club soda, stir gently, and garnish.

FRENCH ORGASM

Enjoyable, to say the least

- 6 ounces white wine
- 1/2 ounce Cointreau
- 1/2 ounce Roses lime juice
- Club soda

Pour wine, liqueur, and juice into glass filled with ice. Top with club soda to taste and stir gently.

GRAND CHAMPAGNE

Two French favorites join hands. Bitter orange peel from Haiti plus vanilla and spices give Grand Marnier its cachet

- 3 drops Grand Marnier
- 6 ounces champagne
- Orange twist for garnish

Pour liqueur into glass, top with champagne, and garnish.

HILLARY WALLBANGER

Hubby Harv knows she likes white wine more than vodka

- 3 ounces dry white wine
- 1 ounce Galliano
- 3 ounces orange juice

Pour ingredients into glass filled with ice and stir.

THE JACKIE LEE

A lively play on the Gin Fizz

- 1/2 ounce gin
- 1/2 ounce Pernod
- 4 ounces champagne
- 1 ounce club soda

Pour gin and Pernod into glass and stir. Top with champagne and club soda.

KINGSTON KOOLER

Percolates like reggae

- 3 drops Jamaican rum
- 6 ounces champagne
- Lemon twist for garnish

Drop rum into glass, top with champagne, and garnish.

KIR

Created by Canon Félix Kir, mayor of Dijon, in the 1850s

- 8 ounces dry white wine
- 1/4 ounce crème de cassis
- Lemon twist for garnish

Pour wine into glass. Add cassis, stir, and garnish.

KIR ROYALE

The Kir gone bubbly

- 2 drops crème de cassis
- 6 ounces champagne
- Lemon twist for garnish

Drop cassis into glass, top with champagne, and garnish.

LEMONBERRY

Iced white wine kissed by two liqueurs

- 6 ounces white wine
- Crushed ice
- 1/2 ounce Chambord
- 3 drops limoncello
- 1/2 ounce club soda
- Lemon twist for garnish

Pour wine into glass filled with crushed ice and add liqueurs. Top with club soda, stir gently, and garnish.

LIMONCELLO COOLER

With the prized liqueur from Italy's Amalfi Coast

- 1/2 ounce limoncello
- 1/2 ounce club soda
- 6 ounces champagne

Pour liqueur and soda into glass and top with champagne.

The Bordeaux Dinners

Wine is to an establishment like The Four Seasons as beluga caviar is to the fussiest gourmet—only the best will do. The wine list presented to diners is a fantastic array of nearly 400 selections from France, Italy, and the length and breadth of the United States. And, naturally, certain wines and wine-based cocktails are also served at the bar.

Wine has also been the centerpiece of the restaurant's private Bordeaux Dinners, which feature tastings of certain vintages. The dinners got their start at a legendary affair held on January 18, 1973, the purpose of which was to introduce to Americans various Georges Deboeuf wines selected by the famous French chef Paul Bocuse. When word got out that Bocuse himself would cook, more than 4,000 callers set the switchboard alight seeking a ticket.

As related by John Mariani and Alex von Bidder in *The Four Seasons—A History of America's Premier Restaurant,* "Bocuse brought his own [ingredients] from France, arriving at JFK Airport with foie gras, truffles, cream, [and] butter." He got them through customs only by choosing a line with "the stoutest customs inspector, believing such a man would appreciate good food and pass him through. After telling the inspector the truffles were only after-dinner chocolates, Bocuse sailed through." The dinner was a resounding success.

Bar patrons at The Four Seasons benefit indirectly from the Bordeaux Dinners whenever one of the chosen wines is well received and finds its way to the bar. The bar wines tilt toward the continental, but that doesn't mean customers can't enjoy a glass of, say, California chenin blanc, Long Island merlot, or Australian or Chilean shiraz.

LONDON EXPRESS

The English like it dry

- 6 ounces dry red wine
- 1/2 ounce Cointreau
- 1/2 ounce
  crème de cassis
- 1/2 ounce dry vermouth

Pour ingredients into mixing glass. Add ice, stir to chill, and strain into glass.

THE MATADOR

A fiery concoction the color of a bullfighter's cape

- 4 ounces
  Tio Pepe dry sherry
- 2 ounces Punt e Mes
- 2 ounces tomato juice
- 3 dashes Tabasco
- Lime wedge for garnish

Combine all ingredients except garnish in mixing glass. Add ice and stir to chill. Pour contents into glass and garnish.

MIMOSA

The drink that launched a thousand brunches

- 2 ounces orange juice
- 4 ounces champagne

Pour orange juice into glass and top with champagne.

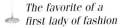

MISS LINDA'S PLEASURE

The favorite of a first lady of fashion

- 1/2 ounce vodka
- 1/2 ounce Chambord
- 3 drops lemon juice
- 5 ounces champagne

Combine vodka, liqueur, and juice in glass and top with champagne.

MOTHER OF PEARL

Flavored with the Japanese honeydew melon liqueur

- 1 ounce Midori
- 1 ounce pineapple juice
- 4 ounces champagne

Pour liqueur and juice into glass and top with champagne.

NOUMÉA COOLER

Named after the seductive colonial French capital in the South Pacific

- 4 ounces cranberry juice
- 1/2 ounce
  passion fruit puree
- 6 ounces champagne
- Orange twist for garnish

Combine juice and puree in mixing glass. Add ice and shake. Pour contents into glass and top with champagne. Stir gently and garnish.

PASSION FIZZ

We're talkin' passion fruit

- 4 ounces white wine
- 2 ounces
  passion fruit puree
- 1 splash dry vermouth
- Lemon twist for garnish

Combine wine, puree, and vermouth in mixing glass. Add ice and shake. Strain into glass and garnish.

PORT PLEASANT

A creamy holiday delight

- 2 ounces port
- 1 ounce cognac
- 1/2 ounce light cream
- 2 dashes dark
  crème de cacao
- Nutmeg for sprinkling

Combine liquid ingredients in mixing glass. Add ice and shake. Strain into glass and sprinkle with nutmeg.

PORTUGUESE DAISY

Ruby port dresses up

- 2 ounces ruby port
- 1 ounce brandy
- 1 ounce fresh sour mix
- 1/2 teaspoon grenadine
- Lemon slice for garnish

Combine all ingredients except garnish in mixing glass. Add ice and shake. Strain into glass and garnish.

RED WINE REFRESHER

Bubbling with lemon-lime and ginger

- 4 ounces red wine
- 2 ounces Sprite or 7-Up
- 2 ounces ginger ale
- Lemon twist for garnish

Pour wine into ice-filled glass. Top with soft drinks, stir gently, and garnish.

RICK'S WHITEWATER

Surging over "rocks"

- Crushed ice
- 4 ounces white wine
- 1/2 ounce triple sec
- Sprite or 7-Up

Fill glass with ice, pour in wine and triple sec, then stir. Top with soft drink to taste and stir gently.

SANIBEL COOLER

Like a gentle ocean breeze

- 3 drops blue curaçao
- 1 drop Southern Comfort
- 6 ounces champagne
- Orange twist for garnish

Combine liqueurs in glass. Add champagne, stir gently, and garnish.

SEÑOR VALDEZ

Coffee meets champagne

- 3 drops Kahlúa
- 6 ounces champagne

Pour Kahlúa into glass, add champagne, and stir gently.

SPRITZERS

Officially, a spritzer is a drink that's half wine, half club soda. But we're leaving the amount of soda (and the glass) up to you. And though these recipes call for ice, one served straight up is no less a spritzer—and a less watery one, at that.

 ## WHITE WINE SPRITZER

The spritzer at its most basic

- 8 ounces white wine
- Crushed ice
- Club soda
Lemon twist for garnish

Pour wine into ice-filled glass. Add club soda to taste, stir gently, then garnish.

 ## RED WINE SPRITZER

A spritzer with something extra

- 6 ounces sweet red wine
- Crushed ice
- Club soda
- Sprite or 7-Up
- Lemon slice for garnish

Pour wine into ice-filled glass. Add equal parts club soda and soft drink to taste, stir gently, and garnish.

 ## RASPBERRY SPRITZER

Flavored with red raspberry

- 4 ounces white wine
- 1/2 ounce framboise
- Crushed ice
- Club soda
- Lemon slice for garnish

Pour wine and liqueur into ice-filled glass and proceed as in White Wine Spritzer.

CHAMBORD SPRITZER

For those who prefer black raspberry

- 8 ounces white wine
- 1/4 ounce Chambord
- Crushed ice
- Club soda
- Lemon twist for garnish

Pour wine and liqueur into ice-filled glass and proceed as in White Wine Spritzer.

MADEIRA SPRITZER

An interesting take on the drink

- 4 ounces Madeira
- 1/2 ounce lime juice
- Crushed ice
- Club soda

Pour wine and juice into glass filled with ice. Top with club soda to taste and stir gently.

SWEETHEART

With honey, grapes, and Prosecco, the Italian sparkling wine

- 4 seedless white grapes
- 1 1/2 teaspoons honey
- 1 ounce vodka
- 5 ounces chilled Prosecco wine
- Lemon twist for garnish

Muddle grapes and honey in bottom of mixing glass. Add ice and vodka, then shake. Strain into glass and top with wine. Stir gently and garnish.

TEAR DROP

Nothing to cry about here

- 4 ounces white zinfandel
- 1 ounce peach schnapps
- 1/2 ounce fresh sour mix
- Club soda
- Lemon wedge for garnish

Combine wine, schnapps, and sour mix in mixing glass. Add ice and shake. Pour contents into glass and top with club soda to taste. Stir gently and garnish.

VANILLA SKIES

Not a cloud in sight

- 1/2 ounce Tuaca
- 1/2 ounce blue curaçao
- 6 ounces champagne

Pour liqueurs into glass, add champagne, and stir gently.

WHITE WINE COOLER

A lemon-lime version of the spritzer. See also Spritzers, page 183

- 4 ounces dry white wine
- 2 ounces Sprite or 7-Up
- Lemon slice for garnish

Pour wine into glass filled with ice. Top with soft drink, stir gently, and garnish.

ZOE'S CABERNET COBBLER

Cobbler is an old name for wine-based cocktails

- 6 ounces cabernet sauvignon
- 1 teaspoon superfine sugar
- Crushed ice
- 3 ounces club soda
- Orange slice for garnish
- Maraschino cherry for garnish

Combine wine and sugar in mixing glass, then shake. Pour into glass filled with crushed ice, top with club soda. Stir gently, garnish, and serve with a straw.

PUNCHES

PUNCHES

These sweet and super-fruity recipes are so good we've sized most of them by the glass (punches aren't always prepared in quantity), figuring it's easier for you to multiply them as needed when you want to make a splash at a party. Punch-bowl-sized recipes are found on pages 192–93 and start with Four Seasons specials good for ladling up in—you guessed it—spring, summer, fall, and winter.

ASHLEY'S PUNCH

Inspired by a tall bar patron from Dallas

- 1 ounce
  Southern Comfort
- 1 ounce vodka
- 1/2 ounce amaretto
- 1/2 ounce orange juice
- 1 1/2 ounces
  pineapple juice
- 2 dashes grenadine
- 1 dash Roses lime juice
- Maraschino cherry
  for garnish
- Lime slice for garnish

Combine all ingredients except garnishes in mixing glass. Add ice and shake. Pour into glass and garnish.

BLOOD ORANGE PUNCH

Featuring the orange with "something extra"

- 2 ounces vodka
- 1 ounce Grand Marnier
- 1 ounce grenadine
- 2 ounces
  blood orange juice
- 1/2 ounce fresh sour mix
- 1 teaspoon
  superfine sugar
- Orange slice for garnish

Combine all ingredients except orange slice in mixing glass. Add ice and shake. Pour contents into glass and garnish.

THE FOUR SEASONS

BLUE MOON PUNCH

*With tequila and
much, much more*

- 1 ounce silver tequila
- 1 ounce blackberry brandy
- 1 ounce blue curaçao
- 1 ounce pineapple juice
- 1 ounce fresh sour mix
- 1 teaspoon sugar
- Lime twist for garnish

Combine all ingredients except
garnish in mixing glass. Add
ice and shake. Pour contents
into glass and garnish.

BOMBS AWAY PUNCH

Bursting with flavor

- 1 ounce Absolut Mandrin
- 1 ounce Absolut Citron
- 1 ounce peach schnapps
- 1 ounce orange juice
- 1 ounce cranberry juice
- 1 ounce fresh sour mix
- 1 teaspoon sugar
- Orange wedge for garnish
- Lemon wedge for garnish

Combine and prepare as
in Blue Moon Punch.

BOURBON PUNCH

With five fruit juices, no less

- 1 1/2 ounces bourbon
- 1/2 ounce orange juice
- 1/2 ounce grapefruit juicy
- 1/2 ounce lemon juice
- 1/2 ounce lime juice
- 1/2 ounce pineapple juice
- Orange slice for garnish

Combine and prepare as
in Blue Moon Punch.

BRANDY PUNCH

With plenty of citrus

- 1 ounce brandy
- 1/2 ounce Cointreau
- 1 ounce orange juice
- 1 ounce lemon juice
- 1 dash grenadine
- 1/4 teaspoon
  superfine sugar
- Club soda
- Orange slice for garnish
- Lemon slice for garnish

Combine all ingredients except
club soda and garnishes in
mixing glass. Add ice and
shake. Strain into glass, add
club soda to taste, and garnish.

CAPTAIN MORGAN PUNCH

Think Pirates of the Caribbean

- 2 ounces Captain
  Morgan spiced rum
- 1 ounce Stoli Ohranj
  vodka
- 1 1/2 ounces
  pineapple juice
- 1 1/2 ounces
  orange juice
- 1 splash grenadine
- Lemon wedge for garnish

Combine all ingredients except
lemon wedge in mixing glass.
Add ice, shake, pour contents
into glass, and garnish.

CHOCOLATE PUNCH

No fruit, but who cares?

- 1 ounce Godiva Liqueur
- 1 ounce dark crème de cacao
- 1 ounce white crème de cacao
- 2 ounces light cream
- 1 teaspoon sugar
- 2 ounces club soda
- Chocolate stick for garnish

Combine all ingredients except club soda and garnish in mixing glass. Add ice and shake. Strain into glass and garnish.

COSMOPOLITAN PUNCH

An iced twist on the Cosmo

- 2 ounces vodka
- 1 ounce Cointreau
- 1 ounce orange juice
- 1 ounce cranberry juice
- 1/2 ounce fresh sour mix
- Lemon wedge for garnish

Combine all ingredients except lemon wedge in mixing glass. Add ice and shake. Pour contents into glass and garnish.

CRANBERRY PUNCH

With a little apple thrown in

- 1 1/2 ounces vodka
- 2 ounces cranberry juice
- 1 ounce apple juice
- Sprite or 7-Up
- Orange slice for garnish

Combine vodka and juices in mixing glass. Add ice and shake. Strain into glass, top with soft drink to taste, stir gently, and garnish.

82ND AIRBORNE PUNCH

A salute to the troops . . . and about as potent as it gets

- 1/2 ounce vodka
- 1/2 ounce dark rum
- 1/2 ounce tequila
- 1/2 ounce Cointreau
- 1/2 ounce orange juice
- 1/2 ounce cranberry juice
- 1/2 ounce grapefruit juice
- 1/2 ounce fresh sour mix
- 1 teaspoon sugar
- Lime slice for garnish

Combine all ingredients except lime slice in mixing glass. Add ice and shake. Pour contents into glass and garnish.

BARTENDER'S TIP If you make these punches in quantity, you can shake three glasses at most in a shaker; for three to six glasses, use a large mixing bowl or pitcher, whisking until any sugar dissolves. For parties, get out your punch bowl and calculator and start multiplying. A little historical note: The British invented punch—then only rum, cold water, sugar, and a citrus juice—when they took possession of Jamaica from the Spanish.

ENGLISH PUNCH

*Pimm's and gin host
a tart Italian*

- 2 ounces Pimm's No. 1
- 1 ounce gin
- 2 ounces limoncello
- 2 ounces cranberry juice
- 1/2 ounce fresh sour mix
- Lemon wedge for garnish

Combine all ingredients
except lemon wedge in
mixing glass. Add ice, shake,
and pour contents into glass.

FRENCH PUNCH

Starring a fine cognac

- 2 ounces Rémy Martin
  V.S.O.P.
- 1 ounce cranberry juice
- 1 ounce orange juice
- Sprite or 7-Up
- Lemon wedge for garnish

Combine all ingredients
except garnish in mixing
glass. Add ice, shake, and
pour contents into glass.

GAYNELLE'S
BURGUNDY PUNCH

Red wine meets brandy

- 2 ounces burgundy
- 1 ounce brandy
- 1/2 ounce triple sec
- 1 ounce sour mix
- Club soda
- Lemon slice for garnish

Combine all ingredients except
club soda and lemon in mixing
glass. Add ice and shake.
Strain into glass, top with
club soda, and garnish.

GINGER PUNCH

A well-spiked ginger ale

- 1 ounce vodka
- 1 ounce sambuca
- 1 ounce fresh sour mix
- 1 teaspoon sugar
- Ginger ale
- Lemon slice for garnish

Combine all ingredients
except ginger ale and garnish
in mixing glass. Add ice, shake,
and pour contents into glass.
Top with ginger ale to taste,
stir gently, and garnish.

GREG'S
MILK PUNCH

*Richer than the usual version
of this holiday favorite. Pale-
brown Baileys Irish Cream is
the enricher, with its velvety
texture and hint of chocolate*

- 2 ounces
  Baileys Irish Cream
- 1 ounce white
  crème de cacao
- 1 ounce heavy cream
- Club soda
- Nutmeg for sprinkling

Combine liqueurs and cream in
mixing glass. Add ice and
shake. Strain into glass, top
with club soda to taste, then
sprinkle with nutmeg.

HUDSON VALLEY PUNCH

For Scotch lovers

- 1 ounce Scotch
- 1 ounce dark crème de cacao
- 1 ounce orange juice
- 1 ounce grapefruit juice
- 1 ounce cranberry juice
- 1/2 teaspoon sugar
- Orange slice for garnish

Combine all ingredients except orange slice in mixing glass. Add ice and shake. Pour contents into glass and garnish.

IRENE'S LAST CALL PUNCH

For when you're ready to call it a night

- 1 ounce vodka
- 1 ounce sambuca
- 1/2 ounce Cointreau
- 1/2 ounce pineapple juice
- 1/2 ounce orange juice
- 1/2 ounce grapefruit juice
- 1/2 ounce fresh sour mix
- 1/2 teaspoon sugar
- Lemon wedge for garnish

Combine all ingredients except lemon wedge in mixing glass. Add ice and shake. Pour contents into glass and garnish.

IRISH PUNCH

A great choice every March 17

- 2 ounces Irish whiskey
- 1/2 ounce green crème de menthe
- 1 1/2 ounces fresh sour mix
- 1 1/2 ounces pineapple juice

1 teaspoon sugar

Combine and prepare as in Kentucky Punch (below).

ITALIAN PUNCH

With Prosecco, the Italian sparkling wine

- 1/2 ounce Campari
- 1/2 ounce sambuca
- 6 ounces Prosecco wine
- Orange slice for garnish
- Lemon slice for garnish

Combine Campari and sambuca in glass filled with ice. Top with wine, stir gently, and garnish.

KENTUCKY PUNCH

Galloping fruit flavor

- 2 ounces Maker's Mark bourbon
- 1 ounce limoncello
- 1/2 ounce orange juice
- 1/2 ounce cranberry juice
- 1/2 ounce grapefruit juice
- 1/2 ounce pineapple juice
- 1/2 ounce fresh sour mix
- 1 teaspoon superfine sugar
- 1 splash grenadine

Combine all ingredients in mixing glass. Add ice, shake, and pour contents into glass.

MERRY MELON PUNCH

With the flavor of honeydew

- 2 ounces Midori
- 1/2 ounce orange juice
- 1/2 ounce pineapple juice
- 1 ounce vodka
- 1 ounce fresh sour mix
- 1 teaspoon superfine sugar
- Maraschino cherry for garnish

Combine all ingredients except garnish in mixing glass. Add ice and shake. Pour contents into glass and garnish.

MEXICAN PUNCH

Ay, caramba!

- 2 ounces silver tequila
- 1 ounce fresh sour mix
- 1 ounce pineapple juice
- 1 1/2 ounces orange juice
- 1 1/2 ounces cranberry juice
- 1/2 teaspoon sugar
- Pineapple spear for garnish

Combine all ingredients except pineapple spear in mixing glass. Add ice and shake. Pour contents into glass and garnish.

OSCAR'S MADEIRA PUNCH

Created by a Portuguese chef

- 2 1/2 ounces Madeira
- 1 ounce cognac
- 1 ounce orange juice
- 1 ounce lemon juice
- 1 teaspoon superfine sugar
- 4 ounces chilled champagne
- Lemon slice for garnish

Combine Madeira, cognac, juices, and sugar in mixing glass. Add ice and shake. Strain into glass, top with champagne, and garnish.

PAM'S PEAR PUNCH

Something a little different

- 1 ounce Päron pear vodka
- 1 ounce Poire William
- 1/2 ounce pineapple juice
- 1/2 ounce orange juice
- 1/2 ounce fresh sour mix
- Club soda
- Pear slice for garnish

Combine all ingredients except club soda and garnish in mixing glass. Add ice, shake, and pour contents into glass. Top with club soda to taste, stir gently, and garnish.

PARTY PUNCHES

Some of these party punches are mixed with sorbet—a little of which you might want to add whenever you prepare other punch recipes in this chapter in larger quantities. Don't be afraid to experiment, since one of the beauties of punch is its flexibility.

SPRING PUNCH

The taste of fresh raspberries

- 4 cups vodka
- 4 cups Absolut Vanilia
- 2 pints raspberry sorbet
- 2 cups raspberry puree
- 1 cup grenadine
- 2 cups Cointreau
- 1 cup superfine sugar
- 4 cups fresh raspberries for garnish
- Cranberry juice ice cubes

Mix all ingredients except garnish and ice in punch bowl, stirring until sugar dissolves. Add ice and garnish.

SUMMER PUNCH

Starring rum and tequila

- 4 cups rum
- 4 cups silver tequila
- 1 pint orange sorbet
- 1 pint strawberry puree
- 1 cup superfine sugar
- 1 cup grenadine
- 4 cups cubed fresh pineapple for garnish
- 4 oranges, sliced, for garnish
- Pineapple juice ice cubes

Prepare as in Spring Punch.

AUTUMN PUNCH

Red apples and cranberry

- 4 cups vodka
- 4 cups apple brandy
- 2 cups sour apple liqueur
- 2 cups cranberry juice
- 2 cups apple puree
- 1 cup superfine sugar
- 4 apples, cored and sliced, for garnish
- Cranberry juice ice cubes

Prepare as in Spring Punch.

WINTER PUNCH

Cognac and Grand Marnier meet the mango

- 4 cups Rémy Martin V.S.O.P. cognac
- 4 cups Grand Marnier
- 1 pint mango sorbet
- 1 pint mango puree
- 4 cups sliced mangoes for garnish
- Orange juice ice cubes

Mix liquid ingredients in punch bowl, add ice, and garnish.

HOLIDAY PUNCH

As rich an eggnog as you'll find

- 2 cups white
  crème de cacao
- 4 cups Baileys Irish Cream
- 2 cups Harveys
  Bristol Cream
- 4 cups prepared eggnog
- 1 cup superfine sugar
- 1 or 2 blocks ice
- 1/2 cup nutmeg
  for sprinkling

Mix all ingredients except
nutmeg and ice in bowl. Add
ice and sprinkle with nutmeg.

MIMOSA BEACH PUNCH

From the Hamptons

- 2 1/2 cups Cointreau
- 2 cups vodka
- 2 cups orange juice
- 1 pint orange sorbet
- 1 cup superfine sugar
- 4 oranges, sliced,
  for garnish
- 8 cups champagne
- Orange juice ice cubes

Mix vodka, juice, sorbet, and
sugar in punch bowl. Stir and
add ice. Pour in champagne,
stir once, and garnish.

PLANTERS PUNCH

A Myers's Rum creation (1879)

- 4 cups Myers's rum
- 2 cups Cointreau
- 3 cups pineapple juice
- 3 cups orange juice
- 1 cup lime juice
- 1/2 cup grenadine
- 2 oranges, sliced,
  for garnish
- 1 cup maraschino
  cherries for garnish
- Pineapple juice ice cubes

Combine rum, Cointreau,
juices, and grenadine in punch
bowl. Add garnishes and ice.

PRESIDENT'S PUNCH

With the fruit of the cherry tree

- 2 1/2 cups light rum
- 4 ounces
  cherry brandy
- 2 pints cherry sorbet
- 1 pint cherry puree
- 1 cup grenadine
- 2 cups superfine sugar
- 4 cups fresh cherries,
  pitted, for garnish
- Cranberry juice ice cubes

Prepare as in Spring Punch.

Fruit-Juice Ice Cubes for Punch

Ice made from fruit juice won't water down punch as it melts,
and it adds even more flavor. Make cubes by filling an ice tray
with juice, then freezing. For blocks of ice, pour liquid into
pint-size milk cartons and freeze. Freeze several trays or
blocks so you can keep the punch cold as the ice melts. By the
way, when using regular ice, avoid dilution by choosing blocks.

RASPBERRY PUNCH

Raspberry shares the rocks glass . . . or punch bowl . . . with orange and cranberry

- 1 1/2 ounces raspberry brandy
- 1/2 ounce Chambord
- 1/2 ounce vodka
- 1 1/2 ounces orange juice
- 1 1/2 ounces cranberry juice
- 1/2 teaspoon superfine sugar
- 3 raspberries for garnish

Combine all ingredients except garnish in mixing glass. Add ice and shake. Pour contents into glass and garnish.

SOUR APPLE PUNCH

Tart but delish

- 1 ounce vodka
- 1 ounce sour apple liqueur
- 1 ounce fresh sour mix
- 3 ounces apple juice
- 1 teaspoon sugar
- Apple slice for garnish

Combine all ingredients except garnish in mixing glass. Add ice and shake. Pour contents into glass and garnish.

VANILLA PUNCH

Rich, creamy, spicy

- 2 ounces Absolut Vanilia
- 1 1/2 ounces Captain Morgan spiced rum
- 1 1/2 ounces pineapple juice
- 1 1/2 ounces heavy cream
- 1 teaspoon superfine sugar
- Nutmeg for sprinkling

Combine all ingredients except nutmeg in mixing glass. Add ice and shake. Strain into glass and sprinkle with nutmeg.

YANKEE PUNCH

A cheer for the indomitable Bronx Bombers

- 1 ounce vodka
- 1 ounce Malibu rum
- 1/2 ounce fresh sour mix
- 1/2 ounce peach schnapps
- 1 ounce orange juice
- 1 ounce cranberry juice
- 1/2 teaspoon superfine sugar
- Lemon wedge for garnish

Combine all ingredients except garnish in mixing glass. Add ice and shake. Pour contents into glass and garnish.

SHOTS

SHOTS

Mixing a shot is an either/or proposition: shake and strain, or layer. So we've squeezed more choices into this chapter by condensing our standard directions for shaken drinks to three words: shake and strain. A few other recipes call for layering, the directions for which are given on page 20.

ALABAMA SLAMMER

Yee-haw!

- 1 ounce amaretto
- 1/2 ounce Southern Comfort
- 1/2 ounce sloe gin
- 1 dash lemon juice

Shake and strain.

THE ALCHEMIST

Would've loved Goldschlager

- 1/2 ounce Goldschlager
- 1/2 ounce sambuca
- 1 ounce vodka

Pour Goldschlager into glass, layer with sambuca and then with vodka.

ANGELA'S PASSION

With passion-fruity Alizé

- 1 ounce Alizé Gold Passion
- 1 ounce vodka

Shake and strain.

APPLE BASKET

With three kinds of apples

- 1 ounce sour apple liqueur
- 1/2 ounce calvados
- 1/2 ounce applejack

Shake and strain.

AUTUMN LEAF

With Scotch and two liqueurs

- 1 ounce Johnnie Walker Black
- 1/2 ounce Punt e Mes
- 1/2 ounce Kahlúa

Shake and strain.

AZTEC SKY

Curaçao, from dried peels of Caribbean bitter oranges, is often tinted blue

- 1 ounce blue curaçao
- 1 ounce gold tequila

Shake and strain.

BANKS OF INVERNESS

Loch Lomond calls to you. . .

- 1 1/2 ounces Glenmorangie 18-year-old Scotch
- 1/2 ounce Grand Marnier
- 1 splash water

Shake and strain.

CAMERON'S CHOICE

The South meets Scotland

- 1 ounce Old Grand-Dad bourbon
- 1 ounce Drambuie

Shake and strain.

CHERRY BONBON

Rich, richer, richest

- 1/2 ounce Godiva Liqueur
- 1/2 ounce Cherry Heering
- 1/2 ounce vodka
- 1/2 ounce heavy cream

Pour liqueur into glass and layer with Cherry Heering, then vodka, then cream.

CINNAMON STICK

With Goldschlager, the cinnamony Swiss liqueur containing bits of gold leaf

- 1 ounce Goldschlager
- 1/2 ounce Jägermeister
- 1/2 ounce Absolut Peppar

Pour Goldschlager into glass, layer with Jägermeister and then with vodka.

COCK YOUR BEAVER

Scottish soldiers tilted their beaver-fur hats to the angels

- 1 1/2 ounces Glenlivet 12-year-old Scotch
- 1/2 ounce Southern Comfort

Shake and strain.

DIANA'S ARROW

A zinger from the Roman goddess of the hunt

- 1 ounce Tuaca
- 1/2 ounce maraschino
- 1/2 ounce vodka

Shake and strain.

FOUR SEASONS SHOOTER

Starring some of our favorite fruit liqueurs

- 1 ounce vodka
- 1/3 ounce peach schnapps
- 1/3 ounce Chambord
- 1/3 ounce sour apple liqueur

Shake and strain.

FOURTH OF JULY

White tops the red and blue

- 1 ounce grenadine
- 1 ounce blue curaçao
- 1 ounce light cream

Pour grenadine into glass. Layer with liqueur and float cream on top.

SHOTS

GREEN DEVIL

For those who prefer gin

- 1 ounce gin
- 1/2 ounce Hiram Walker green crème de menthe
- 1/2 ounce Roses lime juice

Shake and strain.

GUINEVERE'S SMILE

Perchance would've pleased the good folk of Camelot

- 1 1/2 ounces Chivas Regal
- 1/2 ounce Baileys Irish Cream

Shake and strain.

ITALIAN LEMONADE

Lemon times three

- 1/2 ounce lemon-flavored vodka
- 1/2 ounce limoncello
- 1/2 ounce lemon juice

Shake and strain.

KATHY'S KICKER

A gin shot

- 1 3/4 ounces gin
- 1/2 ounce yellow Chartreuse

Shake and strain.

JAMAICAN THRILL

A venerable rum with equal parts coffee liqueur and pineapple juice

- 1/2 ounce Myers's dark rum
- 1/2 ounce coffee liqueur of choice
- 1/2 ounce pineapple juice

Shake and strain.

LASER BEAM

Pinpointed pleasure. Spicy Drambuie, which originated on Scotland's Isle of Skye, is made from Scotch and herbs and is sweetened with heather honey

- 1 ounce bourbon
- 1/2 ounce Drambuie
- 1/2 ounce peppermint schnapps

Shake and strain.

LUCKY IRISHMAN

Tastes of licorice and black raspberry

- 1/2 ounce grenadine
- 1/2 ounce green crème de menthe
- 1/2 ounce Baileys Irish Cream

Pour grenadine into shot glass and layer with second, then third, ingredients.

THE McCARVER

The right stuff

- 1 1/2 ounces Glenmorangie 18-year-old Scotch
- 1/2 ounce Grand Marnier

Shake and strain.

MINTICELLO

Limoncello with mint

- 1 ounce limoncello
- 1 ounce whiskey of choice
- 1 ounce white crème de menthe

Shake and strain.

MISTICO MISSILE

Fitted with a premium tequila

- 1 ounce José Cuervo Mistico
- 1/2 ounce peach schnapps
- 1/2 ounce grapefruit juice

Shake and strain.

MOONLIGHT JIG

Foot-stompin' good

- 1 1/2 ounces Irish whiskey
- 1/4 ounce Drambuie
- 1/4 ounce B & B

Shake and strain.

NUTBURGER

Nothing against the liqueur-making monks, mind you

- 1 ounce Frangelico
- 1/2 ounce amaretto
- 1 ounce vodka

Pour Frangelico into shot glass and layer with amaretto and then vodka.

THE OLD RESTING CHAIR

Named for a tune composed by a famed Scottish fiddler

- 1 1/2 ounce Abelour a'bunadh Scotch
- 1 ounce B & B
- 1 splash water

Shake and strain.

ORANGY PEACH

With a bittersweet orange liqueur and peach schnapps

- 1 1/2 ounces whiskey of choice
- 1/2 ounce Punt e Mes
- 1/2 ounce peach schnapps

Shake and strain.

PINEAPPLE BOMB

A Caribbean blast

- 1 ounce Bacardi Black
- 1/2 ounce Malibu rum
- 1/2 ounce pineapple juice

Shake and strain.

POUSSE-CAFÉS

Born in New Orleans during the Gilded Age, these elaborate layered whimsies pushed the boundaries of the after-dinner drink. The colorful striations of spirits and liqueurs create a work of art of sorts, though one that offers only fleeting pleasure. (For layering directions, see page 20.)

CHERRY ALMOND MINT CREAM

A little bit of heaven?

1/3 ounce grenadine
1/3 ounce green
  crème de menthe
1/3 ounce amaretto
1/3 ounce kirsch
1/3 ounce brandy
Whipped cream
  for topping

Pour grenadine into glass and proceed as in Pousse-Café Classique.

CHOCOLATE ORANGE DELIGHT

Rich and beautiful

1/2 ounce dark
  crème de cacao
1/2 ounce Cointreau
1/2 ounce Godiva Liqueur
1/2 ounce vodka
1/2 ounce heavy cream

Pour crème de cacao into a pousse-café glass and carefully layer remaining ingredients in the order listed. Handle with utmost care when serving.

POUSSE-CAFÉ CLASSIQUE

À la française

1/2 ounce green Chartreuse
1/2 ounce maraschino
1/2 ounce cherry brandy
1/2 ounce kümmel
Whipped cream
  for topping

Pour Chartreuse into glass and carefully layer ingredients in the order listed. Top with whipped cream, taking care not to upset the layers.

POUSSE-CAFÉ STANDISH

*A classic of its kind.
One of the ingredients,
kümmel, is a colorless liqueur
with the scent of fennel,
caraway, and cumin*

1/2 ounce grenadine
1/2 ounce white
  crème de menthe
1/2 ounce Galliano
1/2 ounce kümmel
1/2 ounce brandy

Pour grenadine into glass and proceed as in Chocolate Orange Delight.

PORTIA'S CHOICE

A sweet shot

- 1 ounce bourbon
- 1/2 ounce fresh sour mix
- 1/2 ounce sweet vermouth

Shake and strain.

POWWOW

*Taking part: a Kentuckian,
a Scot, and a Dane*

- 1 ounce bourbon
- 1/2 ounce Drambuie
- 1/2 ounce
  peppermint schnapps

Shake and strain.

'QUILABERRY

Tequila and black raspberry

- 1 ounce Chambord
- 1 ounce gold tequila

Pour liqueur into shot glass
and float tequila on top.

ROYAL RUSH

*Raspberry mix with a little
red currant thrown in*

- 1/2 ounce Chambord
- 1 ounce Absolut Kurant
- 1/2 ounce Stoli Razberi

Pour Chambord into shot glass
and float vodkas on top.

RUMMY MINT

And spicy, too

- 1/2 ounce white
  crème de menthe
- 1/2 ounce
  Captain Morgan rum
- 1/2 ounce fresh sour mix
- 1/2 ounce white
  crème de menthe

Shake and strain.

RUMS AWAY

Three rums in one shot

- 1/2 ounce Bacardi Light
- 1/2 ounce Myers's
  dark rum
- 1/2 ounce Captain Morgan
  spiced rum

Shake and strain.

SAN JUAN HARBOR

*With a premium Puerto
Rican rum*

- 1 ounce Bacardi Ciclón
- 1/2 ounce Chambord
- 1/2 ounce orange juice

Shake and strain.

SARAH'S SHOT

*Favorite shot of a customer
from Oklahoma*

- 1 ounce Frangelico
- 1/2 ounce
  Baileys Irish Cream
- 1/2 ounce vodka

Pour Frangelico into glass and
layer with liqueur, then vodka.

SCOTTISH MAIDEN

With an Italian temperament

- 1 ounce Macallan
  12-year-old Scotch
- 1/2 ounce cherry brandy
- 1/2 ounce Punt e Mes

Shake and strain.

SEÑOR COLD

Has a sparkling personality

- 1 ounce Goldschlager
- 1 ounce gold tequila

Pour Goldschlager into glass
and float tequila on top.

SOUR APPLE SHOT

Throw back and pucker

- 1 ounce vodka
- 1/2 ounce sour
  apple liqueur
- 1 ounce fresh sour mix

Shake and strain.

SOUTHERN SHOOTER

A shot with a drawl

- 1 ounce bourbon
- 1 ounce Southern Comfort

Shake and strain.

THE STROLLING PIPER

A Scottish lad, he is

- 1 ounce Abelour
  single malt scotch
- 1 ounce Drambuie

Shake and strain.

TENNESSEE LICHTNIN'

A bolt of Jack and mint

- 1/4 ounce
  crème de menthe
- 1 1/2 ounces Jack Daniels
  Tennessee whiskey

Pour liqueur into glass and
float whiskey on top.

TEQUILA BLUES

No sorrow here

- 1 ounce Azul blue tequila
- 1 1/2 ounces vodka
- 1 1/2 ounces blue curaçao

Shake and strain.

VODKAMEISTER

A classic shot

- 1 1/2 ounces vodka
- 1 ounce Jägermeister

Shake and strain.

WINDSURFER

*Sweeps you away. Tia Maria is
a Jamaican coffee liqueur said
to have been formulated on the
island in the mid 1600s*

- 1 ounce light rum
- 1/2 ounce Tia Maria
- 1/2 ounce heavy cream

Shake and strain.

FROZEN DRINKS

FROZEN DRINKS

Frozen margaritas (page 131) and frozen daiquiris (pages 110–11) are hardly the only icy palette-pleasers in a bartender's repertoire, and the ones on these pages range far and wide. We've sized the recipes for one drink, so double, triple, or quadruple them as necessary—a likelihood, since most are ideal for parties.

ALPINE FROST

With the pleasantly bitter taste of Jägermeister

- 1 ounce vodka
- 1 ounce Jägermeister
- 1 ounce peach schnapps
- 1 ounce heavy cream
- 6 ounces crushed ice

Combine ingredients in blender, blend until smooth, and pour into glass.

BANANA CREAM

A cool way to get your potassium

- 1 ounce Absolut Vanilia
- 1 ounce crème de banane
- 1 ounce heavy cream
- 1 half medium-sized banana
- 6 ounces crushed ice

Combine ingredients in blender, blend until smooth, and pour into glass.

BANANAS FROSTER

For cooling off in a Caribbean cabana

- 1/2 ounce Captain Morgan spiced rum
- 1/2 ounce crème de banane
- 1 medium banana
- 2 scoops vanilla ice cream
- Cinnamon for sprinkling

Combine all ingredients except cinnamon in blender. Blend until smooth, pour into glass, and sprinkle with cinnamon.

THE BIG CHILL

A favorite of the frozen drink fan club

- 1 1/2 ounces dark rum
- 1 ounce orange juice
- 1 ounce pineapple juice
- 1 ounce cranberry juice
- 1 ounce cream of coconut
- 1 cup crushed ice
- Pineapple spear for garnish

Combine all ingredients except garnish in blender. Blend until smooth, pour, and garnish.

THE BLIZZARD

A wallop of flavor

- 1 ounce brandy
- 1 ounce light rum
- 1 ounce
  Baileys Irish Cream
- 1 ounce Tia Maria
- 2 scoops vanilla ice cream
- 1 splash light cream
- Nutmeg for sprinkling

Combine all ingredients except nutmeg in blender. Blend until smooth, pour into glass, and sprinkle with nutmeg.

 BLUE FROST

Simple and elegant

- 2 ounces vodka
- 1/2 ounce blue curaçao
- 1 ounce heavy cream
- 1/2 cup crushed ice

Combine ingredients in blender. Blend until smooth and pour into glass.

 BLUE VELVET

With black raspberry and melon liqueurs

- 1 ounce Chambord
- 1 ounce Midori
- 2 scoops vanilla ice cream
- Whipped cream for topping
- 3 or 4 drops blue
  curaçao for drizzling

Combine liqueurs and ice cream in blender. Blend until smooth and pour into glass. Top with whipped cream, then drizzle curaçao on top.

 CARIBBEAN COOLER

A short trip to Barbados by way of Japan and Germany

- 1 ounce Malibu rum
- 1 ounce Midori
- 1 ounce peach schnapps
- 1 ounce lime juice
- 6 ounces crushed ice
- Thin sliced honeydew
  melon for garnish

Combine all ingredients except garnish in blender. Blend until smooth, pour, and garnish.

 CHARLOTTE'S MUDSLIDE

With vanilla bean ice cream

- 2 ounces
  Baileys Irish Cream
- 2 ounces Kahlúa
- 2 ounces Absolut Vanilia
- 2 scoops
  vanilla bean ice cream

Combine liqueurs, vodka, and ice cream in blender. Blend until smooth and pour.

 CHERRY VANILLA DELIGHT

"Delight" is an understatement

- 2 ounces Absolut Vanilia
- 1/2 ounce Cherry Heering
- 2 scoops
  vanilla ice cream
- Fresh cherry with
  stem for garnish

Combine vodka, ice cream, and liqueur in blender. Blend until smooth, pour, and garnish.

FROZEN DRINKS

CHOCOLATE FREEZES

Satisfy that never-ending craving for chocolate with one of these frozen drinks, two of which are flavored with white chocolate. Lovers of white chocolate may also want to try the recipes for Frosty Blue Umbrella, Frozen Monk, and Peppermint Frost.

FROZEN DRINKS

CHOCOLATE ALMOND FREEZE

Hits the spot

- 1 ounce amaretto
- 1 ounce white crème de cacao
- 2 scoops chocolate ice cream
- Shaved chocolate for garnish

Combine liqueurs and ice cream in blender. Blend until smooth, pour into glass, and garnish.

FROZEN MOCHA

Can you spell luxurious?

- 1 ounce vodka
- 1 ounce dark crème de cacao
- 1 ounce Kahlúa
- 1 ounce heavy cream
- 6 ounces crushed ice

Combine all ingredients in blender, blend until smooth, and pour into glass.

FROSTY THE SNOWMAN

With chocolate chip eyes and a bright red nose

- 1 ounce vodka
- 1 ounce Godiva White Chocolate Liqueur
- 1 ounce heavy cream
- 1/2 cup crushed ice
- Whipped cream for topping
- 2 chocolate chips for garnish
- 1 maraschino cherry for garnish

Combine all ingredients except whipped cream and garnishes in blender. Blend until smooth and pour into glass. Top with whipped cream and garnish with two chocolate chips as eyes and a cherry for the nose.

POLAR BEAR

A vicarious roll in the snow

- 2 ounces Absolut Vanilia
- 1 ounce white crème de cacao
- 1 ounce Godiva White Chocolate Liqueur
- 1/2 cup crushed ice

Combine ingredients in blender. Blend until smooth and pour into glass.

DARK CHERRY DREAM

For Cherry Heering lovers

- 2 ounces vodka
- 1 ounce Cherry Heering
- 2 scoops vanilla ice cream
- 1/2 cup crushed ice

Combine ingredients in blender. Blend until smooth and pour into glass.

 ## FROSTED APRICOT STINGER

Includes apricot brandy and crème de menthe

- 1 ounce apricot brandy
- 1 ounce white crème de menthe
- 1 ounce white crème de cacao
- 1 ounce orange juice
- 1/2 cup crushed ice

Combine ingredients in blender, blend until smooth, and pour into glass.

 ## FROSTY BLUE UMBRELLA

Try on a rainy day in August

- 1 ounce vodka
- 1 ounce white crème de cacao
- 1/2 ounce blue curaçao
- 1 scoop vanilla ice cream
- 2 ounces crushed ice

Combine ingredients in blender. Blend until smooth and pour into glass.

 ## FROSTY NOGGIN

A dandy holiday eggnog

- 1 1/2 ounces light rum
- 1/4 ounce white crème de menthe
- 3 ounces prepared eggnog
- 2 scoops vanilla ice cream
- Whipped cream for topping
- 3 or 4 drops cherry syrup

Combine rum, liqueur, eggnog, and ice cream in blender and blend until smooth. Pour into glass, top with whipped cream, and drizzle with cherry syrup.

 ## FROZEN CREAMSICLE

No stick required

- 2 ounces vodka
- 1 ounce orange juice
- 2 scoops vanilla ice cream
- 2 ounces crushed ice

Combine ingredients in blender, blend until smooth, and pour into glass.

 ## FROZEN LEMON DROP

An icy palate cleanser

- 2 ounces Absolut Citron
- 1 ounce Cointreau
- 1 ounce lemon juice
- 1 teaspoon superfine sugar
- 1/2 cup crushed ice

Combine ingredients in blender, blend until smooth, and pour into glass.

FROZEN DRINKS

FROZEN MONK

Chills out in France

- 1/2 ounce amaretto
- 1 ounce vodka
- 1 ounce Frangelico
- 1 ounce white crème de cacao
- 1 ounce heavy cream
- 1 cup crushed ice

Combine ingredients in blender, blend until smooth, and pour into glass.

LATIN CONNECTION

Italian liqueur, Caribbean rum

- 2 ounces Tuaca
- 1 ounce light rum
- 1/2 ounce Cointreau
- 1/2 cup crushed ice
- Club soda

Combine all ingredients except club soda in blender. Blend until smooth, pour into glass, and top with club soda to taste.

MATTY'S FREEZE

With a touch of passion fruit

- 2 ounces light rum
- 3/4 ounce brandy
- 2 teaspoons passion fruit syrup
- 1 teaspoon lime juice
- 1/2 cup crushed ice
- Lime slice for garnish

Combine all ingredients except garnish in blender. Blend until smooth, pour into glass, and garnish.

MAUI BREEZE

A tropical delicacy

- 1/2 ounce amaretto
- 1/2 ounce Cointreau
- 1/2 ounce brandy
- 2 ounces guava juice
- 2 ounces mango juice
- 1 ounce fresh sour mix
- 1 cup crushed ice

Combine all ingredients in blender. Blend until smooth and pour into glass.

NORMANDY WINTER

A huddle of chilly monks

- 1 ounce Frangelico
- 1 ounce Drambuie
- 1 ounce Bénédictine
- 1 ounce heavy cream
- 1/2 cup crushed ice

Combine ingredients in blender, blend until smooth, and pour into glass.

PEPPERMINT FROST

Serving up holiday joy

- 1 ounce vodka
- 1 ounce green crème de menthe
- 1 ounce white crème de cacao
- 1 ounce heavy cream
- 1/2 cup crushed ice
- Candy cane for garnish

Combine all ingredients except garnish in blender and blend until smooth. Pour into glass and hook candy cane on glass.

FROZEN DRINKS

RASPBERRY POPSICLE

Lip-licking good

- 2 ounces Smirnoff raspberry vodka
- 1 ounce Absolut Vanilia
- 1 ounce raspberry puree
- 1 teaspoon lemon juice
- 1 teaspoon superfine sugar
- 1/2 cup crushed ice

Combine ingredients in blender, blend until smooth, and pour into glass.

ROMAN DESIRE

Hard to resist

- 1 ounce Absolut Vanilia
- 1 ounce sambuca
- 1 ounce white crème de cacao
- 1 ounce heavy cream
- 1/2 cup crushed ice
- Black licorice stick for garnish

Combine all ingredients except garnish in blender. Blend until smooth, pour into glass, and garnish.

SIBERIAN WINTER

Bundle up tight

- 2 ounces vodka
- 1 ounce Frangelico
- 1 ounce heavy cream
- 1/2 cup crushed ice

Combine ingredients in blender, blend until smooth, and pour into glass.

THE SNOW QUEEN

Deigns to amuse you

- 2 ounces vodka
- 1/2 ounce sambuca
- 1/2 ounce white crème de cacao
- 1 ounce heavy cream
- 1/2 cup crushed ice

Combine ingredients in blender, blend until smooth, and pour into glass.

STRAWBERRY BLAST

With vodka and fresh fruit

- 2 ounces Stoli Vanil
- 1 ounce Chambord
- 3 strawberries, halved
- 1 ounce heavy cream
- 1/2 cup crushed ice
- Strawberry for garnish

Combine all ingredients except strawberry in blender and blend until smooth. Pour into glass and garnish.

SWEDISH BLIZZARD

Sweden's famous vodka gets colder still

- 2 ounces Absolut
- 1 ounce Grand Marnier
- 1 ounce white crème de cacao
- 1 ounce heavy cream
- 1/2 cup crushed ice

Combine ingredients in blender, blend until smooth, and pour into glass.

FROZEN DRINKS

TEQUILA FROST

*Who knew tequila could taste
so rich and creamy?*

- 1 ounce silver tequila
- 1 ounce grapefruit juice
- 1/2 ounce honey
- 1 scoop vanilla ice cream
- 1 ounce heavy cream
- 2 ounces crushed ice

Combine ingredients in
blender, blend until smooth,
and pour into glass.

VAL D'AOSTA

*A coffee-flavored drink named
for the region encompassing
the snowy Italian Alps*

- 2 ounces sweet vermouth
- 2 ounces coffee ice cream
- 1 ounce pasteurized
  egg white
- 1/2 cup crushed ice

Combine ingredients in
blender, blend until smooth,
and pour into glass.

TSUNAMI

*Our version of the Tidal Wave,
a favorite of frozen drink fans*

- 1 ounce Midori
- 1 ounce light rum
- 1 ounce orange juice
- 1 ounce pineapple juice
- 1/2 ounce
  cream of coconut
- 1 cup crushed ice
- Lime slice for garnish
- Maraschino cherry
  for garnish

Combine all ingredients
except garnishes in blender.
Blend until smooth, pour
into glass, and garnish.

WINTRY NIGHT

*Turn up the thermostat
and enjoy*

- 2 ounces whiskey of choice
- 1 ounce coffee liqueur
- 1 scoop coffee ice cream
- 2 ounces crushed ice

Combine ingredients in
blender, blend until smooth,
and pour into glass.

HOT DRINKS

HOT DRINKS

Hot alcoholic beverages come into their own in winter, but coffee laced with something extra is a popular after-dinner drink at any time of year. Nevertheless, you'll probably want to enjoy most of the drinks in this chapter when the winter winds blow.

AGAVERO DREAM

The vanilla scent of Agavero, blended from reposado and añejo tequilas, comes from the damiana flower

- 4 ounces hot coffee, sweetened to taste
- 2 ounces Agavero
- 2 ounces light cream

Pour coffee into glass, add liqueur and cream, and stir.

BARBADOS COFFEE

Rich and spicy

- 4 ounces hot coffee, sweetened to taste
- 2 ounces Mount Gay rum
- 2 ounces heavy cream
- Nutmeg for sprinkling

Pour coffee into glass and add rum and cream. Stir, then sprinkle with nutmeg.

ANNIE'S CHERRY PIE

Dessert by the hearth

- 2 ounces cherry brandy
- 2 ounces cranberry juice
- 2 ounces heavy cream
- Cinnamon for sprinkling

Heat liquid ingredients but do not boil. Pour into steamed glass and sprinkle with cinnamon.

CAFÉ CARIBE

Tasting of rum and orange

- 6 ounces hot coffee, sweetened to taste
- 2 ounces light rum
- 2 ounces triple sec

Pour coffee into mug. Add rum and triple sec and stir.

BARTENDER'S TIP Drinks made with hot coffee don't need reheating before serving, but use the microwave or range top for others. For parties, multiply the recipes as needed and serve the drinks in a warm pitcher and steam the glasses or mugs. Steaming a glass simply means heating it, as noted on page 21.

CAFÉ MEXICANO

Flavored with Kahlúa

- 4 ounces hot coffee, sweetened to taste
- 2 ounces Kahlúa
- Whipped cream for topping
- Cinnamon for sprinkling

Pour coffee into glass and add liqueur. Stir, top with whipped cream, and sprinkle with cinnamon.

CAFÉ ROYALE

Rhapsody in a glass

- 4 ounces hot coffee, sweetened or unsweetened
- 2 ounces brandy
- 2 ounces heavy cream

Pour coffee into mug and stir in other ingredients.

CINNAMON ROLL

Enjoy well after the breakfast hour, if you please

- 6 ounces hard apple cider
- 2 ounces cinnamon schnapps
- Cinnamon stick for garnish

Heat cider and pour into mug. Add schnapps, stir, and sprinkle with cinnamon.

FERNET COFFEE

With Fernet-Branca, the Italian digestif

- 4 ounces hot coffee, sweetened to taste
- 1 ounce Fernet-Branca
- Whipped cream for topping

Pour coffee into glass and add Fernet-Branca. Stir and top with whipped cream.

HAZELNUT DREAM

Adrift on a Frangelico cloud

- 6 ounces hot coffee, sweetened to taste
- 2 ounces Frangelico
- Whipped cream for topping
- Chopped hazelnuts for garnish

Pour coffee into glass and add liqueur. Stir, top with whipped cream, and sprinkle with chopped nuts.

HOT APPLE PIE

As good as mom's?

- 4 ounces boiling water
- 3 ounces rum
- 2 ounces calvados
- 1/2 teaspoon cinnamon
- Whipped cream for topping
- Calvados for drizzling

Pour boiling water into glass, followed by rum, calvados, and cinnamon. Stir, top with whipped cream, and drizzle with a spoonful of calvados.

HOT DRINKS

HOLIDAY PARTY WARMERS

The wood in the fireplace is crackling, and the scent of evergreens and cinnamon wafts through the house. There's no mistaking it: The holidays are in full swing. The recipes for these hot holiday punches yield about 8 cups each, so double or triple them as needed.

MULLED WINE

Use claret, burgundy, bordeaux or a similar full-bodied red wine for this traditional treat

- 1 orange, sliced
- Whole cloves
- 1/2 cup sugar
- 2 cups
  citrus-flavored herb tea
- 1 tablespoon lemon zest
- 1 bottle red wine
- 2 cinnamon sticks

Use orange slices and cloves to make citrus wheels (see page 25); set wheels aside. Combine sugar, tea, and zest in a large enameled or stainless-steel pot. Bring to a boil over medium heat, reduce heat to low, and simmer for 15 minutes. Remove from heat and let cool slightly. Add wine, cinnamon, and citrus wheels. Reheat before serving, but do not boil.

SPICED CRANBERRY CIDER

Tart and aromatic

- 4 cups cranberry juice
- 4 cups hard apple cider
- 1/4 cup
  brown sugar, packed
- 3 cinnamon sticks
- 1 1/2 teaspoons
  whole cloves
- 1 lemon, thinly sliced
- Lemon slices for garnish

Combine all ingredients except garnish in a large saucepan. Bring to a boil, reduce heat, and simmer for 15 to 20 minutes. Let cool slightly, then strain into large heatproof bowl. Serve warm, topping each serving with a halved lemon slice.

HOT APPLE CIDER

Warmly traditional

- 8 cups hard apple cider
- 1/4 cup
  Vermont maple syrup
- 2 cinnamon sticks
- 1 1/2 teaspoons
  whole cloves
- 1 1/2 teaspoons whole
  allspice berries
- 1 lemon peel
  cut into strips
- 1 orange peel
  cut into strips

Pour cider and syrup into large saucepan. Tie all other ingredients up tightly in a cheesecloth bag and add to pan. Heat over medium heat. Discard bag and pour cider into serving bowl.

HOT BUTTERED BOURBON

*Beloved by Southerners
of a certain age*

- 2 1/2 ounces
  Wild Turkey bourbon
- 2 ounces apple cider
- Cinnamon stick
- 1 tablespoon
  unsalted butter
- Nutmeg for sprinkling

Combine bourbon, cider, and
cinnamon stick in small
saucepan. Heat, add butter,
and stir. Discard stick, pour
mixture into steamed glass,
and sprinkle with nutmeg.

HOT BUTTERED RUM

The old-fashioned favorite

- 4 ounces boiling water
- 1 teaspoon brown sugar
- 3 ounces dark rum
- 1 tablespoon
  unsalted butter
- Nutmeg for sprinkling
- Lemon wheel for garnish

Pour boiling water into mug,
add sugar, and stir. Add rum
and butter and restir. Sprinkle
with nutmeg and garnish.

HOT BUTTERED WINE

A variation on a theme

- 4 ounces boiling water
- 4 ounces muscatel
- 1 tablespoon butter
- 2 teaspoons
  Vermont maple syrup
- Nutmeg for sprinkling

Pour boiling water into glass
and add muscatel. Add butter
and syrup, stir, and sprinkle
with nutmeg.

HOT TEA TODDY

Not just for Aunt Bertha

- 8 ounces hot tea
- 1/2 teaspoon honey
- 2 ounces gold rum
- 1 pinch cinnamon
- Ginger ale at
  room temperature

Pour hot tea into steamed
glass, add honey, and stir.
Add rum and cinnamon and
restir. Top with ginger ale
to taste and stir gently.

INDIAN SUMMER

As appley as cider gets

- 6 ounces hard apple cider
- 2 ounces apple schnapps
- Cinnamon stick for garnish

Heat cider and pour into
mug. Add schnapps, stir,
and garnish.

IRISH COFFEE

*For St. Patrick's Day, whip a
little green crème de menthe
into the topping, if you like*

- 4 ounces hot coffee,
  sweetened to taste
- 2 ounces Irish whiskey
- Whipped cream for topping
- Crème de menthe
  (optional)

Pour coffee into glass and
add whiskey. Stir, top with
whipped cream, and drizzle
with a spoonful of crème de
menthe, if desired.

JAMAICAN COFFEE

Topped with a layer of cream

- 4 ounces hot coffee,
  sweetened to taste
- 2 ounces
  Appleton Estate rum
- 2 ounces heavy cream

Pour hot coffee into steamed
glass. Add rum, stir, and
float cream on top.

LE GRAND CAFÉ

A creamy indulgence

- 6 ounces hot coffee,
  sweetened to taste
- 1 ounce Grand Marnier
- 1 ounce Frangelico
- 2 drops dark
  crème de cacao
- 1/8 teaspoon nutmeg
- Nutmeg for sprinkling

Pour coffee into steamed
glass. Add rest of ingredients
except the last. Stir and
sprinkle with nutmeg.

LEMONY LICK

A frosty day enlivener

- 4 ounces hot lemon herb
  tea, sweetened to taste
- 1 ounce limoncello
- Lemon wedge for garnish

Pour hot tea into mug and add
liqueur. Stir and garnish.

LUIGI'S
ALMOND TRUFFLE

Could substitute for dessert

- 4 ounces hot chocolate
- 2 ounces amaretto
- 2 ounces almond herb tea
- Whipped cream for topping

Pour hot chocolate into
steamed glass. Add liqueur
and tea, stir, and top with
whipped cream.

MINTY APPLE

Cider with mint and cream

- 6 ounces hard apple cider
- 1 ounce
  peppermint schnapps
- Whipped cream for topping

Heat apple cider and pour
into glass. Add schnapps, stir,
and top with whipped cream.

ORIENTAL WARMER

A taste of the Far East

- 4 ounces hot green tea,
  sweetened to taste
- 2 ounces cherry brandy

Pour hot tea into mug,
add brandy, and stir.

PEACH COBBLER

Cider gets peachy

- 6 ounces hard apple cider
- 2 ounces peach schnapps
- Peach slice for garnish

Heat cider and pour into mug. Stir in schnapps and garnish.

PEPPERMINT PLEASER

A double whammy for mint lovers

- 6 ounces
  hot peppermint herb tea, sweetened to taste
- 2 ounces
  peppermint schnapps

Pour hot tea into mug and stir in schnapps.

RED PAGODA

With sake, Japan's rice wine

- 4 ounces sake
- 2 ounces Chambord

Warm sake, pour into steamed mug, and stir in liqueur.

RED VELVET WARMER

Super smooth and creamy

- 4 ounces
  hot raspberry herb tea, sweetened to taste
- 2 ounces framboise
- 2 ounces light cream
- Whipped cream for garnish

Pour tea into steamed glass. Add liqueur and cream, stir, and top with whipped cream.

SPIKED HOT CHOCOLATE

As you like it. We suggest a few additions, but don't let that stop you from trying others

- 8 ounces hot chocolate
- 1 ounce rum, whiskey, peppermint schnapps, or Chambord
- Whipped cream for topping
- Cinnamon for sprinkling

Pour hot chocolate into steamed glass and stir in spirit or liqueur of choice. Top with whipped cream and sprinkle with cinnamon.

TENNESSEE TRAVELER

For whiskey lovers

- 4 ounces hot coffee
- 2 ounces Jack Daniels Tennessee whiskey
- Whipped cream for topping

Pour hot coffee into steamed glass. Stir in whiskey and top with whipped cream.

TIPSY EARL

Earl Grey in party mode

- 7 ounces
  hot Earl Grey tea, sweetened to taste
- 1 ounce
  Harveys Bristol Cream

Pour hot tea into mug and stir in liqueur.

TOASTED MONK

Ain't misbehavin'. The marshmallow is the one that gets toasted

- 4 ounces hot coffee, sweetened to taste
- 2 ounces Bénédictine
- 2 ounces heavy cream
- Toasted marshmallow for garnish

Pour hot coffee into steamed glass and stir in liqueur. Float cream on top and garnish.

TRADITIONAL HOT TODDY

Hot toddies were once believed to be medicinal. Hmmm . . .

- 1/2 teaspoon sugar
- 6 ounces boiling water
- 2 ounces whiskey or gin
- Lemon slice for garnish
- Nutmeg for sprinkling

Put sugar in bottom of mug, add boiling water, and stir. Add liquor and stir. Add garnish and sprinkle with nutmeg.

VELVET ITALIAN

Bella!

- 4 ounces hot coffee
- 1 1/2 ounces amaretto
- 1/2 ounce brandy
- 2 ounces heavy cream

Pour coffee into steamed glass and stir in liqueur, brandy, and cream.

YO-HO-HO

Cider mixed with a tongue-tingling Puerto Rican rum

- 6 ounces hard apple cider
- 2 ounces Captain Morgan spiced rum

Heat apple cider, pour into mug, and stir in rum.

NONALCOHOLIC
DRINKS

NONALCOHOLIC DRINKS

The faux cocktails on the following pages are tailor-made for young-sters, nondrinkers, and designated drivers. The fruit-based drinks, which account for the larger portion of the recipes, not only often pass for the "real thing" but can give you a healthful shot in the arm.

A. J.'S SURPRISE

For your inner child

- 8 ounces milk
- 2 tablespoons chocolate syrup
- 1 teaspoon maraschino cherry juice
- Whipped cream for topping
- Maraschino cherry for garnish

Combine milk, syrup, and juice from bottle of maraschino cherries in glass, then stir. Garnish with whipped cream with a cherry on top.

ANGELIC PEACH

Lifts your spirits

- 2 ounces peach nectar
- 6 ounces Sprite or 7-Up
- Peach slice for garnish

Pour nectar into glass filled with ice. Add soft drink, stir gently, and garnish.

C. J.' S FIZZER

Simple 'n' sweet

- 6 ounces apple juice
- 6 ounces Sprite or 7-Up
- Apple slice for garnish

Pour juice and soft drink into glass filled with ice, stir gently, and garnish.

THE CARRIE NATION

A temperate pick-me-up

- 12 ounces ginger ale
- 1 splash grenadine
- 1 splash lemon juice
- Lemon slice for garnish

Pour ginger ale into glass filled with ice and add juice and grenadine. Stir gently and garnish.

CHOCOLATE-CINNAMON SHAKE

*Chocolate milk dressed
to the nines*

- 8 ounces milk
- 1 tablespoon
  chocolate syrup
- 1/8 teaspoon cinnamon
- Whipped cream
  for topping
- Cinnamon for sprinkling

Combine milk, syrup, and
cinnamon in mixing glass.
Shake and pour into glass.
Top with whipped cream
and sprinkle with cinnamon.

CRANBERRY DELIGHT

*A beverage with a bubbly
personality*

- 2 ounces cranberry juice
- 2 ounces tangerine juice
- 4 ounces club soda
- Orange slice for garnish

Pour juices into glass filled
with ice. Top with club soda,
stir gently, and garnish.

CRANBERRY FIZZER

Foamy and red

- 6 ounces cranberry juice
- 1 ounce fresh sour mix
- 5 ounces club soda
- Lemon slice for garnish

Combine juice and sour mix
in mixing glass. Add ice, shake,
and pour contents into glass.
Add club soda, stir gently,
and garnish.

CRANSODA

*One part soda pop, one part
healthful cranberry*

- 6 ounces cranberry juice
- 6 ounces Sprite or 7-Up
- Orange slice for garnish

Pour juice and soft drink
into glass filled with ice.
Stir gently and garnish.

ELIZABETH THE GREAT

*Created by bartender Greg
for his young daughter*

- 3 ounces orange juice
- 3 ounces cranberry juice
- 1 dash lemon juice
- 6 ounces club soda

Combine juices in mixing glass.
Add ice, shake, and pour
contents into glass. Top with
club soda and stir gently.

FROSTY NIGHT

*Pepped up with peppermint
and lemon*

- 12 ounces Sprite or 7-Up
- 1/4 teaspoon
  peppermint syrup
- 1 splash lemon juice
- Lemon slice for garnish

Pour soft drink into glass filled
with ice. Add syrup and juice,
stir gently, and garnish.

NONALCOHOLIC

FRUIT SMOOTHIES

The small wonder known as the blender transforms fruit into a drink fit for the gods—the smoothie. Experiment with different fruit juices and add either milk or yogurt, if you like. But as you work on perfecting the smoothie of all smoothies, one of these recipes—or the Virgin Colada on page 226—should satisfy.

COCOBERRY

Coconut and strawberry

- 2 1/2 ounces frozen strawberries
- 1 ounce cream of coconut
- 2 ounces pineapple juice
- 1 ounce fresh sour mix
- Strawberry for garnish

Process frozen strawberries in blender, then add juice and sour mix. Blend until smooth, pour into glass, and garnish.

RASPBERRY MINT SMOOTHIE

With syrups of two flavors

- 1/2 cup plain yogurt
- 1/2 cup raspberries
- 1/2 teaspoon raspberry syrup
- 1/2 teaspoon peppermint syrup
- 1/2 cup crushed ice

Combine all ingredients in blender. Blend until smooth and pour into glass.

SANDY'S SMOOTHIE

As effervescent as you desire

- 1/2 cup frozen strawberries
- 1/2 cup frozen peaches
- 1 cup orange juice
- 1/2 cup crushed ice
- Club soda
- Fresh strawberry for garnish

Process frozen fruits in blender. Add juice and ice, blend until smooth, and pour into glass. Add club soda to taste, stir gently, and garnish.

TROPICAL TWISTER

Carries you away

- 1/2 cup pineapple chunks
- 1/2 cup strawberry pieces
- 4 ounces orange juice
- 1/2 cup crushed ice
- Orange slice for garnish
- Strawberry for garnish

Process pineapple in blender, then add all ingredients except garnishes. Blend until smooth, pour into glass, and garnish.

JOHNNY APPLESEED

A drink on a mission to please

- 3 ounces apple juice
- 1 dash bitters of choice
- 9 ounces club soda
- Apple slice for garnish

Pour juice into ice-filled glass and add bitters. Top with club soda, stir gently, and garnish.

JUICY TART

For those with a yen for passion fruit

- 4 ounces passion fruit juice
- 2 ounces tangerine juice
- 2 ounces cranberry juice
- 1 splash lemon juice
- Lemon wedge for garnish

Combine juices in mixing glass. Add ice, shake, pour contents into glass, and garnish.

KAT'S KOOLER

Bottled sparkling water gets a make-over

- 1 splash lemon juice
- 1 splash lime juice
- 1/4 teaspoon superfine sugar
- 8 ounces sparkling water
- Orange slice for garnish

Combine juices and sugar in glass, stirring until sugar dissolves. Add ice and top with sparkling water. Stir gently and garnish.

MANGO FIZZ

Your tropical turn-on

- 4 ounces mango juice
- 1 teaspoon lime juice
- Club soda
- Lime wedge for garnish

Pour mango juice into ice-filled glass and add lime juice. Top with club soda to taste, stir gently, and garnish.

MIKE'S DELIGHT

How to ratchet the flavor of ginger ale up yet another notch

- 1 1/2 ounces orange juice
- 1 ounce lemon juice
- 1 splash grenadine
- 5 ounces ginger ale

Pour juices and grenadine into mixing glass. Add ice, shake, and pour contents into glass. Top with ginger ale, stir gently, and garnish.

THE MOVIE STAR

Quaff while wearing your darkest shades

- 3 ounces tangerine juice
- 3 ounces cranberry juice
- 1 dash lemon juice
- 6 ounces ginger ale
- Orange slice for garnish

Combine juices in glass filled with ice. Top with ginger ale, stir gently, and garnish.

NICK'S FAVORITE

With plenty of fruit

- 3 ounces pineapple juice
- 3 ounces orange juice
- 1/2 ounce fresh sour mix
- 1/2 teaspoon
  passion fruit syrup
- 2 ounces club soda
- Orange slice for garnish
- Maraschino cherry
  for garnish

Combine liquid ingredients in mixing glass. Add ice and shake. Pour contents into glass and garnish.

PAPAYA POP

Two canned drinks make beautiful music together

- 6 ounces papaya nectar
- 1 tablespoon lime juice
- 6 ounces Sprite or 7-Up
- Lime twist for garnish

Pour nectar and juice into ice-filled glass. Top with soft drink, stir gently, and garnish.

PEACH DREAM

Visions of peach and citrus

- 3 1/2 ounces peach nectar
- 2 ounces orange juice
- 1 splash lemon juice
- 1 splash grenadine
- Club soda
- Orange slice for garnish

Combine nectar, juices, and grenadine in mixing glass. Add ice, shake, and pour contents into glass. Add club soda to taste, stir gently, and garnish.

ROOT BEER SWEETIE

Not just for kids

- 3 ounces orange juice
- 1/4 teaspoon sugar
- 9 ounces root beer
- Maraschino cherry
  for garnish

Combine juice and sugar in glass. Stir to dissolve sugar, then add ice. Top with root beer, stir gently, and garnish.

SHIRLEY TEMPLE

The grandmother of alcohol-free cocktails

- 12 ounces ginger ale
- 1 dash grenadine
- Orange slice for garnish
- Maraschino cherry
  for garnish

Pour ginger ale into glass filled with ice. Add grenadine, stir gently, and garnish.

SPARKLING GRAPE

Lime juice gives this tasty grape cooler a boost

- 8 ounces white
  grape juice
- 1 tablespoon lime juice
- 4 ounces sparkling water

Pour juices into ice-filled glass. Top with water and stir gently.

SPICY NIGHT

A variation on the Virgin Mary, perhaps the most famous nonalcoholic drink of all

- 8 ounces tomato juice
- 2 drops lemon juice
- 2 drops Tabasco
- Tonic water
- Lime slice for garnish

Combine juices in glass filled with ice. Add Tabasco and stir. Top with tonic water to taste, stir, and garnish.

SPRITELY APRICOT

Sprite makes friends with the small orange fruit

- 8 ounces apricot nectar
- 4 ounces Sprite
- Lime wedge for garnish

Pour nectar into glass filled with ice. Top with soft drink, stir gently, and garnish.

THE STARLET

Ready for a close-up

- 4 ounces cranberry juice
- 1/4 teaspoon orange syrup
- 4 ounces club soda
- Orange slice for garnish

Combine juice and syrup in glass, then stir. Top with club soda, stir gently, and garnish.

BARTENDER'S TIP No, nonalcoholic drinks don't help your heart in the way researchers say alcohol in moderation does. But fruit juices make up for the loss. A sampling of what they're loaded with:

- **Apricot** The antioxidant beta carotene, plus potassium and iron
- **Cranberry** Vitamin C and hippuric acid (good for the urinary tract)
- **Orange** Great source of vitamin C; also provides beta carotene, folate, thiamine, and potassium
- **Peach** Lots of vitamin A, with some vitamin C and potassium
- **Pineapple** Rich in vitamin C, with good amounts of vitamin B6, folate, thiamine, iron, and magnesium
- **Tomato** Good source of vitamins A and C, folate, potassium, and the antioxidant lycopene

TRIPLE TREAT

Garnished with three fruits

- 4 ounces grapefruit juice
- 1 dash lemon juice
- 8 ounces ginger ale
- Lemon slice for garnish
- Orange slice for garnish
- Maraschino cherry for garnish

Pour grapefruit juice into glass filled with ice, then add lemon juice. Top with ginger ale, stir gently, and garnish.

TROPICAL FIZZER

O. J. gets effervescent

- 4 ounces orange juice
- 8 ounces Sprite or 7-Up
- Pineapple spear for garnish

Pour juice and soft drink into glass filled with ice, stir gently, and garnish.

TROPICAL SPLASH

Comes into its own at the beach

- 6 ounces mango juice
- 6 ounces orange juice
- 1 dash bitters of choice
- Orange slice for garnish

Combine juices and bitters in mixing glass. Add ice and shake. Pour contents into glass and garnish.

VIRGIN COLADA

A chaste Piña Colada

- 4 ounces pineapple juice
- 1 1/2 ounces cream of coconut
- 1 teaspoon lime juice
- 1/2 cup crushed ice
- Pineapple spear for garnish
- Maraschino cherry for garnish

Combine all ingredients except garnishes in blender. Blend until smooth, pour into glass, and garnish.

VIRGIN MARY

This vodka-free counterpart of the Bloody Mary is said to have been born in 1927 in a Nantucket bar

- 4 ounces tomato juice
- 1 splash lemon juice
- 1/2 teaspoon Worcestershire sauce
- Tabasco to taste
- Salt and pepper to taste
- Lime wedge for garnish

Fill glass with ice and add juices, sauces, salt, and pepper. Stir and garnish.

WALT'S SOUR RUBY

With Ruby Red grapefruit

- 2 ounces Ruby Red grapefruit juice
- 1 teaspoon fresh sour mix
- 4 ounces club soda

Combine juice and sour mix in mixing glass. Add ice, shake, and strain into glass. Top with club soda and stir gently.

WILD RAIN

Let it pour

- 2 ounces guava juice
- 2 ounces orange juice
- 2 ounces cranberry juice
- Club soda
- Orange slice for garnish

Combine juices in mixing glass. Add ice, shake, and pour contents into glass. Top with club soda, stir gently, and garnish.

BAR BITES

BAR BITES

It wouldn't be fair not to provide some nibbles to serve at parties, so Four Seasons Executive Chef Christian Albin (see page 236) is graciously sharing a few recipes. And, not surprisingly, these hors d'oeuvres draw on the bounty of the seasons. We start with spring.

TAYLOR BAY SCALLOPS WITH LIME, BASIL, AND SAKE

Bay scallops are smaller than sea scallops, and Taylor Bay scallops are smaller still and eaten raw. Look for them at a fish market. Mirin rice wine can be found in gourmet markets, while sake—the better-known Japanese rice wine—is sold at larger liquor stores.

- 4 ounces whole ginger, sliced
- 1/2 cup sake
- 1/2 cup mirin rice wine
- 2 green onions with tops, chopped
- Juice of 1 lime
- 12 Taylor Bay scallops, shelled and cleaned
- Crushed ice
- 2 basil leaves, cut into narrow strips
- 4 limes, cut into 24 segments

1. Peel and slice ginger. Combine sake, mirin, ginger, and onion in small saucepan and place over medium heat. Simmer until the mixture is reduced by half.

2. Strain the liquid into a bowl, stir in lime juice, and let cool.

3. Clean and open scallops, remove membrane, and put each scallop back on the half shell. Place on serving platter over crushed ice.

4. Spoon sauce over each scallop and garnish with a few basil strips and two lime segments. Serves 4 to 6.

ASPARAGUS WRAPPED IN PROSCIUTTO

Use medium-sized asparagus spears (fresh only, of course) for these easy-but-elegant hors d'oeuvres. If you prefer, substitute thinly sliced smoked breast of duck for the prosciutto.

- 8 to 12 asparagus spears
- 8 to 12 very thin slices prosciutto

1. In large pot of boiling water, blanch spears until just tender—about 2 to 4 minutes.

2. Plunge spears into ice water, drain well, and put in refrigerator until ready to use.

3. Cut prosciutto slices so that they are about an inch shorter than the spears.

4. Position a spear at the bottom of a prosciutto slice and roll it to wrap, leaving the head of the spear exposed. Arrange on a platter and serve. Serves 4 to 6.

ENDIVE WITH GORGONZOLA

Stilton, Maytag, or any other crumbly strong cheese can be substituted for the Gorgonzola. You can also garnish the endive spears with your choice of sprouts—mustard, bean, or whatever suits your fancy.

- 8 ounces cream cheese
- 8 ounces Gorgonzola cheese, divided into two portions
- 1/4 cup port wine
- 5 heads Belgian endive
- Sprouts of choice for garnish

1. Soften cream cheese and half of the Gorgonzola to room temperature. Cut remaining half into small, thin pieces.

2. Cut a small portion off the bottom of each endive head, then separate the spears and place them on a platter.

3. Combine softened Gorgonzola and cream cheese and port in a food processor or blender or mix by hand in a large bowl.

4. Spoon the mixture into a pastry bag with a flat or zigzag tip. Pipe an equal amount of softened cheese onto each endive spear.

5. Top each stuffed spear with a little of the reserved Gorgonzola, then garnish with sprouts.

Makes approximately 24 spears.

SUMMER

FOUR SEASONS CRAB CAKES

Crab cakes, here prepared as mini cakes, are one of the specialties of Chef Albin's kitchen. To shape the cakes, you'll need small metal rings or cookie cutters measuring 2 to 3 inches in diameter.

SAUCE

- 1 tablespoon unsalted butter
- 1 tablespoon all-purpose flour
- 1/4 cup chicken stock
- 1/4 cup milk
- 1/4 cup Pommery mustard
- 1/2 teaspoon salt
- 1/8 teaspoon freshly ground black pepper
- 1 teaspoon mustard seed
- 1 teaspoon ground turmeric
- 1 teaspoon curry powder
- 1/2 teaspoon paprika

CRAB CAKES

- 1 pound fresh crab meat
- 1 dill pickle, chopped
- 1 stick celery, chopped
- 1 egg yolk, beaten
- 6 ounces mayonnaise
- 6 ounces white bread without crust
- 1 tablespoon unsalted butter
- 1/2 tablespoon olive oil

1. To make the sauce, melt butter in a small saucepan and stir in flour until it starts to brown. Gradually whisk in stock and milk and simmer over low heat until thickened, stirring often.

2. Stir in remaining sauce ingredients and cook for 2 or 3 minutes over very low heat, stirring often. Remove from heat and refrigerate.

3. Pick bones out of crab meat. Finely chop pickle and celery.

4. In a medium-sized bowl, mix crab, pickle, celery, egg, and mayonnaise.

5. Tear bread into pieces and put into the jar of a blender. Process to make bread crumbs, then spread crumbs evenly on a plate.

6. Put crab meat mixture into metal rings, pressing it with your fingers to pack firmly. Carefully remove each cake from ring and lay flat on crumbs; turn over and repeat. Continue until cakes are evenly coated.

7. Melt butter in large nonstick frying pan, add oil, and cook cakes over very low heat. Cook until golden brown, turning once. In the meantime, remove sauce from the refrigerator and bring to room temperature.

8. Arrange cakes on serving platter and spoon or squeeze a dollop of sauce onto the center of each one. Makes about 12 mini cakes.

CHERRY TOMATOES WITH SMOKED SALMON MOUSSE

These bite-sized stuffed tomatoes are always a hit, and the mousse is a snap to prepare. Yellow cherry tomatoes could also be used, of course, but they won't be as flavorful as red tomatoes.

- 8 ounces
  cream cheese
- 2 ounces smoked
  salmon, cut
  into pieces
- 4 or 5 drops
  lemon juice
- 3 tablespoons heavy
  cream
- 3 drops Tabasco
- White pepper
  to taste
- 40 red
  cherry tomatoes
  (about 2 pints)
- Dill sprigs
  for garnish

1. Combine cream cheese, salmon, lemon juice, cream, and seasonings in a food processor or blender and process until smooth. Refrigerate for 30 minutes.

2. Rinse cherry tomatoes. With a sharp knife, cut off stem end of each tomato. Remove seeds and pulp with a melon ball scoop and place the tomatoes cut-side down on paper towels to drain.

3. Soften chilled mousse by stirring with a wooden spoon. Pack mousse into a pastry bag fitted with a star tip.

4. Place cherry tomatoes on a tray, cut side up. Pipe mousse into each one and top with a dill sprig. Makes about 40.

CRISP POTATO SKINS
WITH SOUR CREAM AND CAVIAR

For these stuffed hors d'oeuvres, choose round new potatoes. Chef Albin uses Osetra caviar, which is prized for its nutty flavor, but any caviar you choose will lead to scrumptious bites.

- 12 new potatoes
- 2 tablespoons
  olive oil
- Salt and pepper
  to taste
- 1 cup sour cream
- 4 ounces caviar

1. Preheat oven to 275° F.

2. Rinse potatoes well and place on baking sheet. Bake for 35 minutes, then remove from oven and let potatoes cool.

3. Cut potatoes in half. Using a melon ball scoop, remove potato from the skins (save it to use in another recipe). Brush the inside and outside of each skin with oil and sprinkle with a little salt and pepper. Place skins on a baking sheet, cut side down.

4. Preheat oven to 375° F and bake skins for 5 to 10 minutes or until golden brown. Let cool.

5. Once the skins have cooled, fill each one with a dollop of sour cream and top with a teaspoon of caviar. Transfer to a platter and serve. Makes 24.

WHITE BEAN CROSTINI

To prepare these toasts, you could either spend a couple of hours cooking dried white beans (cannellini) or you could opt for a quality canned brand. Chef Albin does the former but you won't go wrong taking the shortcut.

- 16 pieces crusty Italian bread
- 1 cup cooked white beans
- 2 level teaspoons tomato paste
- 1 1/2 teaspoons red pepper flakes, divided into two portions
- Salt and freshly ground black pepper to taste
- 1 medium-sized garlic clove, peeled
- 1 tablespoon fresh rosemary leaves, chopped
- 2 tablespoons unsalted butter
- 1 cup chicken broth
- 2 tablespoons olive oil
- Juice of 1 lemon
- Italian parsley (leaves only), chopped

1. Preheat oven to 400° F. Put the bread on a baking sheet and heat in oven for 3 minutes on each side. Remove and set aside.

2. Drain the beans and combine with tomato paste, 1/4 teaspoon red pepper flakes, and salt and pepper in a medium-sized saucepan. Cook over low heat, stirring often for three to four minutes.

3. Purée the seasoned beans by mashing well with a fork or passing them through a food mill.

4. Finely chop garlic, rosemary, and 1/4 teaspoon red pepper flakes. Melt butter in a saucepan with oil, add chopped ingredients, and sauté for 2 minutes over medium heat. Add bean purée and stir to mix.

5. Heat the chicken broth to lukewarm in a small saucepan and pour into bean purée, and stir well to incorporate. Cook for about 10 minutes or until the mixture is fairly thick.

6. Remove mixture from heat, add lemon juice, and stir well.

7. Spread 1 heaping tablespoon bean purée on each piece of bread. Arrange on a large platter, sprinkle parsley over the toasts, and serve warm. Makes 16.

ZUCCHINI MADELEINES

These savory shell-shaped "muffins" are full of good things, including Parmesan cheese. Madeleine pans are sold at larger kitchenware stores.

- 1 1/2 cups shredded zucchini
- 1/3 cup olive oil
- 3 shallots, peeled and minced
- 5 large eggs, beaten
- 1/4 cup milk or plain yogurt
- 1 1/4 cups grated Parmesan cheese
- 1/2 cup chopped basil leaves, packed
- 1 cup all-purpose flour
- 1 teaspoon baking powder

1. Preheat oven to 400° F.

2. Peel one large or two small zucchini and shred with a large-hole grater. Measure out 1 1/2 cups, place on paper towels, and pat dry.

3. Pour olive oil into a sauté pan and heat. Add shallots and sauté over heat until just limp. Remove from heat and set pan aside.

4. Mix together the eggs, milk or yogurt, cheese, and basil. Add flour and baking powder and mix in a food processor, a blender, or by hand.

5. Pour mixture into large bowl. Fold in zucchini, shallots, and oil, taking care not to overmix.

6. Spray madeleine molds with nonstick spray. Using a small spoon or a pastry bag, fill molds with mixture so that it is level with (or just under) the top of the pan.

7. Bake for 12 to 18 minutes or until light brown. Makes about 36 madeleines.

OYSTERS WITH SUN-DRIED TOMATOES

Chef Albin uses only Hog Island oysters for this recipe, but any oyster will make you swoon when topped with the chef's mouthwatering mixture of sun-dried tomatoes, shallots, basil, and thyme.

- 12 oysters, shucked
- Sea salt
- 1 tablespoon butter
- 1 garlic clove, peeled and finely diced
- 1/2 cup dry white wine
- 2 1/2 tablespoons olive oil
- 1/2 cup chopped sun-dried tomatoes
- 2 shallots, finely chopped
- 3 tablespoons chopped basil leaves
- 2 sprigs thyme, chopped
- Salt, pepper to taste

1. Preheat oven to 350° F.

2. Clean oysters, then place over coarse sea salt in oven-proof dish.

3. Melt butter in a sauté pan and cook garlic until translucent but not brown. Add wine to pan and simmer until reduced by about a third.

4. Add oil, sun-dried tomatoes, shallots, basil, thyme, and salt and pepper. Cook and stir until shallots are translucent.

5. Top each oyster with an equal amount of the mixture, covering it evenly. Bake for 5 to 7 minutes and serve. Serves 4 to 6.

WINTER

PIZZA WITH CARAMELIZED ONION AND GOAT CHEESE

Caramelizing onions takes up to half an hour, but once you've tasted this pizza you might not mind. The recipe calls for drizzling the pizza with truffle oil, although you could use olive or walnut oil instead. Likewise, you can compensate for the time spent caramelizing the onions by using refrigerated pizza dough from the grocery store.

- 1 tablespoon olive oil
- 2 medium-sized Vidalia or other sweet onions, sliced
- 8 ounces goat cheese
- 4 rounds prepared pizza dough, 4 inches in diameter
- Truffle oil for drizzling

1. Preheat oven to 450° F.

2. Pour olive oil into a heavy pot, add onions, and cook until caramelized, or almost brown. Stir often to prevent burning, adding a little water as necessary.

3. Roll out dough rounds and spread onions evenly over the surface. Top each pizza with crumbled cheese, drizzle with oil, and bake for 8 minutes or until lightly browned.

4. Slice each pizza into quarters or eight wedges and serve. Makes 16 to 32 slices.

SMOKED SALMON ROULADE

These salmon rolls are wrapped much like small pieces of candy, then halved. Chef Albin uses Sevruga caviar for the topping, but any type you choose will work fine. And the fire-breathing wasabi mustard? Most supermarkets have stocked it since the sushi craze came along. To blanch the chives so they won't break, plunge them into boiling water for six seconds, then flush with cold water and pat dry.

- 6 slices smoked salmon
- 1/2 tablespoon sour cream
- 1/2 tablespoon wasabi mustard
- 12 chives, blanched

1. One at a time, lay salmon slices between sheets of parchment or wax paper and pound them thin.

2. In a small mixing bowl, combine sour cream and wasabi and stir until mixed.

3. Spoon equal amounts of the mixture into the center of each salmon slice. Roll up the slices and tie off each end with a blanched chive.

4. Cut the rolls in half and top each with a spoonful of caviar. Serves 4 to 6.

RUSTIC CROSTINI

These toasts—topped with a mix of chopped chicken livers, sage, and juniper berries—could have come straight from an Italian country kitchen. The juniper berries can be found in the spice section of gourmet stores and better grocery stores.

- 16 pieces
  crusty Italian bread
- 10 chicken livers
  (cleaned and with
  fat removed),
  equally divided
  into two batches
- 4 fresh sage leaves
  chopped
- 4 juniper berries
  chopped
- 1/4 cup olive oil,
  divided
- 1 whole clove garlic,
  peeled
- 1/2 cup dry red wine
- Salt and pepper
  to taste
- 16 sage leaves
  for garnish

1. Preheat oven to 400° F. Put bread on a baking sheet and heat in the oven for 3 minutes on each side. Remove and set aside.

2. Finely chop half the chicken livers with a sharp knife. Cut the remaining livers into quarters and set aside.

3. Finely chop sage and juniper berries.

4. Heat half the oil in a small heavy saucepan over medium heat. Add the garlic clove, finely chopped livers, sage, juniper berries, and sauté for about 10 minutes, stirring often.

5. Add wine and let the mixture simmer over low heat until it reduces by about a third—about 10 minutes. Remove from heat and set aside.

6. Meanwhile, heat remaining oil in a small heavy saucepan and add the quartered chicken livers. Season with salt and pepper and cook for 4 minutes, stirring often. Remove from heat.

7. Spread 1 tablespoon of the finely chopped mixture onto each piece of bread, then top each with a sage leaf and some of the quartered chicken livers. Arrange on a platter and serve. Makes 16.

CHRISTIAN ALBIN, EXECUTIVE CHEF

Chef Christian Albin continues The Four Seasons's tradition of introducing innovative dishes with a continental flair. A native of Jlantz, Switzerland, he trained at the Hotel Belvedere and the Hotel Drei König in his native land before moving to New York to help launch the Swiss Pavilion restaurant, where he worked under the renowned Seppi Renggli. In 1973 Albin became chef de cuisine at the Restaurant Associates–owned Forum of the Twelve Caesars. Stints at Tavern On The Green and The Four Seasons followed, and in 1990 Albin was appointed as executive chef of The Four Seasons.

In 2000, Chef Albin's efforts led to the restaurant's being honored with a Best Restaurant in America award from the James Beard Foundation, only one of many awards The Four Seasons has received over the last several years.

BIBLIOGRAPHY

Calabrese, Salvatore. *Complete Home Bartending Guide*
New York: Sterling Publishing Co., Inc., 2002

Cunningham, Stephen Kittridge. *The Bartender's Black Book*
Brockton, Mass.: The Bartender's Black Book Co., Inc., 2002

Foley, Ray. *Bartending for Dummies*
New York: Wiley Publishing, Inc., 1997

Foley, Ray. *The Ultimate Cocktail Book*
Liberty Corner, N. J.: Foley Books, 1990

Grimes, William. *Straight Up or On the Rocks*
New York: North Point Press, 2001

Gluckstern, Willie. *The Wine Avenger*
New York: Simon & Schuster, 1998

Herbst, Sharon Tyler and Ron Herbst.
The Ultimate A-to-Z Bar Guide
New York: Broadway Books, 1998

Mariani, John and Alex von Bidder. *The Four Seasons*
New York: Smithmark Publishers, 1999

Mr. Boston Official Bartender's and Party Guide
New York: Warner Books, 1994

Gary Regan. *The Bartender's Bible*
New York: HarperPaperbacks, 2000

INDEX

A

V

ACKNOWLEDGMENTS

The writer would like to thank Four Seasons bartenders
Greg Connolly, Charles Corpion, and John Varriano
for their patience, hard work, and good humor.
He also gratefully acknowledges the help
offered by the following:

Christian Albin, Executive Chef, The Four Seasons
Alex Von Bidder, Managing Partner, The Four Seasons
Julian Niccolini, Managing Partner, The Four Seasons
Ray Foley, Publisher, *Bartender Magazine*
Regina McMinamin
Susan McQuillan
Gammon Sharpley
Declan McGarry
David Olsen, Gracious Home
Beacon Liquors, Manhattan
Nancy's Wines for Food, Manhattan
Schumer's Wines & Liquors, Manhattan